Women's Worlds

Ideology, Femininity and the Woman's Magazine

Ros Ballaster, Margaret Beetham, Elizabeth Frazer and Sandra Hebron

M

MACMILLAN

First published 1991 by
THE MACMILLAN PRESS LTD
Houndmills, Basingstoke, Hampshire RG21 2XS
and London
Companies and representatives
throughout the world

ISBN 0–333–49235–8 hardcover
ISBN 0–333–49236–6 paperback

A catalogue record for this book is available from the British Library.

Printed in Hong Kong

Reprinted 1993

Series Standing Order

If you would like to receive future titles in this series as they are published, you can make use of our standing order facility. To place a standing order please contact your bookseller or, in case of difficulty, write to us at the address below with your name and address and the name of the series. Please state with which title you wish to begin your standing order. (If you live outside the United Kingdom we may not have the rights for your area, in which case we will forward your order to the publisher concerned.)

Customer Services Department, Macmillan Distribution Ltd
Houndmills, Basingstoke, Hampshire RG21 2XS, England

Contents

v

Preface

This book is a collaborative effort. In 1987 all four of the authors participated in a series of seminars called 'Women's Own? Magazines and the Female Reader', organised by the Women's Studies Committee at Oxford University. Although our methods have been collaborative, the four major chapters are based on, and have been developed from, previous work we have each published or researched individually. The historical data on the eighteenth century comes from Ros Ballaster's research, the nineteenth and early twentieth centuries from Margaret Beetham's. The detailed analysis of twentieth-century magazines was carried out and written up by Sandra Hebron; the work with readers and the discussion of theory and method by Elizabeth Frazer. Although much discussion, drafting, re-drafting, and transfer of editing responsibility has had a certain unifying effect, our different writing styles are, we think, still detectable, and rightly so. The theory, argument and analysis are ours collectively – the product of conversations, meetings, phone calls, letters, drafts and criticism.

Our emphasis here is on mass market women's magazines, the 'mainstream' popular form. Thus, small circulation 'alternatives' such as *Spare Rib* or *Shocking Pink* receive relatively little attention. We have attempted to make our methods of analysis, explanatory theory and understanding of the intersection and conflicts of race, class and gender, clear in our first chapter. Subsequent analyses of historical and contemporary magazines offer an unfolding illustration and exposition from this theoretical base. We do not pretend to offer a detailed history, reading or content analysis of women's magazines since their inception. Rather, we have produced a range of critical readings which we attempt to situate historically.

What we have omitted here has been admirably committed by others. Cynthia White provides a detailed publishing history in her *Women's Magazines 1693–1968*, Janice Winship and Angela McRobbie closer readings and analyses of samples from mainstream magazines. We are particularly indebted to Janice Winship's ground-breaking *Inside Women's Magazines*, an examination of individual current titles, which addresses a range of issues to do with women's magazines' constructions of gender. These texts have constituted the point from which our own research began.

We have compiled an appendix which lists the magazines we have analysed and discussed in the body of the text, together with a certain amount of information about their dates of publication, ownership, editors, and so on. Our selective bibliography points to the many more exhaustive analyses and histories.

Our collaborative methods have meant that we have been relatively slow workers. We would like to thank Jo Campling, Dilys Jones and Steven Kennedy at the publishers for their patience and flexibility in dealing with multiple authorship. Our most grateful thanks are due to the women who met for discussions and responded to questionnaires: members of the New College women's group and the Feminist Theory Group at Oxford University; students of the Faculty of English and Humanities at Manchester Polytechnic and Oxford Polytechnic; Doreen Essex, Rosemary Popplewell, Claire Pierce, Sybil James, Jean Gregory, Mina Temple, Alison Jones, Liz Whiteside, Janet Jacobs, Lynne Dewberry. Also to the women who participated in the original seminar series, where discussion was always lively, and which engendered the questions we seek to address in a different format here. Most important of all we wish to recognise the contribution of Kate Mertes who helped to devise that seminar series but had to withdraw from the project of the book. Certain themes central to this book – the making and fragmentation of a female readership, the magazine's construction of an imaginary female community, the politics of fashion photography – were articulated by her in our first discussions.

Our work has been further slowed by a number of practical and emotional problems of the sort that jostle with one another in the pages of the magazines we analyse: the trauma of new jobs, old jobs, commitments to family and friends, the sexual double standard, crises of confidence, the ending, beginning or lack of 'relationships'. If we were to turn to the magazines in search of solutions we would find, as we document in what follows, that our troubles are represented as 'ours', individually, although they are also, by a bizarre and unexplained coincidence, also experienced by millions of other women throughout the western world and through the ages. By contrast, it is our profound conviction that 'our problems' have political and structural roots, that their solutions lie in political struggle and transformation. That so many women have such similar experience is a political matter. The struggle must be in the arena of sexual politics (for sexuality *is* political), the politics of social identity and difference, and the politics of economic relations.

Nevertheless, supportive personal relations have been of immeasurable value and we do not hesitate to thank personally the numbers of people who have given help – intellectual, emotional and personal. We are indebted to: David Beetham, John Campbell, Niki Lacey, Andrew Milton, Jenefer Sargent, Jessica Search (who made dozens of ingenious suggestions for the title), Louise Kanas, Brian Maidment, Jeri Johnson, and Dianne Chisholm.

ROS BALLASTER
MARGARET BEETHAM
ELIZABETH FRAZER
SANDRA HEBRON

Introduction

Feminism and women's magazines

When we began work for this book we realised that our enthusiasm stemmed from our mutual pleasure in reading women's magazines themselves, tempered by the knowledge that this pleasure is by no means pure, unambiguous or unproblematic. The magazine is for us both an object of academic interest and an object of consumption. Reading women's magazines can have exactly the same kind of effect as eating two or more bars of chocolate – the original craving was real but seems in the end to have been for the wrong thing. For all of us, of course, women's magazines have been a continuing presence in our lives but as feminists they have become an obvious subject for analysis and criticism, a staple topic for consciousness raising groups.

The seminar series which prompted this book raised several interesting issues. First, the discussion revolved precisely around the question raised above of why women's magazines are or are not pleasurable for women (and men) readers, and, more particularly, feminist readers. Why, when their contents fill us with outrage, do we nevertheless enjoy reading them? Second, it turned to the vexed question of the ideological function of women's magazines. Most participants felt strongly that the magazines discussed (including the eighteenth- and nineteenth-century ones) offer representations of women which are either downright reactionary or, at least, subtly maintain sexual difference and women's subordination. On the other hand, of course, most of the participants in the seminar, including the authors, identified themselves as feminists who *resisted* the models of femininity in the magazines, although many felt that they had been partly responsible for past 'false consciousness', unfulfillable desire, discontent and disappointment.

Third, and at a more theoretical level, the seminar raised the issue of the relation between literary and social theory in analysis of popular culture. Critical 'literary' readings of magazines have focused on the construction of an implied reader who is simultaneously 'produced' and 'subjected' by the text. These reading techniques have been adopted and adapted in sociological interpretation of the role of popular culture in the reproduction of capitalist and patriarchal social order. However, in both cases the implied reader seems to have been taken as exhaustive for the purposes of analysis and little attention paid to 'her' relation to the historical reader.

We focus, in this book, on the conflict between two 'dominant' analyses of women's magazines common to both these disciplines. Broadly, the first represents the magazine as a bearer of pleasure, the second sees it as a purveyor of oppressive ideologies of sex, class and race difference. In academic criticism – literary, cultural, and sociological – these are two alternative approaches, expounded by different theorists from different conceptual traditions, but, of course, for the actual reader of the magazine at the point of consumption, they can and do exist simultaneously. This conflict suggests another duality at the heart of the woman's magazine. It is at the same time a medium for the sale of commodities to an identifiable market group, women, and itself a commodity, a product sold in the capitalist market place for profit. It is also, of course, a text, a set of images and representations which construct an imaginary world and an imaginary reader. What is the relation *between* the different levels and functions, social and textual, of the women's magazine?

We attempt to look at these questions historically. Journals first began to address women readers as women in the late seventeenth century in England. The nineteenth and twentieth centuries have seen what we have called the differentiation of the female reader – different magazines address different groups of women whether we analyse them as literary texts or as commodities produced for profit. As feminists we resist the implication that all women are the same, that women constitute a homogenous interest group whose consumption patterns are as well-defined as those of, say, hot-rod enthusiasts, or gardeners, or wine connoisseurs. The acknowledgement that the interests and identifications of black or working-class women cannot be subsumed under those of middle-class women is a welcome one. However, just as we must look critically at what it means for *women* as distinct from the entire aggregate of 'the reading public' to be addressed by editors and publishers of magazines in the eighteenth and nineteenth centuries, we must look critically at what it means and whose interests it serves, for example, for black young women to be defined as a distinct *consumption* group by publishers and advertisers in the late twentieth century.

Our argument is organised in four major chapters. Chapter 1 reviews the work of literary and cultural critics, sociologists and social theorists and feminists with regard to popular culture in general and women's magazines in particular. Here, we introduce and discuss the central themes and contradictions that have structured our own analysis, pre-eminent among them the question of the 'stability' of the women's magazine's representation of immutable gender difference. While women's magazines have increasingly inflected their terms of address to women with the specificities of class, race, nation and status difference, they have continued to offer a 'fantasy' of a mythic sexual divide between men and women. This fantasy, however, is always under a threat – sexuality and feminism, in particular, are both potential disrupters of the social order that the women's magazine seeks to confirm.

There is a fairly small existing literature on the women's magazine as such, much of which is little more than anecdotal. We have been much influenced by the structuralist and semiotic analyses of twentieth-century women's magazines offered by Angela McRobbie, Janice Winship, and the early work of Sandra Hebron (McRobbie, 1978a and' b; Winship, 1978, 1987; Hebron, 1983). Kathryn Shevelov provides a suggestive account of the emergence of an address to women in print culture through the medium of the magazine in the early eighteenth century, while Alison Adburgham looks at and surveys the history of the women's magazine from this same point to the start of the nineteenth century (Shevelov, 1989; Adburgham, 1972). Recent feminist work has, of course, been much preoccupied with the study of popular fictional genres associated with a female readership or authorship – romance, gothic, the whodunnit, the photo-strip story. Fiction is a crucial feature of most magazines for women and the reader's true experience, a complex narrative structure in itself, remains one of the magazine's staple media.

The work of (feminist) literary criticism is, then, very relevant here. We have three main reservations about much of the existing literature on women's magazines. First, as we have said, we want to challenge the opposition between an analysis of the magazine as a source of pleasure (to be celebrated) and the magazine as purveyor of a pernicious ideology (to be condemned). Second, these studies have tended to neglect the role of the magazine as a commodity in favour of subjecting it to textual criticism. Third, it is also time that the relation between the reader constructed in and by the text (the *implied* reader) and the actual historical reader who paid her two pennies in 1788 or her one pound in 1988, was properly theorised.

Our own analysis employs close readings of individual samples, but attempts to ground these readings in an historical under-standing of the place and significance of magazines in the making of a modern discourse of womanhood and/or femininity. Dis-course, we would argue, is normative – it shapes the material of social and personal identities, and that of social and personal relations, inscribing social practice, or, more simply, offering people particular ways of both understanding the world and acting in it. Hence, Chapter 1 tries to make clear the authors' understanding of the role and function of discourse and ideology in the manufacture of social identity and difference through a discussion of these terms' recent deployment in theoretical argument. We employ the term ideology throughout our analy-sis, but with reservations. We certainly want to reject the idea of ideology as an all-enveloping and determining force, which shapes people's beliefs, values and actions into the form that best serves the interest of a dominant class. Discourse is neither seamless nor monolithic: textual and cultural analysis of women's magazines, for instance, swiftly reveals multiple contradictions in the repre-sentations of femininity offered within the pages of a single number. Readers are clearly capable of negotiating the complex-ity of the representations and messages they read, see, and hear, and aware of the normative and ideological effects of these representations and messages, even if they do not frame their response in these terms (as the research material with groups of readers in Chapter 5 seeks to demonstrate). Our work attempts to theorise both the activity of this social reader, a knowing and aware subject, and the complexity of the range of texts and discourses which constitute the social world we inhabit, and of which the magazine is only a part.

The historical emergence and definition of the themes of gender, class, nation and race, their articulation in the pages of the magazine and, in turn, their effect on the shaping of the magazine itself structures Chapters 2, 3 and 4 of this book which survey the past three centuries of the women's magazine. At this point we hasten to say that we are not offering a narrative history of the women's magazine, its changing form and content, the appearance and disappearance of particular titles, proprietors, editors and writers. This kind of information is available elsewhere, notably Cynthia White's *Women's Magazines 1693–1968* and Brian Braithwaite and Joan Barrell's second edition of their *The Business of Women's Magazines*. This last, with its thorough cataloguing of the 'births, marriages and deaths' of British titles, is peculiarly symptomatic of the perspectives and attitudes of the producers of women's magazines. Its authors affect a consistently triumphalist tone in celebration of the entrepreneurial and creative business of periodical journalism and publication, fixated on 'success' (signified by a magazine which lasts) and mournful about 'tragedy' (the magazine that folds). Their analysis, unsurprisingly, ignores the politics of the textual world of these magazines, and takes for granted, when it does not actually celebrate, the economic context of the industry.

In contrast, we seek to situate our critical reading of magazine samples in a concrete analysis of the processes by which social relations are forged, contested and maintained. Our historical account of the magazine argues for both continuity and change. In the eighteenth century writers and readers appear to have been actively engaged in a process, or struggle, to establish gender difference as both unambiguous and oppositional, providing 'masculinity' and 'femininity' with different and specific social and textual content. Through the nineteenth and twentieth centuries we see this gender difference institutionalised and entrenched textually in the women's magazine. In Chapter 5 our analysis of sample magazines from 1988 is organised thematically, in order to demonstrate the continuity in thematic emphasis in the magazine – sexuality, domesticity, politics, beautification, and so forth – and the increasingly contradictory nature of the magazine's representation of determining gender difference, fissured with other forms of social identification such as race and class.

The analysis in Chapter 5 incorporates data gathered from tape-recorded discussions about the 1988 sample in particular and women's magazines in general with a small number of groups of women – students, pensioners, professional women. This data has to be used with great caution, of course. It cannot be taken to be statistically representative in any way, and our use of it is informed throughout with an awareness of the complications of method involved in such empirical research. But the material is highly suggestive, indicating the complexity of readers' negotiations with magazines. As readers we do not all bring the same range of interpretative and critical practices to our reading, as our work with different groups of women demonstrates, nor do we use the same interpretative and critical practice at all times. The way one reads *Cosmopolitan* in the bath is not the same as the way one reads it in order to avoid unwanted conversation on a train nor the same as the way one reads it in a discussion group organised by a researcher who is writing a collaborative book on women's magazines. Nevertheless, in all the many and varied contexts in which magazines are read, reading is a *practice*, both institutionalised and rule-governed, and women's reading of magazines is equally subject to certain rituals and structures of understanding, identification and interpretation from which, we feel, the critic can and should generalise.

Our analysis of the 1988 magazines reveals invariance and transformation in the history of the women's magazine. The oppositions of masculine and feminine, public and private, production and consumption, continue to structure the magazine text; sexuality and feminism continue to trouble the smooth surface of its ideological surety. Throughout their history magazines have had to manage acutely contradictory models of masculinity and femininity. Never more so than now, however, when increasing sophistication in technology, marketing and consumer awareness mean that 'successful magazines have to be targeted at market segments based on age and lifestyle' (Braithwaite and Barrell, 1989, p. 139). 'Glossy' magazines like *Cosmopolitan* most obviously tackle the contradictions implicit in this process – constructing women as independent salary-earners with free sexual existences, yet prioritising the heterosexual 'relationship' as the determining force in their social existence. Magazines have turned also to targeting men as consumers of goods other than the car, with the launching of *Cosmo Man* and *GQ*. We do not intend, here, to enter into the debate about whether this exercise is subversive of conventional constructions of masculinity. We want simply to highlight the fact that the contradictory processes at work in gender identification always present in the magazine have become, in the late twentieth century, increasingly manifest. This should not be surprising since the strength of the magazine format from its manifestation has been its rejection of the single, the unified and the monolithic – in other words, its embracing of contradiction. Anything can co-exist with anything on the pages of the magazine (and does). The identification of 'contradiction', therefore, fails to embarrass either editors, writers or readers. Indeed, the form of the magazine – open-ended, heterogeneous, fragmented – seems particularly appropriate to those whose object is the representation of femininity. Femininity is itself contradictory (as feminists have long recognised), but women live with the contradictions. The success of the women's magazine is no doubt connected with its ability to encompass glaring contradiction *coherently* in its pages. In the end, women are not free sexual beings, in the pages of *Cosmopolitan* or anywhere else. The question 'why not?' is one of feminism's most urgent tasks. We hope that this study of women's magazines might make a useful and significant contribution to that project.

1

Theories of text and culture

Part one: critical analysis of women's magazines

The cover of *Cosmopolitan* for January 1988 advertises one of its leading features with the caption 'Men who hate women and the women who love them' The world of the magazine is one in which men and women are eternally in opposition, always in struggle, but always in pursuit of each other; relations between them are beset by difficulty, frustration and failure. Yet, possible solutions like the dissolution of two exclusive and opposed gender categories, or the separation of women from men, or the dismantling of the power structures which now legitimate gender difference, have no place in the women's magazine. The heterogeneity of the magazine form, then, has its limits. Certain solutions and conclusions that might result from its representation of heterosexual relations are clearly not meant to be drawn How does the women's magazine demarcate and delimit its own 'reading' of femininity?

In this section we introduce some of the central themes of women's magazines, as they have been identified by other analysts and our own examination of a sample of magazines from 1988. Critical analysts of the women's magazine attend to two kinds of issue. First, there are those which come under the heading of 'theme' proper, or subject-matter, such as gender opposition, domesticity, royalty, and so on. Second, issues come under the heading of 'formal textual features' to do with layout, the 'tone' of address to the reader, distribution of advertising, fiction, features, and so forth. Of course, formal and substantive features of magazines in practice affect and even positively shape one another.

8

Many analysts have been struck by the intimate tone employed
to address the reader, the cosy invocation of a known commonality between 'we women' (Leman, 1980; Stewart, 1980; Hebron,
1983; Winship, 1978, 1987). Despite status, wealth, class and race
distinctions, the magazine assumes a shared experience between
women: 'It wouldn't matter if Jacqueline Onassis had a billion or a
trillion dollars . . . she is in exactly the same boat as you are when
it comes to raising teenagers' (Lopate, 1978, p. 134). It is not only
the editors and publishers who use this inclusive voice. A crucial
feature of women's magazines is the readers' contributions in the
form of letters, true life stories, the 'make-over'. The voice of the
readers in all these contexts resonates with exactly the same
register of intimacy as that of the professional producers of the
magazine. It matters not at all whether this is because, as readers
frequently suspect, all such contributions may be written by the
professionals themselves. The effect is to make of producers and
reader one group.

Such inclusivity is patently false. The 'ideal' or 'implied' reader
of most women's magazines is self-evidently middle-class, white,
and heterosexual. This inclusivity of address effectively margina-
lises or makes deviant black, working-class or lesbian women.
Here, then, is an example of a formal, textual feature of the
women's magazine – the intimacy of the editorial or journalistic
'we' – which works to define its content or theme, woman.

The construction of women as a homogeneous group, or even a
group at all, is primarily achieved by the invocation of its
supposedly 'natural' opposite – men. From the girl's magazine
to the most popular women's magazines, such as *Woman*, there is
an evident tension between the need to confirm the centrality and
desirability of men in all women's lives and the equally insistent
recognition of men as a problem for and threat to women. They
are lazy, untidy, sometimes violent, require constant maintenance
and upkeep both physically and psychically, are prone to
faithlessness and heart attacks and, in recent years and registering
the currency of a 'popular feminism', sexist and oppressive. This
analysis of men as problematic is congruent, up to a point, with a
feminist analysis of relations between men and women as quasi-
class conflictual relations, relations of domination and oppression.
But only up to a point. For, after all, magazines are part of an
economic system as well as part of an ideological system by which

gender difference is given meaning. They exist primarily as commodities and as the vehicle for advertisements of other commodities. If women are to continue to buy and consume commodities, not only for themselves, but for their families, they cannot also be sold feminist analyses of gender relations. Defining women as 'not men', although it might be a necessary first step and a popular one with political philosophers and social theorists, is evidently not a sufficient one for the women's magazine. If women are to buy and to be, they cannot be defined solely in the negative; femininity has to be given particular content. The magazines' shared version of femininity varies, of course, from historical moment to moment. In what follows, as well as identifying shifts, we point to the instability and non-viability of the versions of female self-hood offered at different points in the history of the magazine. This instability holds both at the level of the components which make up the complex definition of womanhood available in the magazine at any one point and the relation between these components. For example, a dominant and consistent version of femininity offered by magazines, which still has currency in many of the more traditional titles, is that of woman as the repository of the nation's virtue. Virtue is here defined as essentially domestic and private, bound to 'family' ideals of affection, loyalty and obligation, to domestic production or housekeeping. Yet, by dint of their very posing of woman's existence as beset by 'problems' in need of resolution or attention through the medium of the magazine, women's magazines are forced to confront the undoubted realities of 'family' – domestic violence, poverty, illness – which directly conflict with the imaginary ideal projected in such a construction of 'woman'. Moreover, when this definition of woman is one ingredient in an admixture which also includes the representation of femininity as confident participation in the competitive world of business, as it does in some magazines, its inviability becomes even more glaring.

As well as the contradiction within magazines different magazines continually stress the qualities which distinguish them from their rivals. It is in this light that we must read their own protestations of *exclusivity*, their stress on the *difference* between 'Cosmo girls' or 'Company readers' and the rest of the vast undifferentiated mass of (by implication) boring and convention-al women (Braithwaite and Barrell, 1989, pp. 141–6). The *Cosmo* girl and the *Company* reader is, in reality, distinguished from her sisters by her consumption patterns or, as the industry terms it, 'lifestyle'. Publishers and editors of British magazines can always identify their readers in terms of the Registrar General's socio-economic classes which are demarcated by the criterion of occupation (frequently, in the case of women, by husband's or father's occupation). They are only, however, interested in occupation in so far as it is a determinant of 'lifestyle'. The differentiation of the female reader is then bound up with the exigencies of capitalist markets; collective character is determined by what we (are able to) buy.

The 'lifestyles' portrayed in different magazines are not, of course, coterminous with the actual lifestyle, or consumption habits, of the majority of readers of those magazines. It is a commonplace that *Jackie*, although addressed to girls in their late teens is largely read by eleven- to thirteen-year-olds. The clothes and cosmetics featured in the 'glossies' such as *Working Woman* are priced at a level which puts them beyond the means of the typical reader; features present women who own their own business empires, occupy top executive positions, convert country houses into homes, while the magazine's readership consists mainly of women who work for mediocre salaries in shops or offices (Glazer, 1980). Publishers and editors recognise their readers as 'aspirational', aspiring to be older (in the case of teenagers), richer, thinner, in a higher class or social bracket. Magazine editors know their audience to be largely from the C1–C2 British occupational groups (women with white-collar working husbands or fathers). As one editor at the Oxford seminar which provided the origin for this book put it, 'After all, they are the most numerous'. Magazines hold out to these women the 'opportunity' to spend at A and B levels.

There are complex issues here. On the one hand, most women simply do not have the opportunity to spend the amounts of money necessary to acquire the goods featured. On the other, even if particular commodities are bought, the whole 'lifestyle' may not be. A young woman might buy a wedding dress identical to the Duchess of York's without 'buying' the Duchess of York's values. Yet again, women's magazines include features which stress the message that it is much better to be poor and happy than royal and hounded by photographers, or rich and hooked on drugs, drink or divorce. The expensive commodities displayed in the magazine may, then, not be appealing to aspiration at all, but rather to the realm of fantasy. Either way, for our purposes several points are raised. First, a gap emerges between the reader's social and economic reality and that projected by the text she consumes. This gap vividly illustrates Simone de Beauvoir's famous observation that 'one is not born, but rather becomes a woman' (de Beauvoir, 1960, p. 9). Second, the 'femininity' we are invited to acquire in the process of consuming the magazine is not single, nor simple. The model of femininity extended by the magazine to the reader is severely contradictory, or rather, fragmentary. Perhaps instead of talking of contradiction, we should talk of multiplicity. Third, the woman who is addressed by the magazine text is addressed first and foremost as a consumer, of the message of the text *and* of the commodities which it presents as essential to the business of her 'becoming' or construction.

Notwithstanding the contradictions, tensions and difficulties involved in sustaining it as a coherent project, magazines which co-exist at any given historical moment do share a notion of femininity. Looking at the magazines of the late twentieth century, we can identify certain features which recur. A glance at almost any sample of magazines will suggest that whatever else femininity (and especially female sexuality) might be, it is certainly punishable (Gerbner, 1957; Sonnenschein, 1970). This is most evident in the fiction of 'True Romance' magazines, in which women who succumb to their sexual desires more often than not also succumb to severe psychological torment, illness, and even death, but it is also discernible in features such as the celebrity profile, the 'triumph over tragedy' true life experience, and that perennial favourite, the 'problem page'. The heroines of magazines suffer, appallingly and all the time. If they have positively sinned against the conformist sexual ideology of the magazine, their suffering may be brought to an end by repentance; if their only sin is that of being female then stoical resignation, passivity and 'goodness' will finally bring its reward.

Valerie Walkerdine, in analysing the fiction offered by the British girls' magazine *Bunty*, has pointed out the pattern of suffering at the hands of wicked step-parents, cruel teachers, or nasty bullying enemies inflicted on the magazine's heroines. In these stories the heroine's goodness through adversity is finally rewarded with the restoration of family and love (Walkerdine, 1984). Tania Modleski puts forward a strikingly similar analysis of the heroine's fate in Harlequin or Mills & Boon romances. Here the hero's cruelty and seeming contempt is finally transformed despite himself through the sheer passive virtue of the heroine (Modleski, 1984, p. 17). We might conclude, then, that in the romance structures shared by both popular fiction and the women's magazine femaleness is in itself punishable, but can only be transcended or transformed through the acquisition and display of an excessive femininity. Interestingly, Barbara Phillips argues that this theme is continued in the self-consciously feminist magazine *Ms*. Biographical articles in *Ms* feature a range of women in public life (trades-union organisers, campaigners against rape, etc.) who all 'succeed' because they put other people first and enjoy the intrinsic rewards of selfless devotion to duty and community (Phillips, 1978).

Women's magazines almost without exception situate women (all women) either firmly *in* the domestic sphere or in close proximity to it. Magazines vary between those that encourage women to work the double shift (run a home, raise children, reproduce husband and family on a daily basis, dress and groom spectacularly, climb a career ladder and maintain professional and emotional relationships outside the family circle) and those which encourage them to resist any pressure to leave the home. The latter 'reassert' the value of the domestic sphere, particularly that of maternity, and harp on the high cost to women of pursuing paid work. Thus, *Family Circle* tells its readers that the cost of broadcaster Barbara Walters' lifestyle has been high; she has lost a quantity of softness that other women may not be willing to sacrifice (Phillips, 1978, p. 120). Those magazines which do celebrate the 'independent' woman (*Cosmopolitan*, *Honey*, *Options*) nevertheless run regular features on cookery, interior decoration, parenting (otherwise known as motherhood).

Conspicuous by its absence and in contrast to the pervasiveness of the motif of domesticity is the theme of public and civic life, political progress or political institutions. This is not to say that subjects of a 'political' nature never feature in the magazines – they appear in three ways. First, discussion of 'issues' such as ecology, rape, incest, and homelessness invariably speaks to readers' 'personal' concerns about the quality of their family life or their children's future. Second, fairly frequent interviews with politicians, their wives, or leading public figures attend to their domestic setting and environment. Passions and convictions are discussed only in the context of an enquiry into the conflicting demands of job and family, a revelation of 'personality' through a discussion of taste in clothes, nightlife, friends. *Reality* is clearly the world of the family; that of civic virtue, the production of a collective life outside the family, political struggle, is quite unreal. To learn the truth about a politician is to learn the details of his or her domestic existence. Third, many of the weeklies now carry information about legal and political rights, more often than not presented as political goods for consumption. Policy, according to the magazine, is subject to the same laws of supply and demand as fashion. Laws on women and taxation are evaluated in the same manner as the respective merits of different kinds of washing-machine. Once again the forging of community cannot be understood as a public and civic process.

At the heart of the women's magazine lies the paradox that 'natural' femininity can be achieved only through hard labour. Most recently, this discourse of gender acquisition has had to negotiate with the problem of *feminism*. Chapter 5 discusses the various strategies of rejection and co-optation adopted by different magazines in more detail. Ours and others' readings of magazines crucially shows the discourse of gender that structures the genre to be intertwined with those of race, class, nation and age. Magazines acknowledge or construct social class differences in terms of 'lifestyle' or consumption, but consistently deny the existence of structured class or race conflict, offering only personal or moral resolutions to problems proceeding from these stratifications. Racial difference in particular is barely acknowledged in the contemporary British women's magazine. We are, to a woman, assumed to be white; when addressed at all, blackness is not understood as a political but an aesthetic category, taken on a par with the 'divisions' between women of dry and greasy hair, large and small breasts.

The feminine virtues of passive goodness, personal service to others and devotion to the domestic sphere by definition preclude women from productive activity in the public sphere. In the eighteenth century men read and circulated journals in the coffee-houses of London which also served as a distribution outlet for publishers. With the advent of magazines addressed to women, publishers developed means of distributing their product to the family home, to be read and circulated in the drawing-room. Women came to be conceived of as that phenomenon much beloved of the contemporary marketing man, the *final* consumer. The complete separation of coffee house from tea table, the public from the private is, of course, a myth. The writing of this myth continues throughout the nineteenth and twentieth centuries. Advertisers now conceive of women as primary consumers; their recycling of images of domestic bliss and eschewal of any civic or public values serves to maintain the continual circulation of that myth.

And consumption is, undeniably, pleasurable. We must take care not to overdraw the picture of a population sated on pure consumption, the distopian nightmare of the theorist of mass culture of the post-war era, which we go on to discuss in the following section. The pleasure of consumption and that of the fantasy of possibilities of infinite consumption is central to the success of the magazine form and we cannot afford simply to reject it as cultural brainwashing.

How, then, have social, literary and cultural theorists understood the function, effects and agency of popular or mass forms such as the women's magazine? Our discussion so far has not presupposed any specific theory about whether and how magazines work, whether and how they affect their readers or are material factors in the construction of a social reality. Nevertheless we have employed a number of concepts, among them 'gender relations', 'discourse' and 'ideology', which are compatible with some social theories and not with others, so already we have begun to pre-empt the question of 'how magazines work'. The following section offers a review and assessment of a variety of theoretical frameworks that might seem appropriate to the analysis of women's magazines and an outline of our own 'preferred' reading of the workings of mass culture in so far as it illuminates our study here.

Part two: theories of text and culture

A range of theoretical traditions and methodologies have been or might be used to provide an account of the history and construction of the women's magazine. Some of these theories originate in political theory and sociology, others proceed from literary and cultural studies. One of our preoccupations in the development of this book was the tensions and difficulties that such a meeting produces, made clear in the different traditions from which our own interest and work in the women's magazines stemmed. Our purpose here is to discuss the relative merits of the perspectives we have found useful, to evaluate the small amount of existing material on the women's magazine and to elucidate the theoretical concepts and methodological approach we employ in our subsequent analysis.

Mass culture

Theories of mass culture traditionally contrast with those of popular culture in interpreting the former as the imposition of alien class values on an oppressed group and the latter as a more authentic expression of shared values from within the group. Neither formulation seems to us ultimately satisfactory as a means of designating the genre of the women's magazine. We can dismiss early, however, the suggestion that the women's magazine, at least in its contemporary mass-market form, can be understood as a form of authentic 'popular' culture produced by women solely in women's interest. The decision whether or not to designate it as another aspect of an oppressive 'mass culture', at least as mass culture is presently conceived, is more difficult.

The most influential theorists of 'mass culture' have been members of the Frankfurt School, the small body of social and cultural philosophers who, during their exile in the United States from Nazi Germany between 1933 and 1949, provided the backbone of the Institute for Social Research. Shaped by reaction to the horrors of fascism, which was distinguished, of course, by unprecedented success in mobilising the masses, Frankfurt school theory as expounded by writers such as Theodor Adorno and Max Horkheimer views capitalism, despite its ostensible conflict with fascism, as reliant on the same strategies in securing mass acquiescence and uniformity to achieve its ends. Mass culture 'impresses the same stamp on everything', forming a 'filter' through which people view the world prior to their experience of it (Adorno and Horkheimer, 1977, p. 349). Although mass culture and art are both bought and sold as commodities, a truly transformative art can transcend market relations, refusing assimilation into bourgeois reality.

For Adorno and Horkheimer the working classes under capitalism learn acquiescence at work, the rhythms of their lives dictated by technology and management. Denied the creative pleasure of production, they can only perform the same acts of passivity in their leisure culture. As should be clear from this account, Frankfurt School theory concerns itself largely with 'mass' experience in the context of paid labour and industrial capitalism, rarely turning its attention to *women* as consumers of mass culture. The analysis interests us, however, because its influence can be clearly seen in some feminist criticism of the women's magazine. In her influential feminist manifesto, *The Female Eunuch*, Germaine Greer expands on Adorno and Hork-heimer's identification of the degradation of 'love' into 'romance' under mass culture, to point to romance's place in the continuing oppression, humiliation and defeat of women. For Adorno and Horkheimer, the downgrading of love is one symptom of a wider process of class domination directed toward the production of political quietism among the working classes: for Greer, romance is pivotal in the oppression of a different class, a sex class of women.

Greer's argument is structurally similar to that of the Frankfurt School. Ideology works by strategies of distortion, through the imposition of false consciousness. She looks forward to the retrieval of an authentic eroticism, unsullied by the stamp of mass culture's reductionism. With reference to the romance's primary signifier, the kiss, she concludes that an understanding of the 'mystical kiss of the romance . . . more properly . . . as orgasm' is misguided: 'What happens in the romantic view of sex is that the orgasm comes to signify a kiss, not vice versa' (Greer, 1971, p. 184). Mass culture, then, dictates how we experience desire. Authentic sexuality (orgasm) is supplanted by romance (the kiss). Naturally, material sexual relations have a part in this analysis, as do material social relations under capitalism for the

Frankfurt School. Real life does not match up to the desires produced by romance, for heterosexual relations are more commonly experienced as boredom and brutality rather than wine and roses. But an understanding of (romantic) ideology as false consciousness results in Greer's final rejection of women as political agents in favour of anger at their willing victimage. Her sympathy comes to lie with the men who treat with contempt the servile woman who has swallowed such transparent lies (Greer, 1971, p. 95, 183, 288). Here, too, Greer's analysis resonates with that of the Frankfurt School where the exposure of capitalist duplicity engenders contempt for or despair at working-class credulity. Implicitly, then, social analysts, intellectuals, feminist theorists alone can see social reality, sex and class relations, as it is and see it whole.

There are metaphysical and epistemological difficulties in this position which later refinements of the theory of ideology and mass culture have attempted to solve: Is it really defensible to see 'the masses' as the victims of brainwashing? And from what ground outside of the prison of ideology can the intellectual's interpretation be validated? Human agency except on the part of a manipulative and self-seeking ruling class of capitalists or men is erased. Crucially, this formulation of mass culture seriously underestimates the amount of conflict endemic in social existence – things simply do not go as smoothly as the analysts predict (Abercrombie *et al.*, 1980, p. 189). Theories of 'socialisation' postulate people as passive receivers of pre-set ideas, values and roles. How, then, is it that, even with the knowledge of contradictory desires and conflicting values, political action may not take place? Conflict exists *within* as well as *between* subjects. Readers of the women's magazine may be able to identify quite clearly the contradictions inherent in the text's image of the 'ideal' woman, indeed they frequently point to the impossibility of the 'superwoman' whose competence extends across home, work and sexuality, but this does not, on the whole, propel them into taking action to resist or reject the institutions that endorse such representations. Here, then, it seems we need a more sophisticated account of the human subject's relation to social and cultural images than that of passive enslavement. It is, we suggest, through contemporary theories of ideology and discourse that such an account becomes possible.

Ideology and discourse

Specification of what we mean by 'ideology' and 'discourse' has been the most difficult and divisive problem for us in our collaborative composition of this book. Both terms are inflected differently in different disciplines, and are contested from different political standpoints. For social and literary theorists, we suggest, ideology is used in three, sometimes mutually exclusive, ways. First, it refers to a coherent and systematic body or set of ideas about the social world and social relations. 'Pacifism', 'liberalism', 'marxism' and 'feminism' might then be understood as ideologies. Second, and more technically, 'ideology' is used, specifically for marxists, to designate a particular aspect of social reality. Marx distinguishes economic relations, the material and fundamental 'base' of the social order, from the relations engendered through law, political institutions, culture, social relations and ideology, the 'superstructure' which provides a means of ordering and representing economic and social relations to the society that lives within them (Marx, 1859, p. 389). Crucially, changes in the economic base *determine* those in the superstructure. Hence, ideology is always dictated by dominant material interests. Third, ideology is, for many marxists, not merely one element of the superstructure, but rather a *meta*-superstructural force, which conditions and shapes other superstructural elements. Ideology works to stabilise and legitimate the economic base. Most importantly, it is to be distinguished from *scientific* representations of the economic relations which engender a superstructure. While science lays bare, or attempts to lay bare, reality, ideology serves to disguise and mystify it. This normative and efficacious reading of ideology has been employed in distinct and contrasting ways. For Lenin and his most sophisticated interpreter, Louis Althusser, ideology is a necessary and inescapable feature of any viable society. For others, such as Georg Lukács and Antonio Gramsci, ideology is essentially mystificatory, functioning to mask inequality and injustice: social transformation should be directed toward the production of an ideology-free future.

Feminist theorists have always taken the concept of ideology very seriously: ideas, norms, values, representations of gender difference exercise considerable influence, perhaps even more so than economic inequity, in maintaining women's subordination.

Feminist analyses of 'the ideology of femininity' provide an illuminating and impressive body of research, cutting across the boundaries between social sciences, history, literary and cultural studies. However, a viable account of the relation between an analysis of gender ideology and that of class ideology remains a contested area for feminists and marxists alike.

Some theorists assume that men have interests in oppressing women analogous to their class interests: it is in the interests of all men to exploit women's labour or women's sexuality (Delphy, 1984; Dworkin, 1982). Thus, the ideology of femininity works to mystify relations of exploitation and oppression between men and women, to legitimate male domination. Gender relations, here, operate independently of class relations and hence the marxist principle that relations of *production* alone (excluding domestic labour, sexual services, and parenting) generate and explain all forms of social relation. On the other hand, it might be argued that the interests of capitalism are served by the oppression of women through ideology. The naturalising of women's domestic labour and of 'motherhood' ensures the reproduction and maintenance of both bourgeois and proletariat classes: antagonism between men and women in the home can deflect attention from fundamental class antagonism in the workplace. Gender relations may then be dependent on class relations. Either way, in orthodox marxist analysis gender relations are superstructural or epiphenomenal, not fundamental to a social formation.

In contrast with both these positions we argue that the historical emergence of capitalist class formation is inextricably bound up with the emergence of particular definitions of masculinity and femininity, in turn tied to those of race and nation. Class relations, in other words, are not simply defined by relations of production in the factory or other capitalist workplace; they are also structured and anchored by antagonistic gender relations. We insist that gender relations *are* antagonistic and, moreover, not merely functional for a class formation. 'Femininity' has been used as that against which 'man' defines himself in societies of all stripes – feudal, agrarian, slave and class based. Gender distinctions have generated, and been seen as crucial for, social order in pre- and post-capitalist societies alike. Of course, in different societies, femininity and masculinity, though always constructed in opposition, will be accorded different meanings and content.

Our argument is that the conditioning is not all one way – we cannot say that the distinctive meanings of masculinity and femininity we identify in women's magazines are accounted for by the exigencies of modern classes alone. The making of modern class antagonism is as much conditioned by the making of modern gender antagonism as vice versa.

In this section we consider a number of distinct accounts of 'ideology' which have been suggestive for feminists in explaining the oppression of women and which we consider important for an understanding both of the women's magazines' complicity in, and capacity for resistance to, this oppression. We begin with what might be termed 'the dominant ideology thesis', well exemplified in the work of the Frankfurt School. Dominant ideology might be understood as a set of beliefs about and representations of social *definition* reality which serve the interests of a ruling class, imposed more or less intentionally on subordinate groups in order to avert dissent or revolt. There are several problems with this account, not least the inference of 'brainwashing' techniques we outlined earlier in relation to the concept of mass culture. How, in any case, do we measure people's subscription to or rejection of ideological 'false consciousness'? Quantitative sociological research itself (in the form of questionnaires and so forth) is notoriously inclined to mould responses toward the production of unambiguous belief statements couched in a terminology already designated by the researcher. More open-ended interview and ethnographic methods indicate that people hold very shifting, ambiguous, and even downright contradictory 'views', and that they are conscious of a variety of possible ways of looking at and understanding the world. Our own work with readers of magazines supports this.

In our analysis we have not abandoned the notion of ideology. We do think it has advantages over certain kinds of 'discourse theory', for reasons we outline in more detail later, but specifically in that it addresses the relations between different kinds of power – discursive, economic and social. However, we would argue that the assumptions of the 'dominant ideology thesis' – that ideology is unitary, and that it is explicable solely by reference to class interests – must both be rejected. Certainly, it is difficult to establish from a reading of numerous magazine texts, or from research into readers' beliefs and values, what the dominant ideology of femininity actually says. Is it that women are properly subordinate to men? Clearly, this *is* an insistent image. Women are most frequently understood as acting in the service of men, as secretaries, cooks, mothers and wives. On the other hand, women's magazines devote considerable space and energy to asserting the intrinsic and equal value of the feminine sphere. They are also much addicted to visual and verbal images of powerful women in square-shouldered suits carrying briefcases and hailing taxis, leaving their men standing. Women's magazines contain, within single issues and between different titles, many competing and contradictory notions of femininity.

In response to these difficulties inherent in interpreting ideology as a coherent belief system imposed on naive oppressed groups, theorists have attended to the structuring of experience and appearance in order to explain why people believe what they do (Sayer, 1979; Mepham, 1979). A useful analogy here is with a physical phenomena like the rainbow. In one sense rainbows are illusory in a way that the chair I am sitting on is not. Nevertheless if I see a rainbow, which I might accept is not 'really there', it is not because I have defective perception, rationality, or consciousness. I see a rainbow because that is the way the physical world looks, and science can tell me why. In the capitalist world inequality looks just, exploitation looks like fair exchange, and social theories like marxism can tell me why. Under patriarchy, the sexual double standard looks natural, housework seems not to be like other forms of work, and feminism can tell me why. A difficulty remains, however. This account postulates an ultimate reality, the appearance of which has been distorted, but which the analyst or the scientist can explain. In the case of the rainbow, philosophers of physics cannot ultimately agree about what is really there: in the case of social oppression, philosophers of social science have hardly begun to enquire about what is really there in the case of inequality and injustice (Chalmers, 1982; Benton, 1981).

Rather than understanding ideology as residing in 'people's heads' in the form of a belief system, or out in the objective world, as appearances, structuralist theorists have come to argue that it is best understood as inhering in discourses, or in texts – books, films, magazines, and so on. Louis Althusser's late essay 'Ideology and Ideological State Apparatuses', has been taken as a starting point for this understanding of ideology as discourse. For

Althusser, although ideology is generated from the deep logical structures of the mode of production, it is produced and manifested through human subjects. Whereas the analyses of ideology we have met so far take it that the human subject is a 'given' upon which ideology acts to brainwash, hoodwink, or mislead through the presentation of spurious appearances as reality, Althusser and subsequent discourse theorists such as Michel Foucault reject this dualism between subject and world. We understand and experience ourselves as individuals with unity of consciousness, rationality, will and so on, only because we are 'hailed' as such by ideology. Our subjectivity is given content – proletarian, female, bourgeois, black – by virtue of being positioned within a social and political formation that seems to 'recognise' us as such through ideological state apparatuses such as the family, education, the church, and the mass media. Behind them stand the coercive or 'repressive' state apparatuses of police, army, legal system, and state punishment. 'Reality', then, is primarily shaped by concepts and categories of *language*. Central to Althusser's method is the rejection of the idea that the *concepts* of Marx's work are to be judged by reference to an independently existing *empirical reality* they might be taken to describe (Benton, 1984, p. 38).

It is precisely this line of thought that has led to some of the most significant developments of, and departures from, Althusser's work (Macdonnell, 1986, pp. 60–81). 'Neo-Althusserian' discourse theorists point out that he remains committed to the idea of ideology as *disguise*, representing scientific method as the only means to get behind the veil of appearance. Ultimately, we must ask: 'What is there to "reality" except for language?' It is only within language, already structured by ideology, that we can seek to provide an account of what is 'really' going on in capitalist or patriarchal society. This kind of linguistic 'determinism' seems to substitute one form of victimisation for another. An image of a naïve proletariat hoodwinked by a nefarious bourgeoisie is replaced only by that of the human subject trapped by a web of linguistic structures (Barrett, 1980, pp. 86–93; J. Thompson, 1984, pp. 96–98). Agency becomes another linguistic illusion.

Although Althusser's original essay poses problems for feminists in its assertion that ideological state apparatuses function to uphold the capitalist class order paying no attention to the question of gender 'interpellation' in the production of the human subject, feminists have adopted and adapted his argument. If reality is constructed or, at least, known through discourses, then there is no reason to take class division as the primary and determining social division. We can acknowledge, then, that the structuring discourse of gender (and other differences such as race) is every bit as powerful as the discourse of class. Indeed psychoanalytic theory would suggest that gender difference is the most basic and fundamental social and psychic structure. The turn to language is crucial here: for feminist psychoanalysis, the origins of gender ideology lie in the very acquisition of language (Mitchell and Rose, 1982, p. 31; Cameron, 1985, p. 20). Language and meaning themselves are predicated on difference: the child who acquires language does so by learning to recognise difference (from the mother), a difference signified by the phallus, or lack of it.

Phenomenological sociology has also been critical of acceptance of the 'facts of experience' as having any privileged status and come to focus on the means by which people *construct* such facts – how they account for and come up with 'descriptions' of their social reality (Garfinkel, 1969; Stanley and Wise, 1983, pp. 138ff). On the whole, the question as to why we have certain categories, concepts and understandings of 'experience' rather than others has tended to be neglected, in favour of studying the rules and procedures which govern their application and employment. Crucially, questions of the distribution of *power* have been shelved. Why is it that some social groups are able to make and insist on definitions that are oppressive to other groups? Why, for example, are men able to dismiss behaviour that a feminist wishes to define as 'sexual harassment' as 'just a joke' or an act of 'chivalry'? Or, more importantly for our purposes, why is it that the popularity and ubiquity of the women's magazine does not make its valorisation of the 'feminine' a discourse of 'power' in contemporary society?

There are clear parallels between the contention that ideology (for Althusser) or discourse (for Foucault) constructs human subjects and the literary critical concept of the 'implied reader'. Sociology and the study of social identity here collapses into textual criticism. The study of the 'implied reader' constructed in and by the text of advertising, novels, newspapers, legal speech, or television *is* the study of social actors. The fact that different texts, or genres, construct different implied readers can be taken as evidence of the split and fragmentary nature of human subjectivity (as opposed to the Cartesian 'cogito' which postulates the self as undivided and indivisible entity or locus of experience, cognition and rationality). This formulation of subjectivity as radically split resonates with both feminist experience and theory: women are addressed as sensible mothers of three by one magazine, single pursuers of the ultimate sexual fix by another, as feminists by a third. In its own terms though it cannot account for our negotiations with or struggles against these conflictual positions. If we confine our social analysis to textual interpretation we neglect the area of readers' resistance to the subjectivities postulated by the magazine texts. Moreover, such an account of textual subjectivity alone cannot explain differences of power and effect exercised by different texts in different contexts – why, for example, do more women read *Cosmopolitan* than *Spare Rib*? or, why does *Cosmopolitan* appear less interesting or affecting to the reader in her early thirties than it did in her early twenties?

It is here that the inadequacies of a notion of 'discourse' as opposed to that of 'ideology' are clear. Discourse theory at its best insists on the *institutional* coherence and implementation of discursive categories such as 'masculinity', 'femininity', 'madness', 'criminality' in the process of securing social dominance. At its weakest it can only trace the tangled fissures of power in a complex social formation, at the expense of an account as to why particular discourses or representations come to dominate and not others. For Michel Foucault discourses are tied to, indeed structure, *practices* – the incarceration of 'criminals', the treatment and designation of 'the mad'. We can easily extend this thesis to embrace the way particular definitions of femininity structure particular social roles and practices for women – housewife, nurse, professional invalid, prostitute. For the purposes of analysis, if we tie together discourse, institution and practice, the boundaries between one discourse and another remain fairly clear. But in any one social phenomenon, such as the women's magazine, elements of several discourses will be employed – those of psychotherapy, medicine, fiction, photography, humanism, and so forth. Properly speaking, the 'discourse of the women's magazine' employs and carries elements of a variety of discourses. However, such density of reference and discursive variety does not imply that the women's magazine does not ultimately work to secure male dominance or women's oppression. Just the reverse in fact. We would argue that it is precisely such mobility and complexity that enables the magazine to maintain its hegemonic position in women's lives. In our analysis of a single phenomenon, the women's magazine, we try to be precise in our terminology. By referring to the 'discourse of the women's magazine' we intend the term in its widest sense, tying together varieties of discourses, practice, and institution, the specific conjunction of which at different historical moments serves to produce and contribute to an ideology of femininity that, contradictory as it is, confirms relations of gender and class dominance in the social reality we inhabit.

Semiotics

It is a simple point that there is nothing in nature which dictates that a magazine should be called a 'magazine'. Semiotics, the study (or science) of signs, offers an account of why this is the case, in its insistence that words do not have intrinsic meanings, but signify concepts in an arbitrary (though not random) differential fashion. Beyond this, however, semiotics takes from the pioneering linguist, Ferdinand Saussure, the assumption that language has a determining, rather than purely functional, role in our perception and understanding of the world. For example, a variety of terms exist that seemingly 'designate' something we might call 'reading matter': book, pamphlet, magazine, journal, newspaper, and so on. I recognise a 'book' by virtue of its difference from these other concepts, not because of some set of fixed characteristics that mark it as such. Saussure's point is that this difference is not natural: my awareness of it is engendered by the existence of differentiating terms in language. Native speakers of a language which lacked this distinction would not 'see' or articulate this difference.

Further, semioticians point to the social or mythic meanings of linguistic signifiers such as the word 'book'. Semiotics meets ideology theory in the work of Roland Barthes, specifically in his influential essay 'Myth Today'. Here, Barthes designates a second order system of meaning, whereby the linguistic sign (the conjunction of the signifier and signified) itself becomes a signifier, clustered with other 'mythic' concepts or signifieds (status, civilisation, love, enmity, etc.). Umberto Eco, in response to sceptical empiricists, points out that a seemingly simple signifier like a 'button' has a wealth of meanings beyond designating its functional usage: it can be a sign of civilisation ('savages' do not have buttons), of status, wealth, membership of social groups, fashion culture (the fly-buttons on a pair of Levi-501s) (Eco, 1984, pp. 110 ff). A button, then, is far from being a 'knob or disc sewn to garment to fasten it by passing through buttonhole' as the *Concise Oxford Dictionary* defines it. Language is understood by semiotics as a system of signs (the conjunction of signifier and signified) which mediates experience. Everything in culture, then, has significatory potential and can be subjected to the semiotician's 'reading'.

Myth, like ideology in Althusserian usage, is described as offering a way of making sense of the world and one in which reality is understood as constructed rather than reflected. We face here the same problem as that outlined earlier with regard to ideology theory: that is, 'who is to say what is real and what is apparent?' or 'who is to say what this means?' The ambiguity runs deep in Barthes's interpretations of cultural icons such as the advertisement and the film-star in his *Mythologies* essays because of his declared commitment to indeterminacy of meaning. If anything can mean potentially anything, how are we to account for the fixing of particular mythic associations in culture, if not by the invocation of an extra-textual determining structure of power relations?

Barthes's insistence on 'inter-textual' reading to some extent resolves this difficulty. Our understanding of a text is always informed and structured by our prior understanding and use of other texts. With respect to the women's magazine, this returns us to the question of an 'implied reader'. A moment's thought reveals that the reader implied in a particular text – a year's issue of *Woman*, for example – does not coincide with any embodied social person. The principle of inter-textuality suggests that embodied person's social identity is nevertheless textually constructed, taking the term 'text' in its broadest sense and taking into account that embodied persons inhabit a world which consists of a multiplicity of texts.There is no *pure Woman* reader; subjects' reading of *Woman* will be informed by their consumption of a complex matrix of other texts: from romance fiction to the Brontes, *The Times* to the tabloids, soap opera to Shakespeare. However, if reality is structured by language, and difference is central in fixing meaning, then gender difference takes on a quite distinct appearance from the mere biological distinctions of sexual difference with which traditional social theory works. The exact content of masculinity and femininity are not fixed, but linguistically shaped. In turn, femininity comes to signify a multitude of things at the level of myth. Semiotics has joined with psychoanalysis in some important contemporary theories of gender, which have nevertheless attracted criticism because they make of gender *the* paradigm for difference, only shifting the emphasis from biological to psychic origins. That is, they understand 'language' as a deep psychic matter, rather than social one.

Nevertheless, by far the most significant and perceptive body of work on women's magazines has been developed under the theoretical aegis of Barthesian semiotics, the structuralism of Althusser, and especially the social theory of Antonio Gramsci, in the shape of materials from the Birmingham Centre for Contemporary Cultural Studies. The work of Angela McRobbie, Janice Winship and Sandra Hebron seeks to mesh a semiotic awareness of structure and sign with a marxist analysis of social hegemony (McRobbie, 1978; Winship, 1978; Hebron, 1983). Hegemonic order, as defined by the Italian communist Antonio Gramsci, secures consent from subordinate classes to the rule of the dominant through the mobilisation and naturalisation of the values and culture of the dominant class (Gramsci, 1988, p. 324). Gramsci's own preoccupation lay in outlining the work communism had to do if it was to defeat capitalism and secure its own ideological hegemony in mid-1930s Italy. More recently, cultural studies has employed his terminology in the attempt to ascertain why subordinate classes fail to secure hegemony (Hall and Jefferson, 1976, pp. 38ff). This Gramscian perspective has helped to contain the semiotic nightmare of endlessly proliferating meaning in the interpretation of mass or popular forms such as the women's magazine by providing an account of the means by which some readings come to be *preferred* over others.

Stuart Hall points to the fact that the transformation of meanings at the connotative level (or Barthes's so-called second order) is an *active* process. While any one cultural text offers a multiplicity of meanings to its reader, ultimately not just *any* meaning can or will be drawn from it. Readings are 'structured in dominance', offering a pattern of 'preferred' options in line with the 'preferred' institutional, political and ideological order (Hall, 1980, p. 134). This preferred reading legitimates existing inequalities, exerting a normative influence on the consumer, *but* it is possible for the reader to reject it. This might explain, then, feminists' sense, in their relation to the women's magazine, of reading to some extent 'against the grain'. We might add to this the complication that texts that assert their oppositional status in relation to a dominant order, such as *Spare Rib*, offer a different preferred reading, a feminist one.

   ✦ Semiotic theory encourages critics to focus on and emphasise formal features of text and meaning. In contrast to simply scrutinising texts for ideological content, or enquiring into their resonance with deep psychic structures, semiotic analysis explores the arrangement and deployment of contents as well as *what they say*. Advertisements for perfume in a women's magazine acquire their cultural significance (frequently the 'mythic' suggestion of luxury, pleasure, release, romance) by virtue of their juxtaposition with other materials such as articles about child abuse, other advertisements for instant sauce mix or sanitary towels, recipes for coq au vin, etc. The physical appearance of a sign is crucial to its meaning, also. The 'serious' significance of the problem-page in a teenage girl's magazine is indicated by the fact that it is printed in black and white rather than in full colour (McRobbie, 1978, p. 29).

   This analysis extends also to the cultural significance of *which* text we display as an indicator of our status and selfhood in society. Texts, like other cultural artifacts such as shoes, have social meanings. Simply to read women's magazines, as opposed to another kind of text such as a novel or a newspaper, is a choice that supposedly indicates something about its reader, just like the choice between wearing flat lace-ups or stilettos. Second, to read one title rather than another – to choose, say, *Vogue* over *Woman's Own* – defines the reader even more closely, as a participant, in the publisher's terms, in one lifestyle rather than another. Further, each magazine offers its readers a particular way of making sense of the world. The magazine has a dual focus, referring both to the world outside itself, and to itself in the world. 'To prove that *Company* isn't afraid to tackle the biggies, this month's Loose Talk asks what you think about religion . . .' (*Company*, December 1988).

Pleasure, textuality, liberation

Feminist critics interpret the formal features of mass cultural forms addressed to women not only in terms of the meaning and construction of signification, but in terms of the way that different textual forms resonate, or not, with female desire, with the shape and texture of women's lives, with that difficult entity termed women's 'pleasure'. Michèle Mattelart, for example, comments on the congruence between the repetitive, open-ended form of women's popular culture (soap-opera and the magazine in particular) and the rhythmic, cyclical nature of women's lives. Cyclical temporalities are disparaged and devalued in masculinist cultures which privilege teleology and closure, thus alienating women from dominant culture; only in popular culture are feminised patterns of temporality and narrative indulged (Mattelart, 1986, p. 16). In an analogous argument, Tania Modleski identifies soap-opera's resistance to closure and privileging of 'private' domestic rhythms over public event as congruent with women's pleasure (Modleski, 1984, p. 111).

It is important to resist claiming that cyclical or open-ended form is *essentially* a female quality, rather than a culturally learned distinction of gender. However, we would argue that the formal elements of the women's magazine are fundamental to its commercial success and the kinds of pleasure it offers its reader. One of the most striking features of the magazine is its heterogeneity, juxtaposing different genres, mixing print and photography, offering a range of characterised 'voices'. It does not demand to be read from front to back, nor in any particular order, and its fragmentary nature is admirably suited to women's habitual experience in modern society of the impossibility of concentrated attention (distracted by calls on their time from men, children, the conflicting demands of work and home). The magazine's periodicity, its regular appearance once a month or once a week, allows both open-endedness (continuing series or features) and routinisation, confirming its readers in a way of life where leisure, like work, is regulated in time (Beetham, 1990).

We take seriously these arguments about the congruence of the magazine form with the nature of women's experience and the importance of exploring formal elements in order to explain the specific pleasures it offers its readers. Yet a recognition of this pleasure does not lessen, nor is it lessened by, an acknowledgement of the magazine's role in perpetuating women's oppression. An attention to the 'pleasure' of the magazine must, however, challenge and supplement the account offered by the theories of ideology and mass culture we outlined earlier. Psychoanalytic method has come to dominate accounts of textual pleasure in literary and cultural studies and with it the presumption that pleasure is always already sexual, that sexuality is the paradigmatic form of pleasure.

Roland Barthes's *The Pleasure of the Text* differentiates between what he terms the text of pleasure (*plaisir*) and that of bliss (*jouissance*). Barthes values reading pleasure in terms of the demands made upon the reader for *active* engagement with the text. Narrative pleasure is analogous to the pleasure of male orgasm, a journey that explores uncertainty and anxiety but is finally offered relief in the form of narrative closure. The agony and disruption of sexual excitement is embarked upon in order to reach satisfaction. In contrast, 'bliss', an unsatisfactory translation of the French term 'jouissance' with its wider connotations of an active, free, but crisis-ridden dissolution of subjectivity and ecstasy, might be understood as a peculiarly feminine form of pleasure/orgasm (Irigaray, 1981, pp. 101ff). Free of narrative event as such, what 'happens' in the text of bliss happens in the reader's engagement with language itself, with indeterminacy of meaning, without crisis-point or closure (Barthes, 1976, pp. 11-13).

Clearly, Barthes's coinage and the focus of other psychoanalytic and semiotic theorists such as Julia Kristeva are directed toward disclosing the disruptive effects of the modernist literary text. If popular forms, such as the women's magazine, fit anywhere in this analysis it is in Barthes's category of the 'prattling text', employing an 'unweaned language: imperative, automatic, unaffectionate' (Barthes, 1983, p. 404). Barthes's characterisation of the prattling text is here reminiscent of Herbert Marcuse's dismissal of the texts of popular culture, which 'In [their] immediacy and directness . . . impede conceptual thinking; thus, impede thinking' (Bennett, 1982, p. 44; Marcuse, 1968). Raymond Williams also comments, specifically with regard to women's magazines, on the imperative and didactic quality of popular culture: 'who can doubt . . . that here, centrally, is *teaching*' (Williams, 1966, p. 15).

For Barthes, then, *jouissance* in reading stems from readerly *production* and cannot be generated by the prattling text of pleasure, where didacticism and imperatives impede the reader's participation and action. The paradigmatic form of pleasure here is, then, production. This raises two issues. First, we would point out with respect to magazines that 'reading' a magazine involves a number of pleasures of action and participation – reading ahead, reading back to front, creating one's own narrative. Second, the analysis of pleasure as production is unreasonably narrow, dismissing as 'inauthentic', or inherently conservative, the pleasure of consumption rather than production, of affirmation rather than negation. In contrast, Judith Williamson argues for the pleasures of consumption, specifically for women, although she is alive to the political limits of such pleasure. The pleasure of *choice* in consumption is evidently a partial illusion: 'we don't choose what is available for us to choose between in the first place' (Williamson, 1986, p. 230). However, she recognises that 'Consuming products does give a thrill, a sense of both belonging and being different, charging normality with the excitement of the unusual' (p. 13). Marx's analysis of the fetishism engendered in and from commodity production provides a framework for the understanding of such excitement in Williamson's work, but she insists that such pleasure should not be dismissed as simply a debilitating effect of capitalist culture. Williamson's account of popular culture captures what is obviously an important aspect of the pleasure of the magazine – not the *jouissance* of engagement with difficult language, nor the relief of narrative closure, but the excitement of consumption, both the actual consumption of the magazine as commodity and the potential consumption of the commodities it promotes in advertising (Lovell, 1987, p. 16).

Tania Modleski points to the proximity of pleasure and fantasy, complicating an interpretation of the satisfactions of popular culture as pure commodity fetishism. Romantic and gothic fiction, she suggests, resonate with feminine hysteria and paranoia. The manifest content of the Harlequin romance, the pursuit of heterosexual union, conceals and represses deep anxiety and ambivalence in relation to rape, validating the desire for power and revenge (Modleski, 1984, p. 48). Ultimately, we would argue, Modleski understands women's consumption of popular fiction as a form of addiction, the point at which pleasure dissolves into pain. Valerie Walkerdine's discussion of *Bunty* stories suggests that they speak to fantasies already present in the child's subconscious – the desire for the good parent in particular (Walkerdine, 1984, p. 168). In a different context, Frederic Jameson has challenged the Frankfurt School account of mass culture to claim that the texts of popular culture manage 'dangerous and protopolitical impulses . . . initially awakened within the very text that seeks to still them'. Despite their immediate ideological function these impulses 'resonate a universal value' in that they stem from deep unconscious structures (Jameson, 1981, pp. 287–8). Jameson's preoccupation here is with the management of class conflict in film but his attention to the political signification of unconscious desire is surely suggestive for a feminist reading of popular culture's management of gender conflict.

There is a paradox, however, in Jameson's attempt to incorporate a psychoanalytic and marxist perspective in relation to popular culture. For the psychoanalyst, the deep unconscious structures that generate desire and pleasure are pre-given and untransformable. By contrast, for materialist marxism and feminism, social and political transformation would enable the transformation of desire and pleasure. The theorists we have discussed in this section extend the possibility of producing new and differently structured fantasies which might negotiate desire and conflict without reconfirming gender inequity – fantasies which do not, for example, encourage little girls to displace their anger onto imaginary others ('bad people') or to direct it back upon themselves. We might use female desire to build an alternative feminist future and aesthetic. Nevertheless, the prospects for such psychic transformation seem slim, if the conflicts and desires in question are as deep-seated, the family drama as universal, as psychoanalytic theory would suggest.

In response to this preoccupation with negative ideological effect, which has spawned a large body of fault-finding political criticism of art, literature, popular culture, sexual practice and social relations, some theorists protest the radical and liberationist potential of pleasure itself. A feminist critique of patriarchy's control of women through sexuality must not be allowed to foreclose on a recognition of female sexual pleasure, despite its proximity to sexual danger (Vance, 1984; Weeks, 1985). Should feminists and left-wing critics attend to the progressive possibilities that inhere in a consumer culture? (Lovibond, 1989). Some might argue that a heterogeneity of style and culture enables the expression of alternative and multiple sexualities and subjectivities.

This argument rests on a belief in the triumph of subjectivity over social determinism. The dominant order attempts to impose tidy social identities on us, to tame our desires, to socialise our behaviour. Eroticism, however, dissolves social identity, boundaries between self and other, takes us beyond the realm of social control. In resistance to the dominant order's attempt to impose uniformity through the reduction of all social being to the dictates of the commodity, individual subjects seize upon the commodity as a symbol of transgression and transformation. Cosmetics and clothes can be employed in anti-social ways, resisting the 'preferred reading' of gender-coded dress or conventional models of beauty. The cultural products which engender or trigger *jouissance* cannot, then, be condemned out of hand as the bearers of a repressive ideology.

This position is fundamentally opposed to the traditional philosophical pursuit of control – the Kantian validation of *plaisir*, cool contemplative pleasure, against the oppressive irrationalism of a *jouissance* that dissolves selfhood (Mercer, 1986a, p. 58). The celebration of transgression and that of its opposite, the rational unity of the subject, remain twin central and contradictory motifs of western philosophy. Under the influence of Freudian theories of subjectivity, some feminist theorists have turned to a celebration of the dissolution of self-identity as the exercise of feminine power. The striving for autonomy, unity, erectness (all central Enlightenment concepts) are understood as masculine qualities that are finally destructive and alienating, while feminine fluidity and non-self-identity offers the possibility of liberation from oppressive social structures and norms (Irigaray, 1981).

We might doubt, however, whether an understanding of pleasure as inherently disruptive of selfhood (even if the self is finally reintegrated through narrative closure/male orgasm) is exhaustive. There are pleasures which confirm personal identity and integrity rather than challenge. Familiarity, comfort, affirmation, integration, as women's magazines repeatedly prove, *are* pleasurable. The women readers of magazines we interviewed also pointed to another form of pleasure, that of knowledge or the pleasure of the critic. When talking about magazines, women endlessly, and delightedly, parody and mimic them, displaying their own literacy in and mastery of its generic conventions. Barthes mentions the critic's pleasure only briefly and disparagingly, dismissing it as a form of voyeurism. For us, this does not capture the importance of a sense of participation won from familiarity that marks readerly pleasure.

A second position that allies pleasure and liberation understands popular culture as the authentic product of working-class or female experience, which is, nevertheless, in capitalist society liable to be hijacked, distorted and sold back to its 'owners' as a commodity. Thus, football might be 'read' as a spontaneous expression of co-operative energy amongst the working class which has now been packaged, capitalised and made into a mass spectator (i.e. consumer) 'sport'. Carnival, now a best-selling commodity of the tourist and leisure industry, in its original setting and form may have acted as a vehicle for opposition to social hierarchy and for the expression of utopian images of power inversion (Bennett, 1986, p. 17).

Critics of this analysis point to the inherent weakness of an 'authentic' culture that can be so easily co-opted into commodity culture and to the intrinsic conservatism of an event such as carnival which challenges dominance one week in fifty-two and may in fact serve to reconfirm social position through the exploration of its opposite (just as the little girl clonking around in her mother's shoes 'learns' her own dependency rather than challenging the institution of parenthood or ideology of femininity) (Mercer, 1986a, p. 60). Further, we might note that neither the working class nor women have ever inhabited a cultural space free from the determinations of other classes, sexes, and cultures. Rather, cultures are forged in the context of class, race and gender relationships, antagonisms and alliances. Culture, then, is always contested and in process. The pleasures which women's magazines offer their readers are not simply liberating nor simply repressive but themselves participate in and contribute to this constant making and re-making of cultural definitions. Our historical analysis pursues this idea in detail.

Subjectivity and the gaze

The theories of textual pleasure we have so far outlined emphasise the pleasures of narrative (tension and release) and the pleasures of poetics (play and plurality). Evidently there are pleasures in the magazine form which are not encompassed in these accounts – visual pleasures, or what has been termed the pleasure of the *gaze*. Traditionally, women have been understood as the object of the gaze, which makes the case of the woman reader who is presumed to take pleasure in looking at the magazine model an interesting one (Mulvey, 1975–6; Kaplan, 1984; Holland, 1983; Gamman and Marshment, 1988).

Observation in western culture is clearly understood as a form of power, and the respective roles of observer and observed are as a result insistently metaphorised in western philosophy in terms of gender division. The scientist is masculine, the nature he observes feminine. Woman is object, man subject. As Jean-Paul Sartre recognised, however, the tragedy of becoming a subject, of adopting the position of the looker, is that the subject is always vulnerable to the possibility of becoming an object for others, of being looked at himself (*sic*) (Lloyd, 1984, p. 94). Psychoanalysis employs the Freudian concepts of voyeurism and fetishism to account for this gendered construction of subjectivity through the exercise of the gaze (Kaplan, 1984, p. 322). In both cases, however, the erotic component of the gaze is emphasised – it is, then, sexy to be masterful.

In the face of the vulnerability that Sartre identifies in this construction of a masterful selfhood, feminists have argued that social institutions and practices devote themselves to the maintenance and bolstering of men's subjectivity (Dworkin, 1982, p. 13). Man accrues to himself the privilege of being the one who looks through his exclusive control of property rights and the social institutions of science, medicine, art and culture. The corollary of this institutionalising of the gaze as male is that that which is looked *at* is feminised. For women the project of transcending objectification/feminisation and becoming subject/ masculine is fraught with difficulty, whereas for men to become lookers is to become properly masculine, to inhabit their 'natural' social identity. Objectification is never, even potentially, escapable for women. Women learn early to think of themselves as objects of the gaze and imaginatively to take up the masculine position in order to look at themselves as men might look at them (Berger, 1972, pp. 42–7). Men by contrast, notwithstanding Sartre's exposition of their existential tragedy, do not necessarily experience themselves as objects. Given modern social conditions and institutions, men are more liable to experience their subjectivity as intact, safe, and unified and to do so through the experience of objectifying women.

We cannot fail to be impressed by the fact that *all* the newsagents' shelves display images of women, from top-shelf pornography to 'special interest' magazines for car-owners, photographers, deep sea fishers and computer buffs. All magazines, including women's magazines, have pictures of women on the cover (Winship, 1987, p. 9). Given what has been said about the gendered nature of the gaze, what are we to make of this with regard to the women's magazine in particular?

Laura Mulvey's ground-breaking essay on Hollywood film argues that no other position than that of male looker is available to the film audience. Thus, women find themselves in the split position of looking at the women on the screen from a masculine subject position. In response to Mulvey's thesis, feminist critics have attempted to argue for the presence of a subversive *female* gaze (Gamman and Marshment, 1988). Might women have an independent relationship with women represented on screen? The most obvious relationship would be one of identification, with the strong, brave or witty female character. All too frequently of course such representations are enclosed in a narrative frame whereby female independence is defeated, through death or marriage. More boldly, Patricia Holland has argued that the 'page three' girl or topless model of the daily British tabloids extends to women readers an image of an independent sexuality that undercuts the dominance of a myth of romance, demonstrating the earning power of female sexuality (Holland, 1983). If we reject the assumption that women only look at women in terms of identification, however, we must entertain the possibility that the woman magazine reader's gaze may in fact be desirous. She may desire the woman represented, rather than to be *like* the woman. In other words to what extent do we wish to read the female gaze as lesbian? The proven failure of the 'male pin-up' in the women's magazine, experimented with in *Cosmopolitan*, would suggest that the female gaze must be interpreted either as the adoption of a masculine subject position in relation to the female image, or as an indicator of the continuing symmetry of the terms 'woman' and 'commodity', even for women themselves.

As we proceed with our historical analysis of women's magazines we shall have a great deal more to say on the matter of women's relationship to images of other women. Here we want simply to draw attention to a shift in the debate on women and the 'gaze' away from Mulvey's focus on formal technique and the circumstances of production in order to 'read off' the position of the reader in relation to any given visual 'text'. Later responses to Mulvey's argument have stressed the possibilities for reading and viewing in resistance to the 'preferred reading' produced through such formal and generic strategies. Lesbian desire, for example, can rarely be identified as inscribed as a possible 'reading' of a typical Hollywood film or a Mills & Boon romance. Nevertheless, women may project lesbian desire onto these texts. Moreover, they may be able to adopt more than one subject position in relation to the female image they are consuming, that split focus that John Berger identifies as characteristic of women's experience of subjectivity. It will be obvious that we would resist the assumption that readers are simply victims of the ideology inscribed in the texts they consume. Just as critics may reach different conclusions about the subject position constructed in and by a text according to the theoretical perspectives they bring to it, so readers will bring a variety of perspectives and knowledges to bear in their acquisition of pleasure in reading. However, such perspectives, we would suggest, are neither random, nor purely subjective.

The practice of reading

The body of social research into how, when and where readers, particularly women readers, read is to date surprisingly small

(Radway, 1987; Holland, 1975; Taylor, 1989; Frazer, 1987; Barker, 1989). Within the discipline of literary criticism, however, reader response theory has become increasingly sophisticated and significant (Fish, 1975; Iser, 1978; Jauss, 1982; Tompkins, 1980). For critics interested in the reading process the problem lies in relating their specific accounts of reading (made by the professional who is trained to read literary texts in particular ways), not just to the variety of different interpretations made possible by the text itself, to the different expectations and skills of a range of readers. Both Iser and Fish construct a prototypical, largely dehistoricised reader who embodies the critic's own engagement with the text. Jauss, in contrast, insists that the dominance of one reading of a text over another lies in the shifting 'horizon of expectations' possible in any one historical moment. In his concept of 'interpretative community' Fish also reaches toward a communal and historical account of the reading process, but in both cases the debate is conducted on an abstract rather than specific level. Moreover, reader response theory has in the main been developed in relation to the texts of 'high' culture and on the assumption that gender (along with most other social markers) is not a determining factor in the reading activity (Jacobus, 1986, pp. 83–6).

By contrast, social and cultural research on the practice of reading has focused on exploring the methods of reading employed by specific social groups. With regard to women's magazines, research has been confined to readings of women's and girls' magazines in the context of an exploration of ideology, discourse or semiotics. Such work has three points of reference: the text, a theoretical framework and methodology, and the critic's analytic reading. Ethnographic research shows that reading magazines is an important pastime in the daily lives of women and girls (McRobbie, 1978b), and cultural theorists attempt to determine the political and sociological significance of such texts in the acquisition of gender identity.

This focus necessarily demands an attention to circumstances or context of reading (or viewing or listening) – what Colin Mercer has called 'occasions of reading' (Mercer, 1986b, p. 184). The researcher into women's magazines must be aware of the different meanings that will emerge from any one title or text dependent on the conditions under which it is 'read': under the desk at school, in

the bath, on the train, over coffee, and so forth. More importantly, perhaps, reading in modern society is understood to be a
private and *solitary* pursuit and, it has been suggested, has
peculiarly strong connections with the construction of private
family life (the sphere of femininity) and the building of bourgeois
hegemony (Corrigan and Gillespie, 1977). Out of the many texts
available for readers' consumption in commodity culture, the
women's magazine is one of the few that is still, although not
always, read collectively. Women pensioners exchange magazines
and sections of magazines amongst themselves, schoolgirls read
Just Seventeen together on the bus.

Research into reading that draws on readers' own accounts of
their responses has concentrated on the process of interpretation –
the means by which readers make (or fail to make) meaning from
a text. A famous example is I. A. Richards's analysis of his
undergraduates' interpretations of poetry (Richards, 1929). Norman Holland interprets five students' responses to a short shory
by Faulkner, taking texts to be the transformation of a writer's
unconscious wishes and fantasies in orthodox psychoanalytic
fashion (Holland, 1975). Work such as this has been criticised
for being 'biassed', for eliciting responses that confirm the critic's
own theoretical perspective by posing certain 'tendentious' questions (Culler, 1983, p. 64). It is not, we would argue, the 'bias' that
is problematic here, but rather the unwillingness to recognise and
admit that no research can offer an 'objective' or 'universal'
account of its object. Readers' readings and their reported
experience are no more nor less authentic than that of the critic
or writer.

This does not mean, however, that reader research should be
discounted altogether. Talking to readers has proved invaluable in
this book, not least in revealing that no reader can or does occupy
the imaginary position of 'naive' or 'ideal' reader, produced in and
by the ideology of a single text. 'Ordinary' readers and critics
produce readings structured and shaped by social context and
shared cultural meanings. What reader research does offer is an
outline of the range of possible ways of reading and making sense
of texts and, perhaps more important, the limits and range of
discourses available to talk about them.

The work of Janice Radway in compiling and assessing the
responses of a specific group of women readers of romance novels

provides an important insight into these discursive limits. Questions designed to elicit interpretations of particular texts, she reports, were almost invariably responded to with descriptions of the pleasure of reading itself, particularly as an 'escape' from the living-room, television and family (Radway, 1987, p. 87). This interesting phenomenon has several possible implications for theorists of reader response. First, it may be that the kind of reading activity engaged in by critics is an acquirable skill not engaged in, in the normal course of events, by everyone. Second, it might mean that the process of making meaning goes on whenever a reader reads, but that it is not easy to articulate – that it goes on at some level of consciousness to which the researcher cannot gain access. Third, and most challenging of all, it may mean that the process of making meaning, or interpretation, is not the most important aspect of reading. Radway's respondents alert us to the possibility that the literary and formal aspects, even the content, of texts may not be their most important characteristic for readers.

However, this does not explain why women choose to read romantic fiction or women's magazines to 'escape' domestic pressures and enclosure, rather than a newspaper or Tolstoy. It is, then, crucially important to consider whether there are *specific* and *shared* pleasures for women in the magazine, as well as how reading and pleasure may differ from reader to reader. But there are complex methodological issues which mean that 'data' of this sort must be approached with caution. Traditional social science distinguishes between *raw data* and data which is interpreted, ordered and encoded by the social scientist. In our view (in line with other critics of traditional social science), this distinction cannot be sustained. Data gathered by social scientists is always already encoded. This is obviously the case in our own research, which largely took the form of recordings of groups of women talking about women's magazines. The accounts we have gathered are, of course, dictated by conventions of what it is possible to say about women's magazines, what one says to a researcher, how talk is conducted in a discussion group, during an interview, or when filling in a questionnaire.

Women's talk about magazines does, however, tell us about the discourses about magazines and the reading of magazines available in our culture. Experience is, then, constructed discursively and not irreducibly individual. This does not mean that there is no diversity within and between these discourses, from feminist political condemnation to feminist claims for community and support, from the representation of magazines as a source of information and education to the representation of them as vehicles for fantasy and 'escape'. These, and others, form a repertoire on which women are able to draw when they articulate their experience of magazines.

In our commitment to some form of sociological investigation into the varying means by which different women read and understand the magazine text, we are not committing ourselves to a simplistic picture of a unified subject determined by social, cultural and symbolic context. On the contrary, it is central to our argument that, although subjects characteristically invoke unity of consciousness or strive for it, they evidently hold split and fragmentary positions. Cultural texts and discourses are material factors in the construction of such fragmentary states of being and it is the researcher's responsibility precisely to attend to the contradiction and conflict that inheres in subjectivity.

We are committed, then, to the analysis of the *social* reader. Our method, however, is still based mainly upon our own readings of magazines, readings shaped by our social and historical circumstance. It is only in Chapter 5, when we turn to contemporary magazines, that we are able to draw upon other women's accounts of their reading to complement our own. The voices of women readers of the eighteenth- and nineteenth-century magazines are, unfortunately, not available to us. It may be that our engagement with texts *is*, as psychoanalysis predicts and describes, the exercise of unconscious desires and drives, but, if this is the case, we need a social account, an account of economic circumstance, political power, cultural hegemony, to explain why. Our readings attempt this wider historical explanation.

We are interested above all in the interaction between real historical women and the genre of magazines for women. We embarked on this project with the desire to explore the relationship between the genre, the femininities constructed in its pages, the discourses it employs, and the making of that historical reader. We begin, appropriately enough, with the beginning of magazines for women, with the eighteenth-century periodical.

2

Eighteenth-century women's magazines

In 1745, a correspondent to *The Female Spectator* wrote seeking advice from its editorial board on the respective merits of three suitors for her hand. Bellamonte opens her letter with the declaration:

> Dear Female Sage, I have a vast opinion of your Wit; and you may be convinced of it by my asking your Advice; – a compliment, I assure you, I never paid to my own Mother, or to any other Soul besides yourself. (vol. 2, p. 105)

Here, it appears, we have a form and tone instantly recognisable to the twentieth-century reader of women's magazines. The magazine functions as surrogate 'family', providing an intimate and private space for the discussion of issues to which even, or perhaps especially, a mother cannot be made privy. The next three chapters outline the appearance and development of the women's magazine from the late seventeenth century to the present day. Despite the striking continuity this early example of the 'agony column' illustrates, we will also seek to highlight and analyse significant *differences* in the history of the construction of a new genre directed at the woman reader.

The history of the women's magazine is intimately connected to a larger history of modern representations and discourses of femininity. Indeed the magazine for women only becomes possible with the emergence of a consensus, which we locate in the late seventeenth to early eighteenth century, that gender difference, rather than distinction of status or wealth, is the primary arbiter of social power for women. This is not to suggest that gender was not a significant register of social inequality prior to this period, but that it was at this historical moment that it came to be articulated as such. The history of modern patriarchy's construction of 'the feminine', and women's relationship, resistance and submission to that ideological construction, is, however, neither linear nor absolute. It is, rather, a history of struggle and contradiction. Women's magazines have, since their first appearance, registered and responded to such conflicts within ideologies of gender. In order to trace this history, we have chosen to consider a small number of influential publications in some detail. These we take to embody certain 'key moments' in the making of a genre. We concentrate on the dynamic process of exchange in the discourse of the women's magazine by which the genre is developed in relation to new ideological formations of femininity and, in turn, offers its female readers ways of negotiating and defining themselves in relation to those formations.

Any attempt to provide a material account of the readership of women's magazines before the mid twentieth century faces some specific problems. It is not easy to establish who bought, let alone actually read, many of the periodicals we discuss. Until the establishment of the Audit Bureau of Circulations in 1931 there was no central record of the gross circulation figures of periodical publications. We have very limited evidence, beyond the inevitably aggrandising claims of the magazines themselves, of the number of consumers – in the sense of purchasers – which any individual magazines commanded prior to this date. Even where publishers' figures and records are available they rarely indicate the ratio of men to women purchasers, or the different social classes to which men or women readers belonged. In late-twentieth-century Britain the majority of women's magazines are purchased over a shop counter. In previous centuries they were bought largely by subscription, a pattern still common in the United States. Where they do exist, early publishers' records, especially subscription lists, are therefore a potentially valuable source of information on the class and sex profiles of magazine readers of different historical periods. Here, too, difficulties arise however. Because men were the primary wage or salary earners it is more than likely that they would have subscribed to magazines on behalf of their wives or daughters.

If we seek to discover not just who bought but also who *read* these magazines, further problems emerge. Actual numbers of readers of magazines are notoriously hard to establish. This is because they command so many 'hidden' readers – those who do not subscribe to, or buy, the magazine, but have access to it by some other means. In the twentieth century these readers are most commonly other family members and friends, but in earlier centuries they would have included the domestic servants of those who could afford the full subscription. This potential for cross-class readership of the same magazine was increased by the fact that throughout the eighteenth and nineteenth centuries, periodicals appeared in bound annual volumes, as well as the weekly or monthly parts. With the establishment of lending libraries in the mid eighteenth century, those who could not afford the full cost of the magazine could borrow it for a minimal sum (Ellegard, 1957). More significantly, perhaps, the magazine was not always consumed in its original periodical form but rather under the same conditions as a single, double or triple decker novel. These factors, compounded with the absence of reliable market research or empirical data on readers and the separation of the 'ideal' or projected reader from the 'actual' or material reader, make readership figures and profiles in these eariler periods even more difficult to establish than those of modern magazines.

In the last chapter of this book we set out our arguments for resisting the obvious temptation to collapse the historical reader into the ideal reader of the magazine, in the absence of other forms of data. To put it briefly, because women's magazines define their readers as 'women' they embody definitions of what it means to be a woman in a culture at any given historical moment. However, we know that a contemporary woman reader often does not feel she matches the image projected by the magazine. She may be 'fat' and forty, whereas the magazine defines femininity in terms of being slim and young; she may be childless, whereas the magazine defines mothering as central to womanliness. Furthermore, we know from market research that substantial numbers of men read women's magazines, which, of course, position them as women (Mintel, 1986). We must assume, then, that magazines of earlier periods functioned in a similar way in relation to their readers. We can only interpret them as evidence of the discursive constructions of femininity available to and normative in their period of publication, just as we do in relation to magazines of our own period. Another constant is the magazine's continuing status as commodity. Moreover, its history has always been a smaller part of the growth of the print market as a whole. The magazine's methods of finance and distribution have, however, undergone significant changes through the centuries, as the last few paragraphs have made clear. There are other shifts we chart in the next two chapters. It was not until the mid nineteenth century that advertising became a crucial source of revenue for magazines; throughout the eighteenth century they were maintained on their sales figures alone. The introduction of advertising on a large scale in the magazine radically altered the appearance of the women's magazine as well as its normative representations of femininity. Likewise the growth of periodical publishing as an industry has led to increasing professionalisation and specialisation within the genre. Twentieth-century women's magazines thrive on the *appearance* of 'amateurism', particularly in the use of readers' 'true-life stories' and letters. Eighteenth-century magazines maintained themselves in reality by drawing upon their readers as an unpaid resource for material.

Another common phenomenon of the eighteenth- and nineteenth-century periodical press which has altered is the power of the individual proprietor, publisher or editor. Unlike the newspaper barons of today, the press men of the past could combine the roles of editor, journalist, publisher and proprietor. This was true in all areas of the print industry, of course, but the fact that it was men who were likely to have the economic and discursive power in publishing has particular implications for magazines addressed to women. Some of the leading women's magazines were conceived, financed and published by one man as, for example, was George Robinson's *Lady's Magazine* (1770–1830). Samuel and Isabella Beeton's *Englishwoman's Domestic Magazine* (1852–79) offers an example of production by a husband and wife team but one in which the man played the leading public role. Male editors frequently wrote the bulk of the magazine under a variety of different, often female, personae. As late as the 1890s the 'advanced' magazine, *Woman*, was being written in large part by its editor, Arnold Bennett, who adopted a series of pseudonyms including 'Barbara', 'Marjorie' and 'Marguerite'. Most modern women's magazines, in contrast, are edited by women although a few, such as *Woman*, make much of the persona of a sympathetic male 'editor'. However, aside from the interesting question of how editorial persona functions to establish readers' relationship with the magazine, the modern editor's role cannot be equated with the economic and ideological power these early male 'magnates' wielded over the content, style and structure of their magazines.

The shape of the women's magazine has, then, been dictated both by changing ideological conceptions of the status and condition of women and by general, not specifically gendered, causes – such as changes in print technology, government intervention in the press, the emergence of other new forms of periodical publication and improvements in marketing techniques. Such changes are not, however, without their effects in the construction of modern gender ideologies; indeed the dominance of the modern conceptual division of women into consumers and men into producers could not have been possible without these sorts of technological advance under capitalism. The history of the development of the women's magazine as a commodity is also the history of the construction of woman as consumer, and it is the peculiar and specific relation of these two factors that gives the women's magazine its distinct and separate place within the economic and ideological determinants of the publishing industry.

Addressing women

On 27 February 1693 the first number of the *Ladies' Mercury* was published in London with a direction to its readers that:

> All questions relating to Love etc., are desired to be sent in to the Latine-Coffee-House in Ave-Mary-Lane, to the Ladies' Society there, and we promise that they shall be weekly answered with all the Zeal and Softness becoming to the Sex. We likewise desire we may not be troubled with other Questions relating to Learning, Religion, etc.

The first magazine addressed exclusively to women, claiming female authorship and focusing entirely on issues designated as appropriate to 'the Fair Sex', had come into being, and not inappropriately it took the form of a 'problem page'. The *Ladies' Mercury* was a spin-off publication from the highly successful question and answer periodical, the *Athenian Mercury*, brainchild of a maverick publisher named John Dunton. The *Athenian* entertained the public for six years from 1691 to 1697 with answers to 'all manner of Nice and Curious Questions in Divinity, Physick, Law, Philosophy, History, Trade, Mathematick & c . . . proposed by Either Sex' (vol. 3, no. 19, 3 October 1691, Q.1). The *Ladies' Mercury* had a less auspicious history, surviving for only four short numbers. However, the *Athenian* continued to provide a fortnightly 'women's page' and, from the 1690s onwards, all new periodical publications seem to have felt obliged to address or placate their 'fair readers', while a number dedicated themselves wholly to the latter's interest.

Women's magazines did not develop as an adjunct to magazines addressed to men. It is our contention that the emergence of the early modern 'magazine' as a form went hand-in-hand with the development of a specific address to female readers as a definable 'special interest' group. From its first inception, in its earliest form as the single-essay periodical, the magazine's publishers and authors felt obliged to attract the attention of female readers by invoking their interests as discrete and important.

The periodical that, along with its successor the *Spectator* (1711–14), was to dominate magazine writing through the eighteenth century as a model of bourgeois taste and thinking, Joseph Addison's and Richard Steele's *Tatler* (1709–11), made, in its first number of Tuesday 12 April 1709, a clear commitment to female readers. The fictional author of the *Tatler*, an amorous and pompous elder statesman of the coffee-house named Isaac Bickerstaff, announced his resolve 'also to have something which may be of entertainment to the Fair Sex, in Honour of whom [he has] invented the Title of this Paper' (vol. 1, no. 1, p. 15). By the tenth number (Tuesday 3 May 1709), readers were introduced to Bickerstaff's half-sister, Jenny Distaff, who figured as an occasional correspondent in his absence. Distaff represented her brother's project as a benevolent attempt to inform women about contemporary political events and debates in the world beyond the domestic enclosure of the drawing-room, informing them that her 'brother Isaac designs, for the Use of Our Sex, to give the exact

Characters of all the Chief Politicians who frequent any of the Coffee-Houses from St. James to the Change' (vol. 1, p. 89).

Only a year after Isaac Bickerstaff laid down his pen, Addison and Steele introduced the *Spectator*, a daily rather than thrice-weekly paper, which also oriented itself toward a female market, claiming that 'there are none to whom this Paper will be more useful, than to the female World' (vol. 1, p. 46). Addison goes on to complain that women's 'Amusements seem contrived for them rather as they are Women, than as they are reasonable Creatures. . The Toilet is their great Scene of Business, and the right adjusting to their Hair the principal Enjoyment of their Lives' (vol. 1, p. 46). Here too, then, the magazine offers to alleviate the triviality of women's domesticated existence, by bringing the world into their living-rooms, if not their living-rooms into the world. However, in the fourth number of the same paper (5 March 1711), its co-author, Richard Steele, took a somewhat different approach toward his female readers. He promised them a 'Woman's Day' once a week, in which Mr Spectator would 'lead the Young through all the becoming Duties of Virginity, Marriage and Widowhood' while 'endeavour[ing] at a Stile and Air suitable to their Understanding' (vol. 1, p. 21). He hastens to add that this does not mean any depreciation of the journal's high intellectual standard:

> I shall take it for the greatest Glory of my Work, if among reasonable Women this Paper may furnish Tea-Table Talk. In order to do it, I shall treat Matters which relate to Females as they are concern'd to approach or fly from the other Sex, or as they are ty'd to them by Blood, Interest and Affection. (vol. 1, p. 22)

Whereas Addison's comments suggest that the *Spectator* will act as a spy or surrogate for women in the larger political world of the coffee-house and government from which they are debarred, Steele's imply that it will provide a guide or counsellor for them in the domestic world of love and affection that is their 'proper' realm. This seeming conflict should not stand merely as testimony to the different visions of the journal's co-authors. It is, rather, symptomatic of a division that characterised periodical address to women until late in the eighteenth century, between the 'society' periodical (concerned mainly with party political and aristocratic scandal) and the domestic journal (modelled on the conduct book and centering on the concerns of home, hearth and the pursuit of marital happiness). It might also be understood as a division that continues in the women's magazine today. Does the women's magazine provide a women's perspective on a political and social order from which they are generally alienated, or an alternative female community that centres on issues generally assumed to be women's especial concern such as family, home and love?

This last perspective, that of the domestic journal, was finally to triumph in eighteenth-century periodical publication for women, and the history of that triumph is also, in many respects, the history of changed conceptions of sexual and class difference in early modern social structure. Indeed, in the eighteenth century, magazines acted as central media for the shaping and expression of populist interests and taste. In particular they were instrumental in the development of a bourgeois leisure industry habitually represented as 'feminine'. The fascination with defining 'proper' femininity exhibited by the *Tatler*, *Spectator*, and a host of other less influential periodicals, whether explicitly identified as 'for the ladies' or not, was central in the formation of early modern class as well as gender ideology.

Any assessment of the ideological gains and losses that inhere in the contested conceptions of femininity for women as producers and consumers within the newly emergent magazine industry must take into account the material and ideological conditions which brought the magazine into being in this period. In the next section, therefore, we go back to trace the rise of the magazine as a publishing genre. We then turn to look in more detail at the growth of magazines for women, paying particular attention to two of the more successful ventures in the field, the *Female Spectator* (1744–46) and *The Lady's Magazine* (1770–1830).

The rise of the magazine

According to the *Oxford English Dictionary*, until 1640 the word 'magazine' referred exclusively to a storehouse for arms or supplies. In the seventeenth century it came to be employed in booktitles to refer to 'a storehouse of information' or miscellany. Not until the eighteenth century, and specifically with the first publication of the *Gentleman's Magazine* in 1731, was it used to denote a periodical publication directed toward a general reader-ship. What, then, were the reasons for the emergence and success of this particular brand of periodical literature in the early eighteenth century?

Throughout the seventeenth century the British public gained its news information from newspapers, broadsides and pamphlets. The periodical essay paper, and later the magazine, offered a quite different mode of consumption for the 'news'. The first of these most commonly took the form of a single-sheet, long prose essay, written by one author. The magazine or 'miscellany', by contrast, at least pretended to multi-authorship and offered a variety of not necessarily interrelated items. Both these forms were marked, however, not by the claim to be the first to provide the public with an account of contemporary events at home and overseas, but by being the first to pass comment on, interrogate, challenge and explore the import of these current affairs. As Isaac Bicker-staff, fictional editor of the *The Tatler* (1709–11) puts it, the singularity of the periodical journal lay in its aim to instruct the 'worthy and well-affected Members of the Commonwealth . . . after their Reading what to think' (*The Tatler* vol. 1, p. 15).

There were pragmatic reasons for this shift in emphasis in the treatment of news. On a purely practical level, the magazine appears to have been born as a response to government legislation. In 1712 the Tory government endeavoured to control the flood of political propaganda in cheap large-circulation news-papers by imposing a Stamp Tax of a penny or a halfpenny on every copy of a single- or half-sheet publication. It also introduced a tax on paper and advertisements (a major source of revenue for newspapers). Newspapers and single-essay periodicals (such as the *Spectator*) effectively doubled in price, but publishers succeeded in finding a loophole by expanding the length of such productions beyond the single sheet so that they qualified as pamphlets and were taxed at the lower rate of two shillings per impression. These new six-page journals compensated for the paucity of material by switching to weekly or monthly rather than daily, twice and thrice weekly publication and padded the text with commentary, literary extracts and reviews, popular fiction, readers' letters, and so forth. In 1725 the Whig government headed by Robert Walpole tried to prevent this evasion by requiring the use of stamped paper (taxed at a halfpenny per sheet) in all journals and newspapers. Weekly journals now reduced their print size to save space, reduced the number of pages from six to four, and raised their price to two pence per copy. The *Gentleman's Magazine* found another ingenious loophole here, in that the tax applied only to publications engaged in transmitting 'news'. Edward Cave, the magazine's publisher and creator, produced a forty-eight (later forty-six) page journal once a month at the price of sixpence, pieced together out of the best extracts from weekly and daily papers accompanied by the claim that he was only *reprinting* the news. This tactic also evaded the copyright law of 1710 regarding reprinted material in that it applied only to publications in volume form, so that extracts, abridgements and serial publications were exempt from duties.

The magazine, then, appears to have been the result of some clever manipulation on the part of the new demagogues of print culture in response to what they saw as invasive government legislation. However, it also met the needs of a large body of readers. Cave's *Gentleman's Magazine* survived for twenty-seven years. Robert Mayo estimates that the publisher, George Robinson, through his ownership of the *Lady's Magazine* (1770–1830) and *Town and Country* (1769–96), cleared a profit of twelve thousand pounds a year (Mayo, 1962, p. 421). The savings on Stamp Tax and copyright payments alone would not produce this kind of profit or longevity without the added determinant of large circulation. In the early to mid eighteenth century, improvements in communications of both road and mail between London (Britain's publishing centre) and the provinces, along with decreasing paper and publication costs, made it possible for the magazine to reach a far larger audience than newspapers and single-essay periodicals had done previously. Moreover, the magazine was eminently suited to a provincial audience, providing an extensive update on political and social changes along with fiction and other forms of entertainment in a (relatively) cheap and accessible form (see Fergus, 1986, pp. 43–4). The first number of the *Gentleman's Magazine* declared its aims to be:

in the first place to give Monthly a View of all the Pieces of Wit, Humour or Intelligence daily offer'd to the Publick in the News-Papers (which of late are so multiply'd, as to render it impossible, unless a man makes it a business to consult them all) and in the next place, we shall join therewith some other matters of Use, and Amusement that will be communicated to us. ('Introduction', vol. 1, n.p.)

The miscellaneous form of the magazine incorporated features of both the single-essay periodical and the newspaper, reprinting reports of births, deaths and marriages, current events at the same time as it provided political commentary, theatre and literary reviews and synopses, short fiction, and moral argument. However, it lacked the aesthetic and ideological coherence of the single-essay periodical, culled as it was from a variety of sources.

The emergence of the miscellany or 'magazine' in the mid-century was a register of political change as well as changes in the economics of publishing. As J. M. Downie has demonstrated, in the years following the Glorious Revolution of 1688 the periodical press was instrumental in the formation of party political discourse (Downie, 1969). From the election of a Tory government in 1710 to the death of Queen Anne in 1714, Swift's Tory *Examiner* and the Whig *Medley* were engaged in a bitter struggle to rewrite political history according to their opposing party ideologies. Addison and Steele made no secret of their Whig sympathies in the *Tatler* and *Spectator*. Lady Mary Wortley Montagu, in her short-lived periodical *The Nonsense of Common-Sense* (1737–38), critiqued the misogyny of the Tory and country Whig opposition paper *Common-Sense*. The fact that Montagu's journal only ran for nine issues might suggest that by the 1730s the exclusively party political journal was no longer viable or popular. More generalised class conflict seems to have become the focus of the magazine's political discussion rather than party conflict. By this point, magazines, if they were vehicles for a coherent ideological position, represented a broad bourgeois consensus, the result of long years of Whig mercantilist government under Robert Walpole (Goldgar, 1976).

Literary study has traditionally identified the magazine with the novel as part of an attempt to satisfy the demands of a newly formed literate and leisured bourgeois reading public, eager for entertainment and amusement but without access to the formal education in the classics that would have made other literary forms, such as Augustan verse satire, available to them (Davis, 1983; Mayo, 1962; Richetti, 1969; Watt, 1957). We do not wish to fundamentally challenge this interpretation, but we would argue that attention to the 'woman question' which figured so large in all periodical publication throughout the eighteenth century might reveal more complexity in this history of complicity between the rise of bourgeois hegemony and the development of 'popular' narrative forms that both cater to and shape the ideology of a class. Such a reassessment has begun to take place in recent feminist analyses of the novel (Poovey, 1984; Armstrong, 1985). But the significance of the magazine, and in particular the women's magazine, in the simultaneous 'feminisation' of culture and the development of a dominant bourgeois ideology in Britain from the mid eighteenth century onwards, has yet to be assessed.

The single-essay periodical: tattling and spectating

We deal here with two periodicals of the early and mid eighteenth century which claim female authorship and address themselves to a female readership: the *Female Tatler* (1709–11) and the *Female Spectator* (1744–46). Both were, probably, written by a single author and consisted of a long single essay. Both, as their titles suggest, were produced in response to a leading male-authored journal and both solicited the support of a female readership in their critique of and challenge to masculine control of periodical literature. As earlier comments on Addison's and Steele's famous periodicals have implied, the customary invocation to a female reader in the 'man's' periodical probably signified something other than a selfless interest in alleviating the boredom of the leisured bourgeois lady. Rather, we suggest, the condition of the bourgeois woman, condemned to a life of triviality and mundanity as a result of her enforced alienation from the public world of politics, business and trade, was employed as a metonymic substitute for that of her male counterpart, one of 'the Fraternity of Spectators who live in the World without having anything to do in it', 'the Blanks of Society' (*Spectator*, vol. 1, p. 45). Like the Spectator himself who, having made his money in the city has retired to the country, bourgeois women have no declared 'interest' in government and politics. Addison and Steele, as Terry Eagleton and John Barrell have argued, succeeded in turning the apparent alienation of a class into an asset (Eagleton, 1984, pp. 9–27; Barrell, 1983, pp. 17–50). The bourgeois gentleman emerges as the ideal arbiter of political morality because he has no material interest in its processes. The positioning of the bourgeoisie is essentially a feminine one, tattling and spectating rather than acting in the world of politics, defined precisely by its inactivity, identified as a class precisely because of, rather than in spite of, its supposedly 'apolitical' stance.

The most successful of a number of journals produced in response to the *Tatler* was the *Female Tatler* which ran in a variety of forms from 8 July 1709 to 31 March 1710. Its ostensible author/editor was a Mrs Phoebe Crackenthorpe, 'a Lady that knows everything' who insists in the first number that her 'Design is not to Rival his [Bickerstaff's] Performance, or in the least Prejudice the Reputation he has deservedly gain'd'. Mrs Crackenthorpe develops an almost exact feminine mirror to the *Tatler* itself. She suffers similar difficulties with her manservant, Frances, to those undergone by Bickerstaff with his Pacolet. Her journal appears thrice weekly on those days that Bickerstaff's does not. Whereas Bickerstaff controls his operation from Will's Coffeehouse, Mrs Crackenthorpe sets up her 'Scandal-Office' in her drawing room, where, she says in the first number, 'half the Nation visits me, where I have a true history of the World'.

The *Female Tatler*, like many eighteenth-century journals, has a complex publishing history. A version of the magazine was published by Benjamin Bragge from 8 July 1709 to 31 March 1710, but in the eighteenth number the author announced her plan to transfer to the publishing house of Anne Baldwin. Through numbers nineteen to forty-four, two rival issues emanated from both Baldwin and Bragge. Numbers forty-five to fifty-one (19 October to 2 November 1709) continue from Baldwin alone. On 4 November 1709, 'A Society of Ladies' took over the editorship, concluding their work on 31 March 1710 (numbers fifty-two to one hundred and eleven). Moreover, the real identity of the author behind Phoebe Crackenthorpe is still in dispute (Anderson, 1931; Graham, 1936–7; Harrington Smith, 1951–2). Despite the fact that in July 1709 a Whig paper, the *British Apollo*, clearly cited Thomas Baker as the journal's author, strong claims have been made for Delarivier Manley, a Tory propagandist and the most well-known writer of scandal fiction during the reign of Anne. The figures behind the 'Society of Ladies', who took over in November 1709, were certainly not all female. Bernard Mandeville, satirist and philosopher, and Susannah Centilvre, playwright, are known to have been part of the group.

Whatever the sex of her creator, Phoebe Crackenthorpe remains one of the first instances of a female journalistic persona who trades on her femininity as a means of access to social power. The *Female Tatler* was a party political paper, a Tory riposte to the Whiggish ideologies of its male counterpart, but its themes were almost wholly feminocentric. In its two year life it addressed, among others, issues of women's education, female learning, prostitution, the moral import of the stage, and the new phenomenon of the actress. The second number (11 July 1709) refuted accusations of triviality, claiming that the paper was 'not an impertinent Rotation of Chit Chat but a well-grounded Design, divertingly to lead People into good Moral Instruction whose intent in reading this Paper might be only to find out some invidious Reflection, or laugh at an idle Story'. Specifically, the paper insisted that 'women's issues' were a matter for political, indeed party political, concern. The *Female Tatler* marks a sadly short-lived moment in the history of the women's magazine when party politics and contemporary 'scandal' could be claimed as the special provenance of the woman writer and reader. By the 1770s, and with the first appearance of the *Lady's Magazine*, such an equation had become impossible and any attempt to introduce 'politics' into the domestic environs of its women readers was met with immediate and vociferous complaint. The drawing-room that served as Phoebe Crackenthorpe's 'Scandal Office' came to be viewed as a sanctuary from, rather than a magnet for, political debate.

Eliza Haywood's periodical, the *Female Spectator*, was instrumental in the transformation of the women's magazine from scandal shop to domestic retreat. Published in twenty-four monthly numbers from April 1744 to March 1746 with two numbers omitted, Haywood's magazine amalgamated some of the best features of the single-essay periodical and the newly developed popular 'miscellany'. Where the *Tatler* and *Spectator* on average ran to sixteen hundred words per issue printed on two sides of a single half-sheet in double columns, the *Female Spectator* took the form of a six page 'book' in single columns of some six thousand words at a cost of sixpence. Despite these typographical and presentational differences, the *Female Spectator* did imitate its male counterpart. Haywood provided herself, like Addison and Steele, with a fictional circle of informed contributors. The *Spectator*'s six men were replaced by four women, introduced in the first number by their leader, the Female Spectator herself. 'I shall,' she writes, 'in imitation of my learned Brother of ever precious Memory, give some Account of what I am, and those concerned with me in the Undertaking' (vol. 1, p. 2).

The contrast between the two editorial boards is striking. If the *Spectator*'s gentlemen contributors embodied the diversity of profession among men of the educated classes in the early eighteenth century (two peers, a lawyer, an army officer, a farmer, and a clergymen), the ladies make us aware of the lack of professional choices available to women of those same classes. The ladies are defined by their marital status – a widow, a wife (Mira), and a virgin daughter (Euphrosine). Significantly, only the anonymous editor herself is defined autonomously without reference to a man, husband or father, in the only 'profession' available to the respectable middle-class woman, that of writer.

Like Phoebe Crackenthorpe, the Female Spectator is a well-defined journalistic persona, a woman of the world who 'never was a Beauty' and who, in her maturity, has come to regret the 'Hurry of promiscuous Diversions' that filled her youth (vol. 1, p. 2). This may be a concealed reference to the personal history of Haywood herself, who, in the 1720s, was notorious as a producer of erotic novels and scandal fiction (Whicher, 1915). However, the Female Spectator converts her disreputable past into an asset for a woman editor, asserting:

> whatever Inconveniences such a manner of Conduct has brought upon myself, I have this Consolation, to think that the Public may reap some Benefit from it; – the Company I kept was not, indeed, always so well chosen as it ought to have been, for the sake of my own Interest or Reputation; but then it was general and by Consequence furnished me . . . with the Knowledge of many Occurrences, which otherwise I had been ignorant of. (vol. 1, p. 3)

Haywood's editorial persona is a complex one, which seeks to resolve a number of contradictions for the woman writer in this period. Sexual and moral innocence are desirable commodities for the young woman in search of a husband, but they make for tedious copy in the periodical. Haywood conveniently splits her authorial psyche, into the members of her editorial board and a series of imaginary correspondents, as well as the past and present history of the Female Spectator herself, in order to resolve these paradoxes.

The declared aim of the *Female Spectator* is a moral one, but the first number locates the periodical uneasily between a scandal or 'society' journal and a moral conduct book. The Female Spectator announces that she has secured herself 'an eternal Fund of Intelligence' through 'Spies' placed not only in London but in the provincial Spas of England and a number of European cities, but not, she insists, with the 'Design of gratifying a vicious Propensity of propagating Scandal' (vol. 1, p. 6). Yet the twenty-four numbers of the *Female Spectator* contain no contemporary scandal, no veiled references to the sexual and political misdemeanours of the rich and powerful of Court and Commons such as the *Female Tatler* had indulged. It offers instead, month by month, a series of exemplary tales that expose women's vulnerability to male sexual lust, avarice, and marital abuse, from which the Female Spectator draws moral conclusions and advice to her female readers about how to avoid a similar fate. By the fifth month Haywood had introduced a number of (probably fictional) correspondents who write to the Female Spectator seeking advice, suggesting improvements to or criticising the journal. Increasingly, the magazine took the form of two or three lengthy 'readers' letters', followed by the judgement of the Female Spectator and her editorial board. This format allowed Haywood to experiment with male personae. A philanthropic gentleman named Philo-Naturae writes in to encourage women to take up the study of Natural Philosophy, and the editorial board accordingly sets off on a country ramble, magnifying-glasses in hand, in order to report back to their readers about the habits of caterpillars and snails (vol. 3, pp. 141–56, 290–303). John Careful points out the debilitating effects of regular tea-drinking, characterising the vice as 'a kind of Debauchery no less expensive, and perhaps even more pernicious in its Consequences, than those, which the Men who are not professed Rakes, are generally accused of' (vol. 2, p. 95). The Female Spectator dismisses the complaint of expense, arguing that wives have a right to expect a husband of means to supply them with this small indulgence, but concurs with his fears about the dangers of excessive indulgence.

The Female Spectator herself is one of the first agony aunts in British periodical literature. Her first correspondent, Mrs Sarah Oldfashion, declares herself at her wit's end in her endeavour to prevent her headstrong daughter Biddy from taking morning walks in Ranelagh Gardens. The Female Spectator's advice consists of some pious commentary on the wrong-headedness of the younger generation, the remark that Mrs Oldfashion 'will find all her Endeavours for this Purpose unavailing', and a warning not to carry out her project to exile Biddy to a relative's home in Cornwall as likely only to exacerbate her rebellion (vol. 1, p. 271). Ten months later the Female Spectator righteously defends herself from Sarah Oldfashion's reproaches, reminding her of her explicit injunction against Cornwall (vol. 3, p. 176). Biddy, it appears, has eloped with the groom of a neighbouring gentleman in order to escape the horrors of her exile.

This example demonstrates that the *Female Spectator*, despite its professed moralistic aims, was not repressive in its attitudes toward female education and equality. Indeed, a letter from one Cleora in book ten, pointing to women's continuing slavery to men through ignorance, inspires an impassioned meditation from the editor on the necessity of education and, in particular, philosophical training for women (vol. 2, pp. 230–4). However, like most discussions of the value of women's education conducted in eighteenth-century magazines, pamphlets, tracts and novels of the eighteenth century, it is seen only as a commodity that would enhance women's prospects on the marriage market: 'supposing her an excellent Oeconomist, in every Respect what the World calls a notable Woman, methinks the Husband would be infinitely happier were she endued with other good Qualities as well as a perfect Understanding in Household Affairs' (vol. 2, p. 234).

The *Female Spectator*, then, offers an example of the new 'domestic' magazine that came to dominate women's periodical literature from the mid eighteenth century onward, concentrating on the struggle to achieve marital happiness and perceiving 'women's issues' as determined solely with regard to this single 'career'. In many ways it provides a 'conduct book' in regular periodical form, for its female readers (Hodges, 1957; Koon, 1978-9). It carried no needlework patterns, recipes, medical or childcare advice, as did later examples of the form, focusing almost exclusively on the trials and tribulations of 'romance'. Yet, we can see in the *Female Spectator* a departure from the conventions of the single-essay periodical of the early eighteenth century and a shift toward the new miscellany structure combined with the development of a genteel, didactic editorial voice which was to become the hallmark of the later *Lady's Magazine*. Eliza Haywood probably wrote every word of the magazine herself, but through a variety of personae she succeeds in creating an atmosphere of intimacy and female community. Whether all her correspondents were fictional creations or not, the magazine broke new ground in presenting itself as a medium for women's concerns, a conduit for dialogue and exchange between women produced collectively by women. Specifically, it created an artificial imaginary community in which its readers could participate from the isolation of their homes. Like the editorial board, the Female Spectator's readers are invited to consider themselves as 'several Members of one Body, of which [she is] the Mouth' (vol. 1, pp. 5–6). Also, like the board in their supportive editorial practices, the appearance of consensus is produced by insisting that 'everyone has the liberty of excepting against, or censuring whatever she disapproves' (vol. 1, pp. 71–2).

A letter exchange in book eight of November 1744 reveals the extent to which the magazine was seen to have departed from the conventions of the single-essay periodical and its customary manner of addressing the female sex (or, if we take the correspondents to be the fictitious creation of a single author, the extent to which Haywood herself saw it as such a departure). Curioso Politico, writing from White's Chocolate-House, accuses the Female Spectator of reneging on her promise of the first number to provide extensive commentary on British and European current events. Expectant readers, he argues:

> instead of that full and perfect Account of the most momentous Actions you made them hope . . . find themselves for several Months together entertained only with Home-Amours, Reflections on Human Nature, the Passions, Morals, Interferences, and Warnings to your own Sex; – the most proper Province for you, I must own, but widely inconsistent with the Proposals of your first setting out. (vol. 2, pp. 118–19)

The magazine, in other words, had failed in its projected task of political organ, ignoring foreign wars, internal national strife and momentous political events in favour of the provision of purely private domestic advice. The Female Spectator, as always, defends herself, insisting that 'the better we regulate our Actions in private Life the more we may hope of public Blessings' (vol. 2, p. 125). Moreover, she makes one of the earliest statements about the distinction between magazine and newspaper, identifying them as the mouthpieces of different sexes:

> Several of the Topics he reproaches me for not having touch'd upon, come not within the Province of a *Female Spectator*; – such as Armies marching, – Battles fought, – Towns destroyed, – Rivers cross'd and the like: – I should think it ill became me to take up my own, or Reader's Time, with such Accounts as are every Day to be found in the public Papers. (vol. 2, p. 123)

With Haywood's *Female Spectator* we see the articulation of a separation between the public and the private spheres on the basis of gender distinction through the association of specific forms with specific genders – the newspaper as masculine and public, the magazine as private and feminine. This is not to say that women's magazines were less 'political' in the broadest sense of the term because of the emergence of a 'domestic' orthodoxy, but rather that female political influence came to be defined precisely by the avoidance of party political statement or commentary.

The *Female Spectator*, then, marked the advent of two major changes in the history of the women's magazine. First, it marked a generic transformation from the single-essay periodical to the miscellany form, and second, it marked a political change from the party journal which included women among its readers as one section of a politically interested public, to the popular women's magazines which defined its readers in terms of domestic enclosure and their absence from or lack of interest in state, as opposed to sexual, politics.

The domestic miscellany: ladies' magazines

The *Female Spectator* came to a close with its twenty-fourth 'book' at the end of March 1746. The editorial board announced their plan to establish a new 'League' with several gentlemen, including Mira's husband, who had discovered their identities.

This may be a reference to the publication in 1746 of two conduct books by Haywood, entitled *The Wife. By Mira, one of the Authors of the Female Spectator* and *The Husband. In Answer to the Wife*. Haywood embarked on another much more short-lived periodical project entitled *The Parrot. With a Compendium of the Times*, which ran for only nine weekly numbers from 2 August to 4 October 1746. *The Parrot* was, however, a return to the format of the 'scandal sheet' perfected by the *Female Tatler*, rather than an emulation of that of the *Female Spectator*. After the latter's final appearance the publisher promptly brought it out in a four-volume octavo edition and the book version ran into six editions until 1756, proving its affectivity as a conduct book as well as ongoing periodical. A seventh and last edition did not appear until 1771.

The period between 1756 and 1770 saw a series of experiments in the production of a miscellany magazine for women readers equivalent to the *Gentleman's Magazine*, which remained spectacularly indifferent to a prospective female readership. The annual 'Prefaces' attached to the *Gentleman's Magazine* made no mention of 'the Fair Sex' and it eschewed all fiction until six years into its life. The first piece of fiction it offered, entitled 'A Story Strange as True', ran from April 1737 to March 1738 (vols 7–9). It opened with an account of a conniving woman who tricks a clergyman into marriage, pursuing him to the Continent, and ended on an amour between a French priest and a sexually voracious Lady Abbess. Clearly, such fiction was aimed to titillate its male readers rather than appeal to the supposedly more delicate taste of their wives.

Robert Mayo remarks that the *Gentleman's Magazine*'s 'typographical ugliness was a badge of its fundamental sobriety and practicality' (Mayo, 1962, p. 168). It sought to attract, in particular, men engaged in commerce and business, keeping them abreast of recent events, facts, advances in knowledge in as abbreviated but thorough a fashion as possible. The woman reader of the magazine in this period was far removed from this profile. Leisured, with a reasonable amount of 'pin-money' to spend, but only poorly educated, her life revolving around husband and home, she sought entertainment, pleasure and, to a certain extent, escape. The popularity of the oriental tale and exotic travel narratives in miscellanies of the period addressed to women are clear indicators of the inexhaustible demand for fantasy among female readers of the time (although surprisingly, the *Female Spectator* conscientiously avoided both forms, sticking firmly to the sentimental domestic tale of the seduced maiden).

Before the first appearance of *The Lady's Magazine* in August 1770 a number of less successful or abandoned projects attempted to move away from the single-essay periodical into the form we now recognise more readily as the women's magazine. One of the earliest attempts was *Records of Love, or Weekly Amusements for the Fair*, which ran for only twelve numbers in 1710. The first (7 January 1710) promised that 'Each Paper will contain something new and diverting, according to the example of the first Novel, without any Personal Reflections or Immodest Obscenities' (p. 15). Each number consisted of a series of short fictions demonstrating the triumph of virtuous love. *Records of Love* proves more interesting in its complex initiatives to enable female subscription, offering reduced rates to subscribers and promising early delivery to the subscriber's house (by 4 p.m. on the day of publication, a Sunday). Bourgeois women readers, unlike their fathers, husbands or brothers, could not rely on a regular visit to the coffee-house to furnish them with printed news and entertainment.

Prior to *Records of Love*, the publisher John Tipper had enjoyed remarkable success with his annual *Ladies' Diary* which sold out of all four thousand copies of its first edition for 1704 by New Year's Day, despite the fact that it cost half as much again as other almanacs offered for that year. The *Diary* was a small four-page sheet, including a calendar, some cookery and medical receipts, beauty hints, verses, moral tales, and a space left blank for personal entries and accounts. By 1706, Tipper had introduced the 'brain-teaser' in the shape of enigmas and mathematical questions provided by his readers, and these proved so popular that by 1710 the cookery and medical features were abandoned in their favour. In 1711, Tipper embarked upon a monthly equivalent to the diary, entitled *Delights for the Ingenious, or a Monthly Entertainment for the Curious of Both Sexes*, and consisting entirely of enigmas, mathematical questions, epigrams, songs, anagrams, and small pieces of verse and prose. It was this kind of material, along with short fiction in the mould that offered by *Records of Love*, that was to become the staple for women's miscellanies or magazines later in the century.

It was not until 1749 that the first full-blown miscellany for women was launched in the shape of Jasper Goodwill's *Ladies' Magazine, or the Universal Entertainer*, a venture which ran uninterrupted at fortnightly intervals from 18 November 1749 to 10 November 1753, only closing with an announcement of the unfortunate author's sudden death. Goodwill was the first of a series of strong-willed male authors and author–publishers who endeavoured to produce a particular 'recipe' for a successful women's magazine in the second half of the century. Despite his prefatory claim for the first volume (published at the year's end with a supplement) that it would be 'a most innocent, diverting and profitable Entertainment for young Masters and Misses', the magazine inclined toward the sensational, particularly in its penchant for trial reports. The first number offered the confession of seventeen-year-old Amy Hutchinson, executed by burning for the murder of her husband at the instigation of her lover, a narrative which itself conformed to the tragic fictions of seduction and betrayal that had proved popular in earlier journals for women. The rest of the magazine consisted of reprinted stories (Goodwill, for example, provides a lengthy summary of Henry Fielding's *Amelia* from January to April 1752 in five parts), home and foreign news, an ambitious 'History of England by Question and Answer', enigmas and poetry. Goodwill did not solicit contributions from readers and the fictional material he employed was rarely original, usually abridged versions of already published novels and reprints of fiction from other periodicals. Aphra Behn's *Oroonoko*, first published in 1688, was serialised in fifteen parts in the fourth volume from 14 April to 10 November 1753 (vol. 4) and presented as the first in a projected series of novels that 'may at the same time, divert and instruct' requested by 'many of [Goodwill's] female correspondents' (vol. 4, p. 115).

The involvement of well-known authors in periodical fiction publication did not stop with reprints of their fiction. Oliver Goldsmith and Charlotte Lennox, both leading literary figures, briefly joined the race to produce a profitable and popular ladies' miscellany, following Goodwill's demise. From September 1759 to 1763 Goldsmith, adopting the female persona of a Mrs Stanhope, edited the *Lady's Magazine, or Polite Companion for the Fair Sex*. He proved, however, particularly averse to publishing fiction and offered his readers only two serial stories and a handful of histories, apologues, and oriental tales. Otherwise, the magazine was a sober piece of work, like Mrs Stanhope herself, privileging history, biography, natural science and news reporting. Lennox's was an equally solemn attempt doomed to failure, entitled the *Lady's Museum*, which ran for only eleven numbers in the years 1760 and 1761. In this case, however, presumably because of her sex, the real author's name was given prominence and was clearly meant to be a selling point. The *London Chronicle* advertisement for the first number (28 February/1 March 1760) described the journal as 'a Variety of Original Pieces in Prose and Verse, for the Information and Amusement of the Ladies. By the Author of the *Female Quixote, Henrietta, &c*' (p. 212). Lennox published a new novel serially in the magazine, 'The Story of Harriot and Sophia', which later appeared as a two volume novel entitled *Sophia* (1762). Indeed, we might speculate that the magazine itself was a vehicle for this novel since it ended with its conclusion and that we might view the *Lady's Museum* as an experiment in expanding into new areas of the fiction market. Like many other writers of magazine fiction in the eighteenth century, Lennox made no attempt to adapt her narrative to the serial structure in which it appeared, simply concluding each instalment when she had filled the space allocated to it.

The first number of the *Lady's Magazine, or Entertaining Companion for the Fair Sex* when it appeared in August 1770 saw the most effective fusion of the disparate features and techniques of different prior miscellanies discussed above. The magazine was first launched by the bookseller John Coote over the name of the publisher John Wheble. In April 1771 Coote sold his interest in the magazine to the publishers Robinson and Roberts, but Wheble did not give up his interest without a fight. He continued to publish his rival version of the magazine, continuing the serials already begun and enlisting readers' support from April 1771 to December 1772. His issue of July 1771 contained a lengthy account of the trial over the right of property for the magazine in which the court found for the plaintiffs (Robinson and Roberts), charging the defendant the nominal sum of one shilling (vol. 2, pp. 41–52). Following the court case, however, Robinson and Roberts seem to have won over the public and Wheble's rival publication was forced to close.

From this point on, the Robinson publishing house had the controlling interest in the two most successful magazines of the late eighteenth century, *The Lady's Magazine* and *Town and Country Magazine, or Universal Repository of Knowledge, Instruction and Entertainment* (1769–96). As Robert Mayo argues, these two magazines were 'the powerful leaders of two divergent tendencies in popular taste – the one increasingly modish, raffish and satirical; the other predominantly decorous, sentimental and moral' (Mayo, 1962, p. 188). Both claimed a readership of sixteen thousand, a remarkable figure in a period where literacy levels and earnings remained low and technology in the printing industry was still underdeveloped. By the last decades of the eighteenth century, however, *Town and Country*, along with other 'society' journals, such as the *Court and City Magazine* (1770–71), *Westminster* (1772–85), *Bon Ton Magazine* (1790–96), seems to have fallen into decline. It was not until 1806 that a successful alternative appeared in the shape of the *Belle Assemblée, or Bell's Court and Fashionable Magazine*. In contrast, the pseudo-genteel and sentimental emphasis of the *Lady's Magazine* spawned a number of imitations in the 1790s, including among the most successful the *Lady's Monthly Museum, or Polite Repository of Amusement and Instruction* (1798–1806), the *New Lady's Magazine, or Polite and Entertaining Companion for the Fair Sex* (1786–95) and the *Sentimental and Masonic Magazine* published in Dublin (1792–5).

The *Lady's Magazine* seems to have struck the right chord with an eager reading public. Its first 'Address to the Fair Sex' that accompanied both first number and volume stated that 'the subjects [the following work] treats of are such as appropriated to the fair'. The address goes on to promise 'elegant patterns for the Tambour, Embroidery, or every kind of Needlework' as well as 'engravings [to] inform our distant readers with every innovation that is made in the female dress' and 'Interesting Stories, Novels, Tales, Romances, intended to confirm chastity and recommend virtue'; '[the] housewife as well as the peeress', the editors pledge, 'shall meet with something suitable to their different walks of life' (vol. 1, p. A2). The principal novelty of the magazine was its appearance. Unlike the *Gentleman's Magazine* and Goodwill's earlier attempt, the *Lady's Magazine* did not reproduce the close print of the newspaper, except for its appended foreign and domestic news and birth, death, marriage and bankruptcy listings. It was lavishly illustrated with copperplate engravings and supplied pull-out needlework patterns and ·

sheet music for readers' use. Its fifty-odd pages were available at the cheap price of sixpence. It was also the principal purveyor of magazine fiction in the late eighteenth century. At least a quarter of the magazine was taken up with fiction, much of it published serially and 'commissioned' expressly by the magazine. The serial with which the first number opened, 'A Sentimental Journey, By a Lady', was modelled on Laurence Sterne's novel of the same name which had enjoyed enormous success two years earlier but stripped of Sterne's humour and occasional sexual frankness. Amounting to eight parts, and twenty-seven thousand words, the serial ran for seven years (from August 1770 to April 1777) and was only 'dropped on account of the desire of many Correspondents' as the editor commented with regret in October 1782 (vol. 13, p. 506). By this stage the lady had traversed most of the British Isles, detailing the sentimental beauties of Henley, Dorchester, Oxford, Bath, Bristol, the southwestern counties, London, Canterbury, Dover and the Midlands. Robinson also made use of trial reports as Goodwill had done, opening the August 1775 number with an account of the trial of Jane Butterfield, who was accused and cleared of poisoning by mercury the man who had engineered her abduction from her home at the age of fourteen, seduced her and forced her to cohabit with him for six years (vol. 6, pp. 395–400). Here, too, the sympathy was with the accused woman whose history was one of abuse at the hands of an autocratic man, and who acquired the status of a sentimental icon.

The opening number of the *Lady's Magazine* had not solicited contributions from its readers and, indeed, its promise to display 'the whole treasure of the Muses' implied that most of its fiction and poetry would emanate from established authors. However, the second number provided a French text with a request for a translation from the readers on the grounds that:

> As the French language is almost universally spoken, and as it is deemed a necessary accomplishment for young ladies, it is requested by several of our friends that we would appropriate about one page of our Magazine to some little essay or tale in that language. (vol. 1, pp. 57–8)

Very soon readers were not simply supplying translations but serial fiction, enigmas, poetry, and letters detailing their thoughts on love, marriage, women's education, and responses to previous articles. According to the comments in the editor's 'To Our Correspondents' section, at least one third of the fiction published between 1775 and 1805 in the magazine was contributed by readers without payment. Indeed by 1784 the editors found it necessary to announce that they could not accept any correspondence unless the postage had been remitted (vol. 14, p. 1).

With regard to serial fiction, the reliance on unpaid amateur contributors caused considerable difficulties and 'To Our Correspondents' (which itself expanded from a half column in the 1770 number to a full page at the front of each issue by 1773) increasingly became a litany of requests for continuations of material. The editors struggled to introduce some order in the chaos by setting deadlines for receipt of material. The issue of May 1771 included a statement that no more enigmas would be accepted unless accompanied by the solution, and a request that literary contributors should send their work 'as early as possible in the month, by which means we shall have it more in our power to oblige them' (vol. 2, p. 486). Despite the undertaking to provide provincial readers with a monthly fashion update, the *Lady's Magazine* had considerable difficulty obtaining a regular correspondent. In May 1775 we find the editors abjectly seeking to contact a Miss Charlotte Stanley who had provided a description of 'Ladies' Dress for May':

> We are obliged to this correspondent for resuming her pen, and we hope she will watch every minute alteration in the female dress, and transmit her observations as early as possible in the month, that our patronesses at a distance from the capital, may have their curiosity satisfied without being tortured by suspence, or rendered uneasy by too long expectation. (vol. 6, p. 235)

No response was forthcoming and in 1777 Miss Stanley was brusquely informed that she had been replaced (vol. 8, p. 618). The new correspondent proved equally unreliable, however, and it was not until 1790 that a regular fashion report was established.

Yet the *Lady's Magazine* appears to have thrived because of, rather than in spite of, its unabashed amateurism. The editors were as haphazard as their correspondents. In May 1775 they admitted to having lost the remaining text of a whimsical serial novel entitled 'The Adventures of Cupid the Little' (narrated by a lap-dog to a gentleman who, by means of an obscure ancient document, has acquired the knowledge of animal language) and requested that the (female) author supply another copy (vol. 5, p. 213). The author did not oblige and readers continued to mourn its arrested development as late as November 1778. However, as one shrewd contributor put it in a letter of November 1770 'if you will but permit us to scribble, you never can have any want; for the desire of seeing our own productions appear, will be encouragement sufficient for the whole sex to purchase' (vol. 1, p. 171).

Despite the many interrupted ventures, including half of the forty essay serials offered by the magazine between 1771 and 1807 which ran to ten numbers or less under various titles such as 'The Female Rambler', 'The Censor', 'The Reasoner', and 'The Lady's Monitor', the *Lady's Magazine* did enjoy some remarkable successes. In particular an essay serial under the title 'The Matron' which opened in January 1774 ran for seventeen years. The Matron was a Martha Grey, a widow who introduces herself as 'in [her] grand climacterick . . . having been deeply engaged in numberless scenes, variegated and opposite, serious and comic, cheerful and afflicting' (vol. 5, p. 34). Mrs Grey regaled her readers with the dynastic fortunes of her son and daughter, both widowed, her foppish grandson Charles, her granddaughters, the flighty Emily and shy Sophia, and comic spinster niece, Miss Pen Partlett. Almost immediately, Mrs Grey's serial essay came to incorporate a problem page in which she gave bracing advice to anxious young ladies trying to decide between lovers, or confused about social protocol, as well as to their irate parents. Her advice column proved so popular that in 1789 it was exported to the United States; the letters and answers were reprinted in a Boston monthly entitled *Gentleman and Ladies' Town and Country Magazine*. Like many agony aunts, Mrs Grey was troubled by sceptics, and in August 1774 we find her roundly dismissing allegations that her correspondents were 'a set of fictitious beings' (vol. 5, p. 434). In many respects Martha Grey recalls the Female Spectator in her stern, often old-fashioned moralism, her frankness, her contempt for modern foppery. In a magazine that frequently printed opposing opinions in the same number (publishing diatribes against the whims of fashion side by side with copperplate engravings of the latest hairstyles, squeezing attacks on the pernicious effects of fiction-reading on young minds between an oriental tale and a letter serial), Mrs Grey's single-essay serial provided a certain coherence and continuity. Another popular feature was the medical advice column, and in particular that of Dr Cook, a gout-ridden retired practitioner who offered his services in September 1774. Cook's choice of topics in his column, 'The Lady's Practitioner', seems surprisingly progressive, covering menstrual pains (vol. 5, p. 578) to sore nipples from breast-feeding (vol. 6, p. 257). Correspondents wrote in requesting his recipes for both restoring and removing hair (vol. 6, p. 537; vol. 8, p. 599). However, like the tight-lacing controversy that occupied so many pages of the *Englishwoman's Domestic Magazine* in the mid nineteenth century (discussed in more detail in the next chapter), it appears that Dr Cook's column occasionally provided a means of indulging prurient sexual curiosity and a more vulgar brand of humour than the magazine commonly sanctioned. In June 1775, for example, we find him pontificating upon the superior beauty and breeding capacities of the redhead:

> Time was when golden locks were looked upon as very beautiful, and even the lass of golden hair was, for that very reason, the more eligible, and preferred before those of the sex who bore any different colour; – but the case is changed, and red hair is not so agreeable; though this I can say, such women have the finest skins, with azure veins, and generally become the best breeders of the nation. (vol. 6, p. 316)

Dr Cook's elderly eccentricity and his status as a medical practitioner, as well as his masculinity, enabled the magazine to broach issues that a female persona could not address, providing a sexual frisson in a magazine that otherwise prided itself on its morality and decorum in contrast with both predecessors and contemporaries.

It is clear that by no means all of the *Lady's Magazine*'s correspondents were female. Jean Hunter's extensive research establishes that contributions with a male signature were never less than a third of the total, and often exceeded those with a female signature (Hunter, 1976, pp. 108–9). The issue is further confused by the fact that most of the contributions were pseudonymous, and it was not until the late 1790s that the magazine began to publish the contributors' real names. Correspondents themselves repeatedly questioned the declared sex of another contributor. In June 1773 a 'Friend to the Fair Sex' complained bitterly:

I confess I do not know under what predicament to address you; for the pieces you publish under the signatures of ladies are so masculine, and those under the signature of gentlemen are so feminine, that my embarras is at least veniable. (vol. 4, p. 313)

Even the sex of the editors, then, was under dispute. While it seems more likely that a man should have concealed his sex under a female pseudonym in order to get published in a magazine expressly designed 'for the Fair Sex', it is also true that the *Lady's Magazine* consistently defined women as the consumers rather than producers of its more edifying material, if not its light fiction. With this in mind, it is possible that some female contributors wrote under male signature in order to join the host of 'friends' and 'admirers' of the sex who regularly enlarges upon philosophical and metaphysical questions of the respective capacities of the male and female of the species, rather than confine themselves to the habitual diet offered by 'female' contributors of epistolary fiction, translation, needlework patterns, songs and cookery receipts. Some women clearly did employ male personae for their contributions. In February 1774, when an irate reader wrote in to take issue with an article representing women as slaves to fashion and assumed its author to be male, the editors added a note that 'by the writer's hand [they were] led to think the author was a lady rather than a gentleman' (vol. 5, p. 64).

Whatever the actual sex of the majority of the *Lady's Magazine*'s thousands of contributors, it is apparent that it was formative in the development of the modern women's magazine. Every feature common to the twentieth-century form we know so well appears at one time or another in its pages; the agony aunt, occasional news reporting with a 'woman's' slant, features on famous women (past and present), cookery recipes, sewing patterns, medical advice, readers' letters, regular contributors. Like the modern women's magazine, and unlike the single-essay periodical, the *Lady's Magazine* was not constructed to be read from beginning to end, but rather according to the reader's interests and priorities, article by article. Also unlike the single-essay periodical, it makes little or no attempt to establish an internally consistent ideological position on contemporary issues. In December 1774 the editor was arguing with respect to the Queen that 'the virtues of her present majesty are living exhortations on her subjects to practice all the tacit duties of domestic life' (vol. 5, p. 626). Only four months later (April 1776), the same editor embarks on another aborted attempt to provide a history of famous women, opening with praise for the heroism of the martial Queen Boadicea without a thought for her failure in these same domestic virtues he had considered so requisite for a female monarch (vol. 6, p. 177).

This inconsistency in the interpretation of proper queenliness is in itself an indicator of changing taste and ideology in the women's magazine. The *Lady's Magazine* was always fascinated by royalty and, in particular, the royal ladies. In this respect, it foreshadows twentieth-century women's magazines' fondness for the 'inside story' on the royal family. However, it moves uneasily between the representation of queens and princesses as classical models of femininity – distant, beautiful, objects of fantasy and idealism for their 'public' – and the now more familiar rhetoric that locates the royal family as an extension of the 'family' of the magazine and its readers – well-known, much loved, and fallible human beings. The history of women's magazines' attention to royal figures would provide enough material for a full separate study. Suffice it to say that the tension registered in the *Lady's Magazine* signifies the incompleteness of the shift from a 'society' to a 'domestic' emphasis in women's magazines of the eighteenth century. The dominance of domestic ideology and its application to the representation of royalty in popular women's magazines was not to be established until well into the nineteenth century and, most significantly, through the development of photographic media which, to some extent, closed the gap between royalty and their public, transforming the former into familiar cultural icons.

Despite the striking symmetries of content, then, the late-eighteenth-century magazine was, in many respects, worlds away from its nineteenth- and twentieth-century successors. In particular, the *Lady's Magazine*, despite its many inconsistencies, consistently defines femininity in terms of leisure as opposed to labour. Its own readers militated against the magazine's provision of cookery receipts as inappropriate mundanity for a magazine that was supposed to provide entertainment and edification. Monthly articles entitled the 'Lady's Handmaid' and 'Confectionary Receipts' ran from its inception to the end of 1774, but were then summarily dropped. In 1780 we find one correspondent enraged by another's request to the editor for some culinary advice; she complains, 'Did the lady suppose you made cooking your study?' (vol. 11, p. 282). Needlework patterns, like cookery recipes (confectionary not Sunday roast), were designed to produce ornament, not useful domestic articles. The doctors' columns, similarly, were rarely solicited for 'practical' advice that might entail labour, such as the rearing of young children, but were viewed as beauty consultants. Mrs Grey was asked to provide advice about the control of amorous or unruly adolescents, but not how to manage a household or economise on domestic expense. Thus, a 'lady' was measured not by her domestic labour, but precisely by the number of leisure hours she had to fill by rehearsing from the magazine's music sheets, dressing according to its fashion plates, reading the morally instructive and fantasy literature it recommended to them.

A correspondent of February 1772 provides the editor with an outline and picture of a dream vision in which she observes the goddess of beauty presenting a Roman lady with a volume of the *Lady's Magazine* while a small boy at her feet reads a pattern for decorating an apron. The correspondent sums up the pleasures of the magazine thus:

> The Magazines which preceded yours were evidently calculated to corrupt the morals and vitiate the taste of the rising generation. Those which were more chaste, were in no respect adapted to the circle of the FAIR. What have we women to do with elaborate discourses on the legend of a piece of rusty metal; or the qualities of an unknown animal; the pretended speeches of a stammering senator, or the description of things invisible?
>
> Our sex was almost overlooked by the almost innumerable doers of Magazines. You first, and only you, thought the ornaments of the species worthy of being made more ornamental; by cultivating their understandings, at the same time as you provided them with rules to preserve, though not to sophisticate, their personal charms. (vol. 4, p. 64)

The correspondent here points to a number of significant features of the magazine that ensured its extraordinary longevity and financial success – its identification of women readers as a 'special interest' group with strictly delimited interests, its attention to female 'pleasure' or 'leisure' rather than labour, its representation of women as above all consumers rather than producers.

In the eighteenth century, then, we can observe in the vicissitudes of periodical literature the 'making' of a female reader provided with her own, gender specific, genre of the magazine. Men may be both readers and contributors to the genre, but the text constructs them as ultimately marginal to its activities. The *Lady's Magazine* offers its women readers a programme of femininity as ornament; becoming feminine is a task to be accomplished through the acquisition and consumption of the magazine itself, but a task wholly identified with the world of leisure, and a task that can be a pleasure, not a labour. The fact that women's magazines throughout the eighteenth century could only define women in terms of their relation to men (as wives, widows and daughters) is not so much an indicator of the increasing dominance of gender being the primary means of constructing identity (as opposed to class or status) as an indicator of the increasing identification of a particular class, the bourgeoisie, with the attributes of a particular gender, the feminine, newly defined wholly in terms of a domestic and private sphere. Women, as the *Lady's Magazine* insistently demonstrates, were perceived as the ornaments of a class, a class defined by its patterns of consumption rather than production, and which sought to display its new affluence and influence as part of its struggle to achieve cultural and political hegemony. This construction of class as gender, and in turn the linking of femininity with leisure and ornament, came to condition the making of the genre.

3

Nineteenth-century women's magazines

The complaint made in the *Lady's Magazine* of 1773 that 'Our sex was almost overlooked by the almost innumerable doers of Magazines' could scarcely have been made a century later. By the mid-1870s there was a well-established sector of the magazine press explicitly targeted at women readers. Still small by modern standards, it grew rapidly in the next thirty to forty years. At least fifty new titles appeared between 1870 and 1900, and although some were shortlived some were to last for sixty, seventy, and even a hundred years, material reminders that today's women's magazine is shaped by publishing traditions as well as by contemporary conditions. No wonder an article on 'Women's Newspapers' written in 1894 began with the comment:

> 'the irrepressible she' meets us at every turn in modern life, and perhaps the multiplication and development of newspapers devoted to her special interests, is not the least significant token of her vitality. (March-Phillips, 1894, p. 661)

By the end of the nineteenth century, then, women were consumers of magazines on a scale unimaginable a century earlier. This is partly, of course, because of the general development of print culture. In Britain, as in America, a truly popular or 'mass' press only evolved in the nineteenth century. Though there may be argument about precisely when a mass reading public first emerged, few historians would dispute either that it had come into existence by 1900, or that the periodical was central to that process (Altick, 1957, p. 135). Print at this point ceases to be the preserve of an elite and becomes available to a majority of the population. Women, as roughly half that population, must by definition have been caught up in the spread of reading to the masses.

General histories of the press, however, have tended to ignore the place of gender in the making of the modern reader, assuming that all readers were male or that masculinity was the norm (Altick, 1957; Lee, 1976; but see Vincent, 1989). The increasing importance of the magazine in this century, as in the previous one, has a close but complex relationship to changing constructions of gender difference. Take, for example, the role of fiction in the general magazine. The association between women readers and fiction, begun in the eighteenth century (Watt, 1957), continued through the nineteenth century, shaping both gender ideology and genre in the shape of the novel (Lovell, 1987). Little scholarly work on the relation between female readers and fiction magazines, whether defined as general or family journals, has been undertaken to date (Mitchell, 1981). However, this connection between fiction and the female reader was an important element in the development of the nineteenth-century periodical press, especially in the latter part of the century with the advent of large numbers of fiction magazines aimed at middle class women, and in some cases, like *The Argosy* and *Belgravia*, edited by women (Ellegard, 1957, pp. 32 ff).

At the most general level, the development of the magazine designed to be read by the middle-class family (men, women and children) was an important element in a wider process of re-defining leisure or pleasure in terms of the rational and the private, or domestic, as distinct from the public. In this ideal the context of the woman-centred home was taken as the norm. Different kinds of magazine located themselves differently in relation to this normative concept of the family with its gender divisions; only a few explicitly identified women as their exclusive readership. However, we would argue both that women were likely to enter the mass reading public in rather different ways from men, and that gender ideology shaped the development of the 'general magazines' as well as those specifically aimed at women.

However, our main concern here is, of course, with precisely with those magazines where women's 'special interests' were not only recognised but the basis for production. In the period from 1800 to the First World War women's magazines became established as an important sector of mass publishing. Contemporaries may have felt that these 'papers' were evidence of the 'irrepressible' nature of femininity. More recent accounts, like Alison Adburgham's, tend rather to see them as instruments of repression, collusive in the narrowing of women's horizons, so that any venture outside of the domestic came to be marked as 'unwomanly' (Adburgham, 1972, pp. 271–2). Such simple accounts do not do justice to the complexity involved in reading these texts. The definition of the female reader of magazines is a contradictory process, in which women's importance is both confirmed and strictly delimited, through which the 'feminine' is both repressed and returns as irrepressible. Before we turn to more detailed reading of particular 'key' moments in the magazine's history and individual publications, we pursue some of the wider issues raised by the emergence of mass market women's magazines in the nineteenth century.

The mass press and the making of the female reader

When we say the nineteenth century saw the emergence of women as the major consumers of magazines we mean this in two senses, economic and ideological. Women bought magazines, and had magazines bought for them. Publishing in the nineteenth century, developed in the context of capitalist industrialisation, depended on identifying or creating markets in order to make profit, as it still does. As the century went on and the periodical press became increasingly pervasive and diverse, publishers recognised the importance of women as consumers both of general periodicals and of those addressed specifically to them.

However, as well as, indeed as part of, making profit for their producers, magazines had also to offer their readers ways of making sense of themselves and the world. Women not only *bought*, they presumably also *read* the magazines. This is the second sense in which women were 'consumers' of the magazines addressed to them. Our study focuses primarily on the ideological aspect of women's consumption – but economics and ideology are always interdependent. Publishers defined women as a target market for print, but this was related to a wider redefinition of femininity in terms of certain kinds of consumption patterns, including the purchase of these magazines.

The economics of periodical publishing in the nineteenth century were complex. Magazines, newspapers and journals were, of course, subject to the same economic determinants as any other product. The industry required investment in machinery and development of distribution and marketing networks, like any other burgeoning industry on which Britain built its economic power in the wake of the first industrial revolution. The growth of the periodical press was inextricably linked with that of a number of other industries, including the railways, the postal system, and the power industries, first gas and then electricity, which provided domestic lighting. Expansion in all these areas combined with such social changes as the concentration of population in cities and towns, the growth of general literacy and the spread of education in response to demands from employers as well as the working class, all made the production of periodicals a growth industry for most of the century. Even when, or perhaps particularly when, the rest of the British economy slowed down toward the end of the century, the print industry continued to expand.

This success generated a history (or myth) in which the expansion of the periodical press was taken as the paradigm of the triumph of the 'free market' (Boyce, 1978, p. 26). As we saw in Chapter 2, government attempts to control access to 'news' by imposing taxes gave impetus to the emergence of the magazine in the eighteenth century. So, too, the battle between publishers and government shaped the form of periodical publication in the first half of the nineteenth century. From the 1790s onward the demand for newspapers and magazines grew in the face of government attempts to restrict it through Stamp Acts and taxes on paper and advertising. These taxes were first reduced and then lifted gradually in the 1840s and 1850s with the last (on paper) only disappearing in 1862. The abolition of all these 'taxes on knowledge', as they came to be called, marked the end of government intervention in the press through taxation. Not only was this moment the signal for a rapid expansion in periodicals of all kinds, it was also a symbolic triumph for the 'free press', a term which was itself a nineteenth-century coinage.

The mass press is, therefore, a press geared to the market economy. The development of special interest magazines for women in the nineteenth century must be situated in the context of the wider growth of the industry as a whole. Publishers sought out new markets, principally by targeting what we would now call 'consumer groups'. Magazines began to address groups of readers by age (children's magazines were, in particular, a new phenomenon), class, region, and, of course, gender. However, by a curious, but very familiar, asymmetry, publishers defined women as a distinct, gender-specific target group while men were not. This asymmetry can only be explained with reference to the ideological, as well as economic, determinants of the print industry. The general reader, like the general category of human being (or *man*), was assumed to be male. Women were a 'special interest' group by virtue of being 'not men', but men could not be similarly defined as 'not women'.

These asymmetries of gender enter into other aspects of the economics of mass publishing, but in rather different ways. Take, for example, the growing importance of advertising in publishing finance. We all know that magazine publishers in the late twentieth century depend on the peculiar nature of a product which enables them to sell the same space twice – once to the reader and again to the advertiser. This method of finance locks the magazine into a system in which it is sold not just as a product but as a vehicle for other products, and its readers are defined not only as consumers of magazines, but consumers in general.

Advertising had been a source of finance for publishers, especially of newspapers, well before 1800. By the 1820s, newspaper proprietors in Britain had begun to work with advertising agents as well as advertisers; the first American agency was founded in the 1840s (Lee, 1976, p. 85; Shuwer, 1966). However, the use of advertising in British newspapers was inhibited by a tax, originally imposed with many others as early as 1712. In periods of political agitation around the turn of the century, further Acts made such taxes more repressive (1797, 1815 and 1819). From 1815 to 1833 the rate was a prohibitive 3s 6d when it was reduced to 1s 6d. Magazines had been exempt from the tax and thus women's magazines, along with its fellows, were beginning to realise the possibilities of advertising from early in the century. *La Belle Assemblée* in 1823 declared itself 'a most respectable medium for advertisers' (quoted in Meech, 1986, p. 4). Yet, by more modern standards, or even those of the 1890s, advertising before the 1850s was relatively unimportant as a source of finance. Joint stock companies or private investment provided the seed capital, and then magazines depended heavily on cover sales for their revenue. Not until the eventual abolition of the tax in 1853 was the way opened for advertising to become central to the economics of publishing in all kinds of periodical.

The change in finance is evident in the appearance of the magazines themselves. In the early decades, advertisements were confined to the covers or the pages at the beginning and end of the number. They were routinely stripped out when the magazine was bound into volume form, and the use of display advertisements or visually interesting material was rare. By the 1880s some of the magazines we consider in this chapter carried as many pages of advertisements as of editorial material, and by the 1890s some even mixed advertising and editorial material on the same page. Display advertisements and visually exciting promotional material became part of the attraction of the magazine, as well as fundamental to its financial viability.

This revolution in the finance of periodical publishing increased the importance of women as a target group. While women earned far less than men, the ideology of the 'family wage' which served to perpetuate this earning inequity, gave women responsibility (if not always power) over the family purse. Women's role as consumers and spenders was, therefore, as today, economically far more important than their collective earning power would indicate. It is no accident that the late-nineteenth-century boom in magazines addressed specifically to women coincided with the increasing importance of advertising revenue in the financing of the periodical press, as we discuss in more detail later in this chapter.

Other aspects of the complex interplay of the economic and the ideological in the production of magazines are evident in the unlikely area of print technology. It was the logic of the market which made producers of magazines and newspapers take the lead in developing improved machinery for paper making, type setting, printing and illustration (Plant, 1974, p. 333ff, 281ff). Even in the 1820s, printing involved hand-set type and hand-operated flat presses on expensive paper. Illustration was by woodblock or engraving. By the 1890s new technologies enabled the production of paper from material other than rags, the rapid setting of whole lines of type, printing on vast rotary presses from rolls of paper, and processes of illustration which made it possible to reduce photographs successfully by the use of the half-tone block.

All the elements of the modern mass press were made possible by these advances. Cynthia Cockburn has shown how ideologies of gender entered into and shaped the material conditions of those who worked in the expanding print industry, resulting for example in the exclusion of women from the best paid work (Cockburn, 1981, pp. 41–58). If we consider the magazines directed specifically at women, we can see evidence that gender ideologies shaped the product, as well as the processes of production.

The techniques which made possible improved picture reproduction affected the whole of the periodical press, but they were particularly important for women's magazines, especially those concerned principally with fashion and dress. According to at least one contemporary, it was in a women's magazine, *The Lady's Pictorial*, that the new half-tone plate method of picture reproduction was first used in a periodical (Shorter, 1899, p. 481). This is hardly surprising, since this magazine was one of a number of 'ladies' papers' which made good illustration a high priority, above all in their fashion-plates. The stress on visual quality went beyond mere technological innovation. It was evidence of the continuing and developing importance of *appearance* in the definition of femininity. In tension with the domestic ideology centred on the maternal and the family was another ideal of the desirable woman which centred on physical beauty. Women's magazines like *The Lady's Pictorial* both carried and embodied the message that the visual was central to the feminine.

Technological improvements do not take place in a vacuum. In this case, they cannot be separated from the crucial changes which took place in financing and organisation in the industry. New machines enabled the rapid and cheap production of material, but they were only economic if used for large runs, and besides, they involved outlay of vast capital sums. Economic pressure was toward larger-scale operations. The evolution of large publishing firms which produced a range of magazines was gradual and continued to be financially risky throughout the century (see the story of Cassells in Nowell-Smith, 1958, esp. pp. 157ff). But it was also inevitable, as was the accompanying differentiation and specialisation of the various roles of proprietor, publisher, editor and journalist.

It was Newnes, the creator of *Tit-bits* in 1882, who first succeeded in building a huge publishing empire based on production of a range of periodicals, financed not only from private investment but also from flotation on the Stock Exchange. He was followed rapidly by Harmsworth and Pearson. These three men had between them, by the First World War, established in Britain a pattern of corporation ownership which has come to dominate twentieth-century magazine publication. All three firms later fed into the formation of IPC, the largest British magazine publishing company of the late twentieth century. Most of the elements of this 'New Journalism' were pioneered in the United States and this was particularly true of financial methods. The purchase of the National Magazine Company by Hearst in 1911 signalled the arrival of United States money on the British publishing scene. More important, it also marked the beginning of the multinational company, that central feature of twentieth-century publishing in general and the women's magazine in particular.

Newnes, Harmsworth and Pearson all recognised the importance of the women's magazine for their financial operations, both because of the market for direct sales to women and as a result of the new importance attached to advertising. In the 1890s Harmsworth established a subsidiary concerned solely with magazines for women. Together with Pearson's *Home Notes*, his penny weeklies – *Home Chat*, *Home Sweet Home*, and *Forget-Me-Not* – were immensely successful. D.C. Thomson entered the field in 1910 with *My Weekly*. These magazines were central to the financial success of their parent companies.

The ideological implications of women's consumption of periodicals were even more complex than the economic. As we have already suggested, the term 'mass press', at its simplest, means the transformation of reading from an elite to a majority practice. In the nineteenth century, this means first the consolidation of a predominantly bourgeois or middle-class press and then a shift to encompass the lower-middle and working-classes. It was not surprising, then, to find issues of class formation entangled with the history of the press as an institution. To contemporaries and historians alike, the nineteenth-century periodical press was a focus for the forging of class identities and a forum for the discussion and enactment of class relations. It is crucial to understand that in the first half of the century, periodical publishing catered increasingly for a bourgeois readership and in so doing it was instrumental in the social revolution which brought that class to political and ideological, as well as economic, dominance. This process was more or less complete by the 1850s and 1860s, with the appearance of the *Daily Telegraph* and a vast range of middle-class magazines.

But the periodical press was not only the instrument for the consolidation of middle-class ideology; it also increasingly addressed itself to the skilled artisans and literate working classes who were invited to 'improve' themselves by participating in print culture. The improving and radical artisan magazines of the 1830s and 1840s extended the range of print which was already offered to the working class in popular penny songs, fictions and sensational newspapers. However, it was not until the 1880s and 1890s that the bulk of the working class had access to a range of magazines and a daily metropolitan newspaper (the *Daily Mail*, established in 1892). Print now emerged as a medium primarily of entertainment combined with information rather than as the route to self-improvement.

Obviously ours has been a highly simplified version of press history, but it will do to indicate the process of broadening the class basis of popular print in which magazines for women were involved. Beeton's *Englishwoman's Domestic Magazine*, for example, was important for establishing the format of the middle-class domestic magazine in the 1850s, a format that was adapted and extended to target working-class women in the period between the 1880s and the First World War. Key moments here were the appearance of *Home Notes* and *Home Chat* in the 1890s and *My Weekly* and *Woman's Weekly* in 1910 and 1911, which set the pattern for middle- and working-class women's magazines for the next fifty years.

Again, the mutual articulation of class and gender relations is evident; in particular, the ideology of domesticity which successfully related class, gender and nation under the idealisation of 'feminine' virtue, was crucial for periodical discourse. The middle-class 'family magazine' was an important sub-genre throughout the century. Some were intended for general reading, others aimed specifically at the Victorian family Sunday market. All assumed the idea of the woman-centred home. Relationships between gender roles and class positions were also implicitly drawn on in artisan magazines of the 1850s, such as *Eliza Cook's Journal* or *The Family Economist*, which aimed at a class dialogue centred around the shared values of self-improvement and domestic virtue. So closely related were the gender and class definitions that any attempt at a definitive map of nineteenth-century women's magazines must run into difficulties over where to draw the boundaries. The middle-class general and artisan magazines which tried to disseminate middle-class virtues to the working class often depended on the same ideology of 'the family' and the domestic as did those magazines specifically addressed to women.

Gender difference, like class difference, both shaped and was shaped by the periodical press. However, gender and class did not operate in similar ways. Historians tracing the development of class identities in the early nineteenth century have seen the cheap periodical press as an important site for the struggle over conflicting class-based definitions of 'knowledge' and 'power' (Hollis, 1970; Wiener, 1969). Historians of gender, however, have found little evidence of a *struggle* over the meaning of femininity in journals or magazines (Adburgham, 1972; Gorham, 1982, p. 18). They argue that although class division in the nineteenth century was perceived as socially produced and historically contingent (a view shared by those from widely different political positions), gender difference was widely regarded as natural and universal – certainly until the 1880s and the emergence of the 'new woman' debate. Unlike men, who were discussed as individuals, or groups, or classes, women were represented as wholly determined by domestic roles and biological functions (daughter, wife, mother) or by their failure to fulfil these roles (spinster and 'old maid'). Periodical readers, whether of general or of women's magazines, were offered a model of femininity as undifferentiated and uncontested, focused on the private and domestic as distinct from the masculine world of politics, law and 'work' (Palmegiano, 1976, p. 5).

In what follows we shall argue that this account is an over-simplification. Domestic ideology was neither monolithic nor static; indeed, it was deeply contradictory. There was tension, for example, between, on the one hand, the ideal of the maternal woman whose beauty was inner and spiritual, and, on the other, the assumption that femininity meant physical beauty. Besides, the domestic model was simply unattainable for many working-class women, especially for the large number of them in domestic service, whose work underpinned the middle-class home. Such magazines as *The British Workwoman* and *The Servant's Magazine* recognised this explicitly. Even for middle-class women the ideal of marriage and the continuing financial support of a husband was not certain, given the demographic imbalance between the sexes, and the chances of the death of a spouse.

Such tensions are apparent in women's magazines through fractures and lapses, rather than by direct address. *The English Woman's Journal* was unusual in making demands for equal access to the public arena central to its project. It lasted for six years (1858–64) and, though it had successors – notably *The English-woman's Review* (1863–1903) – none of them made the impact they sought upon the general public (Rendall, 1987, pp. 112–38; Murray, 1985, pp. 138–42). More typical were the bulk of new magazines for women in the 1880s and 1890s. These were launched during the debate around the 'New Woman', but they rarely addressed themselves to her. Even an ostensibly 'advanced' magazine like *Woman* concentrated on fashion, gossip and fiction, rather than employment or sexuality. In other journals, the New Woman was constantly invoked in her absence – rather as the feminist has been invoked in some domestic magazines of the 1970s and 1980s – but always to show her as aberrant and unfeminine. Many of these magazines defined the interests of the reader in narrow, not to say oppressive, terms; but, as John Stuart Mill pointed out as early as the 1860s, the constant reassertion of the dominant ideal of femininity itself acts as proof that it is neither nature, nor self-evident, nor even secure (Mill, 1912, *passim*, esp. pp. 451ff).

We cannot know for certain how nineteenth-century readers negotiated with, or employed, the contradictions and conflicts of feminine identity as defined by the magazine. We can only speculate from our reading of them and understanding of the reader they seem to construct. Although we can be fairly sure that *some* desire was satisfied – these magazines were bought in large numbers, were kept, and were circulated – to suppose that we can define precisely what pleasure these readers actually got from their reading is somewhat more hazardous. Bearing these problems in mind, we still want to resist collapsing the historical reader into the reader 'constructed' by the text, or interpreting nineteenth-century magazines for women simply in terms of female passivity and oppression.

We aim to approach our sample therefore in the consciousness that, like their first readers, *we* bring our own historical situation to our reading. Moreover, they are our history. Just as the nineteenth century was the period in which the foundations were laid for the pivotal role of the women's magazine in today's publishing industry, so the familiar format and pattern of contents in today's magazine can be traced back to developments in the last century.

The bourgeois ideal: the Englishwoman's domestic magazine

The early nineteenth century inherited from the eighteenth both the genre of the women's magazine, with its gender-defined readership, and specific examples of the form, including the *Lady's Magazine*. Fiction and essays were still a staple, and there were numerous 'Annuals' which made illustration and entertainment their selling-point. But the power of the bourgeois ideal of femininity pervaded the culture of the magazines from the start of the century. The linked processes of defining femininity exclusively in terms of the domestic and strengthening the image of the magazine as 'conduct manual', or guide to feminine existence, were already under way before the new century and were well established when Victoria came to the throne (Shevelov, 1989, pp. 188–9). The evangelical revival in the late eighteenth century invested a new importance in moral and religious teaching, purveyed through tracts, books and magazines like Sarah Trimmer's ponderously titled, *The Family Magazine or a Repository of Religious Instruction and Rational Amusement designed to counteract the pernicious Tendency of immoral Books etc. which have circulated of late Years among the inferior classes of People*.

Hannah More, one of the most influential disseminators of evangelical ideas, advocated women's acceptance of the home as their primary sphere of religious influence. Her message was not without its own internal contradictions, especially in as far as it suggested that women also had a social responsibility for philanthropy outside the home (Davidoff and Hall, 1987, pp. 167ff). However, it was the stress on women's domestic duty which was carried forward powerfully into the rest of the century in general magazines for family reading like *The Saturday Magazine* and later *The Leisure Hour*, in those addressed specifically to women in their general domestic role, like *The Christian Lady's Friend and Family Repository*, and in those which targeted women as mothers, including such magazines as *The Mother's Friend*.

Very different from these serious journals of religious duty and family life were well-established titles from the late eighteenth century which survived into the new era. These included the *Lady's Magazine*, which continued to appear, but gradually declined in importance. In 1832 the *Lady's Magazine* merged with two other turn-of-the-century survivors, *The Lady's Monthly Museum* and *La Belle Assemblée*. In 1847 the combined journal ceased publication altogether, thus marking, according to Cynthia White, the end of an era (White, 1970, p. 41). It is significant that the demise of these older-style periodicals was followed five years later by the appearance of the most successful mid-century magazine, which was to provide a model for future developments in the genre.

Samuel and Isabella Beeton's *Englishwoman's Domestic Magazine* was the grandmother of today's *Woman, Woman at Home* and a host of others. Samuel Beeton produced a monthly magazine for the middle class at the right price (2d) at the right time (1852). After two years, he could claim a sales figure of 25,000 per month, and by the launch of the New Series in 1860 this figure had doubled ('Preface' to New Series, 1860). Isabella had by this point joined her husband and was involved in every aspect of the magazine's production, as she was in their later ventures into the magazine industry. Together they were confident enough to make the New Series both larger and visually more attractive with better-quality paper and a colour engraving of the latest Paris fashions at the front of each number.

Beeton's success was undoubtedly the result of having found the right formula for his bourgeois readership, but it was also a triumph of good timing. It appeared at the moment when bourgeois dominance of Britain became absolutely secure. By 1852, Chartism had been defeated, the economy was booming, and the Great Exhibition of 1851, a visible sign of mid-Victorian prosperity, had signalled the triumph of bourgeois values. Central to the definition of the middle class, as we have already said, was the differentiation and separation of male and female spheres, accompanied by a rhetoric of complementarity. Women were to be confined to home and family; these were claimed to be of equal value to the 'occupations' of their masculine counterparts, but were not, of course, economically rewarded in the same way (Davidoff and Hall, 1987, p. 30). However, the sexual difference which was so marked a characteristic of mid-nineteenth-century middle-class culture was developed within a common ideology of the importance of work, in contrast with the eighteenth-century magazine's definitions of both 'femininity' and bourgeois culture as 'leisure'. Nineteenth-century domestic books and magazines defined women in terms of a series of demanding activities, which could be subsumed under the general category of 'homemaking', conceived of as practical (the running of the household), economic (the managing of domestic finances) and moral (biological reproduction redeemed through the work of spiritual and emotional regeneration and sustenance).

The Beetons' domestic magazine spoke to and for this bourgeois concept of the feminine. Defining his target readers firmly as 'women' rather than 'ladies', Beeton located true femininity in the middle class and, therefore, defined it in terms of the private and the domestic. His magazine was, he claimed, for those who wanted to 'make home happy' (vol. 1, 1852, p. 1). A central element in the Beetons' successful formula was – as the subtitle of the magazine indicated – the provision of 'practical information and instruction' in those matters considered essential to homemaking: recipes, sewing-patterns, tips on gardening and the care of pets, advice on household budgets. Beeton drew here not only upon the tradition of the lady's magazine, but from that other important tradition of writing for women which included the conduct book, the domestic treatise, and the serious, often religious, tracts on women's duties already mentioned. However, the *Englishwoman's Domestic Magazine* drew not so much on the evangelical tradition, as on the work of writers like Sarah Ellis, whose series *The Women of England, Wives of England* and *Daughters of England* represented English middle-class culture as the highest expression of womanliness. Even the Beetons' title indicates how, in common with Mrs Ellis, they related their ideal femininity to class and national characteristics.

The magazine also, however, offered itself to its readers as 'entertainment' or recreation. It included serialised fiction, articles on miscellaneous literary topics, and gossip. It ran competitions, and offered prizes. Nor were these marginal elements of the magazine. The fiction, in particular, occupied an important place in terms of both proportion of space and positioning in the magazine. How, then, does this square with the argument about the centrality of domestic work outlined above?

There are two aspects to our answer. First, 'home' itself had a complex function in mid-Victorian understanding of work and leisure. The whole ideology of separate spheres rested on the belief that men, who had access to both public and private worlds, should find at home their leisure and recreation. Indeed the work and leisure separation was demonstrated in the geographical separation of workplace from home, which came to characterise middle-class life. While the domestic, therefore, represented work for the woman, it meant leisure for the man. Moreover, men's domestic pleasure depended on the illusion that home was maintained without any work other than his. Home, therefore, was both the site of women's work *and* of the denial of that work. A further complication exists, in that for middle-class women, home was also their place of leisure. Confined to the domestic by their gender, they were enabled by their class to enjoy leisure time generally inavailable to working-class men and women. Home was, therefore, the site of leisure for middle-class men, and of work and leisure for women. Indeed, as we have already argued, the magazine was part of the growing leisure industry of the nineteenth century. It was an embodiment of an ideal of rational entertainment which centred on the privatised world of the family. No wonder, then, that the *Englishwoman's Domestic Magazine* formula, a mixture of entertainment and practical work manual, was so successful. The adaptations of the formula in today's women's magazines is a sign of the persistence of the contradictory meanings of home which we inherit, and of the still tangled relationship of domestic work and femininity.

The complexity of the meaning of 'home' as the site of the feminine was matched by contradictory meanings of female sexuality. On the one hand, woman's role was to be beautiful, dressed in clothes which expressed the social status of her husband or father and her own desirability. But the domestic role demanded that her sexuality could only be expressed through maternity. This contradiction is particularly evident in two elements of the *English-woman's Domestic Magazine*, its illustrations and its problem-page. The most immediately striking aspect of the magazine and a major selling-point was the fashion-plate of the latest Paris model facing the front page, and the accompanying paper pattern folded inside the magazine so that you could make up the dress in the illustration, or get it made up for you. This was not an entirely original formula, of course. *La Belle Assemblée* or *Bell's Court and Fashionable Magazine addressed particularly to the Ladies*, which had merged with *The Lady's Magazine*, had used the fashion plate as a draw, giving fashion illustration and corset design a high priority. However, the Beetons took only this one aspect of the paper for their new-style periodical, divorcing it from the rest of the package. They dispensed with the other characteristic features of the 'society' magazine, including articles on politics and science.

The introduction into the domestic magazine of the rather different image of femininity represented by the fashion-plate was a potential source of contradiction. For, after all, the image was that of woman as object of desire; the garments displayed were not suitable to activity or work of any kind. This sits oddly with the ideal of femininity in terms of cookery and gardening notes, even though the reader's task was understood as the supervision of those servants actually engaged in physical labour. By bringing together the fashion-plate with the dress-maker's pattern, the Beetons offered a double pleasure – the pleasure of the attractive coloured plate with its image of the desirable woman, symbol of female beauty and conspicuous consumption, on the one hand; on the other, the pleasure of the fantasy that by her own skills the reader could transform herself into that same woman, the object of the reader's gaze. The contradiction between the magazine as work-manual, directed toward the homemaker, and the magazine as purveyor of pleasure, directed toward the leisured woman, is literally papered over with the paper pattern. The persistence of this method in dealing with contradictory definitions of femininity in today's magazines is striking. It underpins the success of magazines like *Prima* and has become almost a cliche of female reading.

In the 1850s and 1860s, however, it was part of a brilliant but potentially explosive set of strategies by which the Beetons sought to hold together the contradictory definitions of the female reader. Another such strategy was the way Beeton dealt with his correspondents in the magazine's problem-page. The original title for the correspondence column, 'Cupid's Postbag' invited confidences, particularly on romantic and sexual relations, but it almost immediately disappeared, reappearing later as the rather more open, if self-conscious, 'Conversazione'. As its title suggests, the tone of the column was always rather arch. Beeton dealt with the correspondence and adopted the persona of the masterful editor, carrying out the promise made in his opening number, to act as mentor to his female readers (vol. 1, 1852, p. 1). His relationship toward his readers was that of an authority figure who was by definition male and older, more experienced, than the readership which was positioned as female and *therefore* younger, less experienced. This masculine persona was emphasised in the semi-flirtatious tone which sometimes coloured the editorial comments as in this response to a question:

> A correspondent wants to know what a flirt is. Virgin innocence! You know well enough what a flirt is. Did you not – not intentionally, of course – make α, β, γ and δ all fall in love with you, including the young man with the ginger-coloured hair and the lisp. Was it this beguiled and betrayed one who says:
>
> > Woman's love is like Scotch snuff
> > You get one pinch and that's enough?
> > (New Series, vol. 9, 1864, p. 228)

Given this tone, it perhaps should not surprise us that in the 1860s the 'Conversazione' section erupted into a controversy over tight-lacing which can only be described as semi-pornographic. The editor occasionally rebuked those, both men and women, who wrote in with detailed descriptions of the pleasures of tight lacing. He regularly threatened to end the correspondence, but conscious, perhaps, that the notoriety it was bringing the magazine did it no financial harm, he allowed it to continue for over a year, concluding it with a promise of a book based on the letters (New Series, vol. 4, 1867, p. 224). There was a similarly tendentious correspondence on the subject of whipping and the corporal punishment of children and servant girls.

The corset controversy presents in a particularly acute form the complexity of the social definitions of femininity the magazine represented. The corset was not only associated *with* the female body, it became a cultural fetish, a representation *of* the female body. As underwear it also signified undress and had the status of a powerful erotic symbol. However it was also a symbol of respectability. The woman who went out unlaced was either a dangerous feminist and an advocate of rational dress, or a woman who brought into the public world of the streets the body which was only appropriate to the most intimate moments of the home. Of course, outside the bedroom, only the *effects* of the corset were visible, but this play between the visible and the invisible was central to the cultural meaning of lacing. Like tight-lacing itself, the magazine's constraining definitions of femininity carried contradictory meanings.

The Beetons' grasp of the financial potential which lay in publishing for women was evident not just in this magazine, or Isabella's famous *Household Management* which first appeared in book form in 1861. They understood very early that the diversification of the market which had led to the targeting of women readers could be carried further. What about periodicals for young women, for upper-class ladies, or even 'the engaged girl'? The Beetons began exploring this avenue in the 1860s with *The Queen*, a magazine aimed at society ladies, and *The Young English Woman*, full of 'Fiction and Entertaining Literature' of a kind appropriate for 'girls of tender age'. After the death of Isabella, however, Samuel seems to have been unable to keep his publishing empire afloat and sold the titles, mainly to Ward, Lock and Tylor, who continued to exploit the Beeton name and the Beeton ideas for decades (Freeman, 1977).

In the 1880s, more than twenty years after the Beetons had begun the process, this kind of diversification underwent a sudden boom. Lower-middle-class women, upper-class young ladies, 'matrons', were all new 'markets' exploited by publishers. The variations on the basic formula laid down the pattern of twentieth-century publishing in the magazine. We identify three distinct groups of magazines typical of this development: the relatively expensive (Sixpenny) weekly ladies' paper aimed at the upper-class woman; the good-quality middle-class domestic magazine, which cost up to sixpence per month; and the penny weeklies aimed at the lower-middle- or working-class woman. In this selection we are evidently neglecting certain important kinds of magazine publication, including that devoted almost exclusively to romantic fiction. However, in a study of this kind, selectivity is inevitable, and we continue to focus on a few texts chosen as illustrative of key issues, rather than duplicating more general surveys.

Ladies' papers

The particular inconsistencies evident in the *Englishwoman's Domestic Magazine* were less apparent in *The Queen*, launched by Samuel Beeton ten years later. The title was almost immediately sold to Cox, who developed it into a leading fashion magazine of a type which became important in the late nineteenth century and that still continues. *The Queen* (subtitled 'The Lady's Newspaper'), *The Lady's Pictorial*, *Gentlewoman* and other similar 'papers for ladies' shared a number of characteristics which distinguished them as a group. All, apart from Beeton's pioneering venture, were established in the 1880s and 1890s. All continued through the Edwardian era and beyond. They have to be distinguished from another group of magazines which also laid claim to the status of 'lady-ship', the cheap fiction magazines, sometimes described as 'mill-girl magazines' such as *My Lady's Novelette*. These latter were descended from nineteenth-century popular fiction which appeared in penny parts or cheap magazine format and drew largely on gothic conventions in their depiction of gently born maidens threatened by aristocratic villains against a backdrop of gorgeously furnished apartments. They may have had no claim to 'Ladyland', as one commentator complained, but they were unlikely to be confused with those 'ladies' papers' with which we are concerned and which claimed to be read by real-life 'ladies' (White, 1970, p. 70).

The most important characteristic these magazines had in common was precisely that they defined their readers as 'ladies' rather than 'women'. The connotations of the word 'lady' were much debated in the late-nineteenth-century world of women's magazines. When Oscar Wilde was approached to edit Cassell's magazine *Lady's World* he agreed only on the condition that the name be altered to *Woman's World*, a change duly effected in 1887

(Ellman, 1987, pp. 274–8; Nowell-Smith, 1958, pp. 253–9). Whatever the complexities of this debate about the meaning of 'lady', it was a word which always brought class and status meanings to bear on gender definition. Whereas the *Englishwoman's Domestic Magazine* had associated femininity with the ideal of the 'domestic woman', seeking to dignify the emotional and practical work of women in the home, the 'ladies' magazines' marginalised domesticity and focused on definitions which foregrounded appearance, social graces and accomplishments, as opposed to labour. They had little to say on housekeeping, childcare, or gardening. Fashion-plates and detailed accounts of the latest style in dress took priority. Fiction had its place, but was marginalised in favour of brief reviews of recent publications, along with notices of concerts and exhibitions, literary gossip, and interviews with writers. In many respects these ladies' papers continued the eighteenth-century tradition that had defined women in terms of their leisure rather than their domestic skills. It is significant, for example, that when *The Lady's Pictorial* featured needlework it was likely to be embroidery or fancy work, rather than paper patterns to be made up.

It was not that the relation between women and home was entirely ignored in these magazines, but that its representation was quite different from that of either the middle-class journals of the period, like *Woman at Home*, or the cheap popular magazines like *Home Notes* and *Home Chats*. 'Home' in *The Gentlewoman* or *Queen* was not the site of woman's work but the visible expression of her taste and, implicitly, of her status. A persistent feature was the illustrated tour of an aristocratic mansion – what we have come to call a 'stately home' – in which the lady of the house conducted readers round her architectural and artistic treasures. More important, however, were the ever-present articles and advertisements in which, either in high quality pictures or in print, furniture, pictures, books and other cultural objects were paraded before the readers as indicators of taste, culture and (implicitly) wealth. It is difficult without more information on patterns of readership to know quite how to read this material. Were these magazines offering their readers fantasy, or realisable models of good taste? Given that readers respond differently according to their own situation, it seems likely that these articles, like those in *Homes and Gardens* today, offer their readers both at once, as Beeton offered his readers both the fashion-plate and the paper pattern. Here, however, the work of making the connection was hidden.

The importance of the *aristocratic* lady as both the subject and the implied reader of the magazines cannot be overstated. Nor should these magazines be read too simply as a nostalgic endeavour to recreate the older model of the leisured lady. This 'lady' was a new creature, the product of the regrouping of the 'upper ten thousand' families in the period between the 1880s and the First World War. The Court and the Queen played a key role in this process. It is significant that Beeton called his paper after the monarch and invited her patronage. The presence of a woman in the most important public office in the country reverberated through nineteenth-century women's magazines in various ways, dependent to some extent on fluctuations in the standing of the monarchy through Victoria's reign. The construction of Queen as Empress in the last two decades of the century was a redefinition of a bourgeois monarch in terms which excited the press at all levels. Combined with this was the emergence of the Court as the centre of fashion and 'high society' which characterised the Edwardian period, but which began at the end of Victoria's reign. Interest in the Court, aristocracy and specifically the Royal Family is not a twentieth-century invention, nor was it confined to the ladies' papers in the period we are considering here. However, for these papers, court functions, royal personages, and the correct etiquette in Society (with a capital 'S') provided staple copy, gave an excuse for special pull-outs and pictures, and provided endless questions for the correspondence columns – 'Given an elder maiden sister of 32 may a young one of 17 be chaperoned to a ball by the elder sister?' (*Gentlewoman*, vol. 2, 1879, p. 20).

Given this particular definition of 'lady' it is, then, not surprising that the second characteristic common to the 'ladies' paper' was a stress on appearance, dress or fashion. Even Beeton's New Series *Englishwoman's Domestic Magazine* had limited its fashion-plates to one per issue at the front. *Queen* and *Gentlewoman* included several examples of the latest dress styles, all presented in high-quality pictures. Visual appeal was both the medium and the message of these sixpenny magazines, the nineteenth-century equivalent of today's glossies. Unlike the domestic magazine they featured femininity as the object of the gaze, a

definition relatively undisturbed by conflicting ideas of motherhood and homemaking. There were contradictions implicit in the
gorgeous images of anatomically impossible women, but they were
of a different order. Perhaps the most important of these
contradictions was that between the role of the reader as the
one who enjoyed the pleasures of looking, as against the invitation
offered to her to be the one who is looked at, to act as object
rather than subject of the gaze. This is, of course, still evident in
current manifestations of the form: the *Cosmo* girl is offered to the
female reader as both object of the look and model for identification or aspiration.

The third characteristic these magazines share relates both to
the status and class definitions of their readers and to the stress on
female beauty. They were all marked by a heavy reliance on
advertising, especially of 'beauty' products (soap, corsets) and of
high-quality dress shops and places to visit. *The Lady* in particular
came to rely on small classified advertisements to keep it
financially buoyant, a policy it still pursues successfully more
than a hundred years after its establishment. Increasingly, as
marketing techniques, product advertising concentrated on well-
known brand names. The stress on the advertisement as a device
for conveying verbal information – promises or assurances – gave
way to a stress on the visually attractive. Advertisements came to
take up as many full pages as editorial material, which itself was
largely devoted to beautifully produced illustrations. Advertising
pages became an attractive as well as substantial part of the whole.
The definition of 'a lady' in terms of her conspicuous consumption
apparent in the elaborate dresses of the fashion-plate was echoed
in the invitations of the advertisement to transform yourself into
all that was desirable in gender and class or status terms.

Advertising enabled these magazines to keep their cover price
down to sixpence when the costs of production were probably
double that price. In magazines like *Gentlewoman* and *Lady's
Pictorial* where almost half the pages were given over to advertisements, their impact was not simply economic. The advertisements
strengthened the connection made elsewhere between femininity
and looking or being looked at. However, they also made explicit
another element of that definition, namely the link between
femininity and consumption (represented as 'shopping'). True
femininity was, ironically, offered as both an aspect of high

status and something which could be bought: a marriage like those so beloved of contemporary gossip, between the impoverished English aristocrat and the American heiress.

These ideas of femininity differ substantially from those elaborated in the Beetons' mid-Victorian model. They carried forward the eighteenth-century idea of the lady defined by her participation in a cultural life made possible by her economic position, but the way this idea was reworked was very much of its time. In particular, the importance of the visual elements underpinned by new technology and new methods of finance looked forward to the twentieth, rather than back to the eighteenth, century. The pages of advertisement which abutted on the fashion-plates and photographs of the famous 'at home', all worked to tie the knot between ideas of womanliness and ladyship, appearance and shopping. In the 1890s this pattern became evident in women's magazines which offered ostensibly very different models of the feminine. Even an 'advanced woman' magazine like *Woman* relied heavily on advertisements for corsets and Pear's soap to keep its cover price low. It also carried, in direct contradiction to its stated aim, the message that woman's appearance and dress was central to her membership of the class of 'lady', and that both of these depended in turn on her spending power and discrimination as a consumer.

These ladies' papers embodied a model of femininity in which appearance and taste were central. In their pages gender difference was powerfully shaped by class and status. However, the ideal of 'The Lady' as Ruskin had pointed out in 'Of Queen's Gardens', had traditionally included elements of social responsibility as well as grace and taste. The idea of a sisterhood between women based on a common humanitarian concern may seem the antithesis of the obsessive interest in the 'upper ten-thousand' which characterised all these papers (though only *Queen* actually ran a column with that name). And yet, occasionally, evidence of just such a sense of social concern breaks through the pages. As we might expect, philanthropic activity was supported as part of the lady's duty, even if it only extended as far as choosing suitable items for, or running, a stall at a charity bazaar. But it went further than that. The magazines carried reports of meetings, not just of sanitary associations, but of the National Union of Women Workers, the Women's Co-Operative Guild and even, on occasion, of suffrage societies (*Gentlewoman*, vol. 2, 1891, p. 673). The assumption must be that these were of interest to readers, or, indeed, that the readers were actively involved.

The reports assumed a definition of women's role which challenged the traditional model of the lady dispensing charity to the poor on an individual basis. As such they were part of a general movement in the period. Whatever was happening elsewhere, however, the potential for disruption was always ultimately contained. One particularly striking example will illustrate this process. In 1892, the *Gentlewoman* conducted a poll among its readers measuring their attitude to the question of women's suffrage. It claimed a readership of 47,000, out of which 9,459 readers participated in the poll. Of these, 8,301 of these voted 'yes' to votes for women and 1,118 voted 'no' (*Gentlewoman*, vol. 4, 1892, p. 779). This astonishing result made no impact on the magazine. The editor continued to ignore the apparent radicalism among his readers, who also continued to read the magazine and in increasing numbers. By 1900 it claimed a circulation of 250,000 (White, 1970, p. 66) who do not appear to have demanded any more serious address to women's political and public role.

Domestic magazines: the late nineteenth century

Powerful as they were, these ladies' journals did not displace magazines which followed in the tradition exemplified by the Beetons' *Englishwoman's Domestic Magazine*. It was the middle-class-women's magazine, rather than the upper-class-ladies' paper, which provided the model for most of the new periodicals of the post-1885 boom. However, the formula, and the way in which the Beetons, for example, had articulated the relation between class and gender, was not carried forward unchanged; it was adapted for the new situation of the late Victorian to Edwardian period. With the success of penny magazines, aimed at the lower-middle- and working-class woman in the 1890s, the same basic formula was used with minor modifications. Most notably the equation of femininity with domesticity had become so pervasive that it could be presented as natural rather than as essentially middle class.

The most important ·of the few contrary currents to the dominant discourse of the domestic, was the one we have been discussing with regard to the sixpenny papers – a definition of the female reader centred on dress, appearance and social (as distinct from public) life outside the home. Increasingly, too, magazines had to respond to the contradiction between the discourse of domesticity and the economic positions of those readers who were being forced into the labour market, or who had begun to demand the right to 'male' occupations. Almost all these magazines ran occasional articles on women at work. Their letters pages evidence the gap between the image of the dependent woman and the reality of women's lives. The contemporary figure of the 'new woman' who embodied the resolution of these economic and sexual demands was as notable by her absence from the pages of these women's magazines as she was from the aristocratic journals. The problems of defining female sexuality were again addressed obliquely in letters pages, and in the fiction, which tended to deal with love and marriage (in that order).

Woman at Home (sub-titled 'Annie Swan's Magazine') was a sixpenny monthly launched in 1893. It placed itself squarely in the Beeton tradition, in that it explicitly addressed the middle-class woman who was, as she should be, 'at home'. It was among these women, Annie Swan believed, that the best examples of femininity and womanliness were to be found (vol. 1, 1893–4, p. 62). However, *Woman at Home* drew on other traditions of publishing as well. Annie Swan herself was a romantic novelist with a strong following among women readers (as Eliza Haywood of the eighteenth-century *Female Spectator* had been). She was not the editor, despite the feature of her name on the title page and the prominence her columns were given in the magazine itself. The editor was, in fact, one 'Claudio Clear', alias Robertson Nicholl, a Presbyterian minister and well known as a columnist and reviewer. Although his name never appeared in the magazine, Nicholl brought to it both moral seriousness and professional expertise.

Backed by a well-established publisher prepared to spend £1,100 on its launch, *Woman at Home* aimed to 'catch the masses' even though it defined them as middle, rather than working, class (Darlow, 1925, p. 112). To this end it deployed all the latest technological and journalistic methods, claiming that it would be for women what the *Strand Magazine* was for men. The *Strand* occupied a key place in Newnes' publishing house in the 1890s and was regarded as the leader in the new journalism. *Woman at*

Home, therefore, drew on romantic fiction and non-conformist religious journalism and also made use of the methods of 'New Grub Street' in the construction of its female readership. It was an immediate success – the print run of 100,000 copies of the first number sold out and a reprint was necessary. The magazine survived the war and only ceased publication in 1920.

The contents list of *Woman at Home* contains the familiar elements of the homemaker's survival kit: recipes, household hints, advice on health and the care of children, discussion of family budgets. All were there. So, too, were articles on dress accompanied by fashion-plates, although there were no paper patterns. A substantial proportion of the sixty-plus pages were given over to fiction. Annie Swan contributed two fiction series in the 1890s. Like Conan Doyle's Sherlock Holmes series in the *Strand*, each centred around a character who provided the link between the separate stories, though here the central character was always a woman. Apart from Swan's serials, there were always a number of short stories, usually centering around love and marriage, or domestic themes, often an additional serial, and short articles on topics of general interest. It seems that the Beeton formula was being reproduced with a strong bias toward fiction, but otherwise relatively unchanged.

There were differences, however, in content, tone and in the positioning of the reader. The most obvious of these was the magazine's appearance. Printed on glossy paper, crammed with illustrations, many of them reproduced by the new half-tone block process, *Woman at Home* offered its readers visual pleasures of a standard that earlier (and cheaper) periodicals could not achieve. The influence of the ladies' papers was evident in such features as 'The Glass of Fashion' – a series on high society – and 'Brides and Bridegrooms', which featured pictures and descriptions of aristocratic weddings. *Woman at Home*, like the *Lady's Pictorial*, used that characteristic feature of the new journalism, the illustrated interview or illustrated biographical article. Writers, members of the Royal Family, politicians, public figures of all kinds, were presented and made familiar through these articles. Illustration provided a crucial element in the construction of these personalities as simultaneously remarkable, yet ordinary and recognisable.

Unlike the mid-Victorian magazines and like the ladies' papers, then, *Woman at Home* presumed its readers to have an insatiable appetite for stories about the Queen and the Royal Family. But it deployed images of the Royal ladies towards a rather different definition of femininity. Specifically, while it drew on the ladies' papers' assumption that Court and aristocracy were the arbiters of fashion and etiquette (offering accounts of society weddings and illustrated articles on stately homes), its main focus was on the Royal *Family* with the Queen at its centre. The Royal ladies, particularly Victoria itself, were presented not as 'ladies' but as the fulfilment of 'womanliness'. The Queen was a model for all her subjects. She was polite, 'all sincere', even rather attractive but nevertheless 'makes you feel that she is a queen' (*Woman at Home*, vol. 6, 1896–7, p. 590). In the pages of the magazine, womanliness was a quality which knew no barriers of status or rank, transcending without destroying social difference.

The idea that womanliness provided a common meeting ground was demonstrated in the magazine's most important feature, Annie Swan's correspondence columns. She had two: one titled 'Love, Marriage and Courtship' and another, on more general issues, called 'Over the Teacups'. This second title, with its positive endorsement of women's gossip, signals her persona. It could hardly have been more different from that of Beeton – Annie Swan was a true 'agony aunt'. She printed long extracts from her correspondents' letters, rather than simply printing her replies. Her comments and responses combined moral seriousness, personal concern, and tolerance of difference. This persona embodied the qualities the magazine defined elsewhere as central to womanliness. For it would be a mistake to read *Woman at Home* as valuing mainly the practical, or even the financial, aspects of homemaking, despite its recipes and detailed budget advice. Rather, it was the work of personal relationships and moral sustenance which were perceived as woman's most important domestic activity. By dealing with her correspondents as individuals worthy of her attention and concern, by reminding them gently but insistently of the spiritual dimension of their lives, Annie Swan's column enacted the advice it gave.

Her correspondents were not only women, nor were the women always middle-class and at home. She received letters from men, mill-girls and domestic servants. Ironically, given the project of the magazine, a large proportion were desperately seeking paid employment. The model of the financially dependent, though

morally independent, woman was not available to them. Annie
Swan recognised the problem this presented. She herself, as a well-
known author and professional journalist, did not conform to the
model of feminine lifestyle the magazine constructed. Such
contradictions are resolved by the assertion that, whatever the
marginal economic or social differences between them, women's
true heart, like Queen Victoria's 'all gentle, all sincere', was the
repository of society's moral values.

The penny papers

In the early 1890s the rising giants of periodical publishing began
to compete for the 'penny', as opposed to the 'sixpenny', market.
By 1893 Harmsworth's Periodical Publishing Company was
producing two weeklies for women, *Home Sweet Home* and
Forget-Me-Not, each priced at a penny. Both assumed the same
reader as that of the domestic magazines, the middle-class woman
at home. However *Forget-Me-Not* modified the domestic magazine formula slightly by concentrating heavily on romantic fiction
in both serial and short story form. It was ostensibly aimed at the
young woman, especially the engaged girl, and offered 'wholesome
reading', that is, fiction which avoided the sexual frankness of
'new woman' fiction (Advertisement, 7 January 1893). *Forget-Me-
Not* therefore combined the attractions of the domestic magazine
with those of the penny novelettes which contemporaries described
as the staple of the average woman's literary diet. The contradictions implicit in bringing these two genres together did not prevent
the magazine from being successful, indeed they may have secured
its success.

Most of the other new penny magazines established in the 1890s
included fiction, often formulaic romantic fiction, but subordi-
nated it to their other elements, especially their practical guidance
on running the home. In 1894 Pearson brought out *Home Notes*, a
penny monthly, and Cassell's, a long-established publisher,
produced *Paris Mode* at a similar price. The Cassell's magazine
offered excellent value, since it was relatively expensively produced. However, despite its large size and colour prints it could
not compete with cheaper looking but more popular domestic

magazines produced by the new publishing houses. In 1895 Pearson's *Home Notes* was reputed to be clearing a profit of £12,000 a year and Harmsworth, not content with the huge circulation of *Forget-Me-Not*, decided to launch a penny magazine to rival *Home Notes*, called *Home Chat*, which offered a similar formula at a similar price, but on a weekly basis. *Home Notes*, which continued until 1957 when it was merged with *Woman's Own*, and *Home Chat* which lasted until 1958, carried the domestic magazine into a new era and addressed a new and much wider readership. Their relationship back to the *Englishwoman's Domestic Magazine* and forward to today's *Woman* and *Woman's Own* can best be illustrated by a brief account of *Home Chat* as it was in the 1890s.

The magazine's title, and its motto 'East, West, Home's Best' which was run as a sub-title, indicated clearly that the stress in *Home Chat* was on the domestic rather than the fashionable (*Paris-Mode*) or the romantic (*Forget-Me-Not*). *Home Chat* explicitly recognised both in its articles and its fiction that women did go out to paid employment. Articles entitled 'How to Dress for Work' still put the emphasis on gender as the central defining element of women, worker outside the home or not, and still defined femininity in terms drawn from the traditional ideas of female beauty. Nevertheless, the recognition was there. However, the main target of the magazine was obviously the married woman at home. It regularly ran articles on 'Household Hints', home decorating and cooking. Mrs M. Beeton was the cookery writer, and the magazine did not disabuse any of its readers who might have thought she was *the* Mrs Beeton. The reader of *Home Chat* was not only a housewife, she was also the mother of a family. 'Mother Chats', Sister Rachel's articles on the care of children, and a 'Cheery Corner' for the children themselves all emphasised the maternal aspect of this female reader. So, too, *Home Chat's* immediate rival, *Home Notes*, devoted nearly 10 per cent of its editorial space to issues concerned with children and child-rearing. Another, often closely related, element common to these magazines, including the more expensive sixpennies, was the space given to answering medical queries. Health was sometimes linked to beauty: *Woman at Home*, for example, regularly ran a 'Health and Personal Appearance' column. However, many of the enquiries, like the constant presence of advertisements for patent medicines, addressed the problem of women's exclusion from medical knowledge when at the same time they were expected to take responsibility for practical health care and sick nursing in the home. Although it occasionally ran articles on servants, *Home Chats* implied a readership of women who actually did some, if not all, of their own domestic work, as well as 'managing the household'. In this it differed from the Beetons' magazine, and manuals directed toward 'running the home'. The patterns and instructions for 'Children's Dresses for Homeworkers' were quite in the Beeton mode, but weekly menus for 'Tired Housekeepers' broke new ground. More revealing, perhaps, were the advertisements, which not only featured such home appliances as the sewing-machine (for those children's dresses), but also regularly extolled the virtues of brand name 'convenience' foods: Bovril, Oxo, Hartley's marmalades, Farrow's dried green peas, Crosse and Blackwell's soups. All these advertisements appeared in the magazine by the end of the century, along with those for polish and soap, household goods and ornaments.

Like the sixpenny papers, the penny magazines depended on advertising to keep their costs low. Large circulation figures attracted advertising, which in turn ensured low prices, which contributed to large circulation figures, in the familiar spiral which dominates the modern press. Magazines like *Home Chat* integrated the advertisements more fully into the text by including some of them on the same pages as the editorial material, rather than confining them to end or specific pages of each number. Here too, as in the sixpenny papers, definitions of femininity became inextricably related to models of consumption. The message of the advertisers was, inevitably, a mixed one. On the one hand they asserted care of the home as the measure of true womanliness, yet they also implied that it was possible to buy short-cuts to the attainment of good housewifery. Was it possible to be a 'good' woman without having your own stock-pot? Perhaps *Home Chat*, like *Woman at Home*, worked with a model of femininity in which practical domestic skills must be complemented by the social skills needed to keep the family working smoothly, but this was never made explicit. Nor was any resolution offered to that inevitable tension between the advertisements for domestic goods and those for beauty products.

There was no equivalent in *Home Chat* to Annie Swan's correspondence columns and their attempt to aid the reader in her problems with fulfilling the requirements of womanhood. Instead, there were a number of female personae (Mrs Beeton, Sister Rachel, 'Lady Betty and Camilla' and Lady Greville), who addressed the reader with a fairly consistent degree of familiarity or intimacy. The serious tone and commitment to women's moral and spiritual duties which characterised *Woman at Home* was correspondingly reduced, though the magazine offered one regular article, 'In the Shadow of the Cross', which sustained the religious ideal quite explicitly. Instead, the magazine's representation of itself as a space in which women's talk or 'chat' could take place was diffused throughout the magazine, carried by more than one persona rather than being concentrated in a single authoritative voice or readers' contributions.

A remarkable feature of these female personae, given the magazine's target was the persistence of aristocratic names or pseudonyms. For example, the fashion column was written under the double by-line of 'Lady Betty and Camilla'. Advice on etiquette was given by 'Lady Constance Howard'. As we have said, the magazine celebrated the housewife at the same time as it carried the contrary identification of femininity as beauty and social grace. The link between this definition and high society was carried by ideas of 'fashion' and 'etiquette'. As 'fashion' was increasingly associated with conspicuous consumption and the 'upper ten thousand', the persistence of aristocratic personae seems less remarkable. However, it is more surprising to find that the magazine opened with a 'chit-chat' or miscellany over the name of 'Lady Greville' and to find ladies like 'The Countess of Normanton' held up as a pattern of motherhood in the 'Model Mothers' series (29 December 1900, p. 109). Here, as so often, we can only deduce readers' responses from the pages of the magazine itself. Columns apparently written by aristocratic ladies and titled 'Society Small Talk' or 'Boudoir Chat' carried a double promise to female readers. On the one hand they allowed the readers the pleasure of asserting their equality *as women* with those supposedly far above them by any other social measure. On the other, and paradoxically, they offered them a peek into the world of the very rich to which they could never have access. The 'chat' could become 'gossip' about the doings of the great and famous, in which the reader was positioned as outsider or even voyeur, rather than as equal. *Home Chat* claimed to offer all women a quality or 'ladies' ' magazine. Harmsworth used the new methods of finance and production to ensure his mass journal was an excellent pennyworth. But the idea of quality was given a twist by the model of the 'lady' which the magazine evoked. It positioned its readers as 'women' whose shared femininity made possible their 'chat', yet presupposed class and status differences which provided a staple part of that chat. This proved a winning formula. In 1910 the Dundee-based publisher D. C. Thomson launched *My Weekly*, a new and even more down-market version of the domestic women's magazine. Thomson, who had published *People's Friend* as early as 1869, saw the potential of that combination of practical household tips with the creation of an intimate gossipy tone which characterised *Home Chat*. *My Weekly*'s version was so successful that it carried the magazine through two world wars and the revolutions of post-war publishing into the 1980s, still published by the same firm. Its immediate rival *Woman's Weekly* was also launched on very similar lines only a year later: it too still appears. *Woman's Weekly* has done better than survive – it has been Britain's best-selling women's magazine in the late 1980s, although with an average reader age of fifty it seems to be in the process of being overtaken by the re-working of the domestic magazine formula offered by *Best* and *Bella*. In 1989, the editor offered an account of the magazine's continuing success:

> Britain's best selling magazine is not the brashest, the glossiest, or the most action-packed. It's the one that, in the words of so many *Woman's Weekly* readers, 'comes into the home each week like a friend'. The magazine is friendly and unashamedly homely and therein, I think, lies its success: in a changing and sometimes bewildering world, *Woman's Weekly* has been a touchstone of security for generations of women. (Braithwaite and Barrell, 1989, p. 143)

Some of the continuities and discontinuities between the late Victorian to Edwardian period and the late twentieth century are revealed here, not just in the content of women's magazine, but in the place they occupy in our culture.

It is a myth that the Victorian era saw a period in which definitions of womanliness were secure. Rather, as this chapter has suggested, womanliness was ever the site of competing definitions based on generation, class, status and wealth. The domestic women's magazine has always offered an illusion of security to women readers caught up in this conflict – first, by asserting the connection between domestic and feminine virtue, and second, since the 1890s, by explicitly offering itself to its readers as a 'friend'. This intimacy of tone is characteristic of the way that all mass media work, but in women's journalism it takes on a special importance. The magazine presents itself as a space in which being a woman is accepted as unproblematic, and as sufficient qualification for participating in the culture of the magazine. That culture is defined in terms of 'woman talk'. Of course, it also conceals the problem of differences between women, just as the intimate tone conceals the institutions of mass publication which bring the magazine to the reader. However, we would argue that the success of the magazines which deploy this formula tells us something about the way femininity continues to be constructed in our society. The magazine simultaneously creates and offers a solution to the uncertainty generated in readers by the gap between what we are and what we 'ought' to be.

4

1914 to 1988: twentieth-century women's magazines

In this brief chapter we trace the lines of continuity between those magazines of the eighteenth and nineteenth centuries discussed in preceding chapters and their successors in the 1980s, which form the subject of our next. Our concern is to show how the patterns laid down in the past help to shape the modern women's magazine, and also how it has departed from them. Here, as elsewhere in this book, we are limiting our discussion to commercial magazines aimed at women whose shared interest in such texts is assumed to be the result of their shared gender. We, therefore, exclude any discussion of the role of women as writers and readers of 'general periodicals'. Nor do we deal with the rise in the twentieth century of a vigorous press dedicated to feminist and other political positions in which women have banded together to make their voice heard. This means we have not, for instance, considered *Time and Tide*, 'the only woman-run, woman-oriented general political, literary and artistic magazine . . . accepted into the world of "reputable" periodicals' (Doughan, 1987, p. 261). Nor have we offered an analysis of the wealth of suffrage journals which flourished around the turn of the century, nor the even more various women's press of the 1960s and '70s. We have included reference to *Spare Rib*, in part because it is sold in station bookstalls, high street newsagents and so forth, in open competition with the more traditional 'domestic' magazines which are the centre of our focus. We hope that others will develop work already begun in this area, but have chosen to delimit our discussion in order to provide a more detailed analysis of what might be termed the 'mainstream' magazine.

Our argument that the late-twentieth-century women's magazine had emerged in a clearly recognisable form by the start of the First World War might be taken as a denial of the significance of recent history. This would obviously be wrong – a huge variety of changes affected the development of women's magazines between 1914 and the 1980s. Not least, as a part, and an increasingly important part, of modern mass publishing, they were caught up in a more general restructuring of the print industry. Changes in print technology, marketing and distribution were necessitated by wider economic and social changes – two world wars, the depressions and booms of an increasingly global economy, the development of multinational corporations, the expansion and diversification of other mass media, and the growth of the leisure industry. By virtue of the fact that they define their readership in the first instance in terms of gender, women's magazines have also, perforce, been involved in wider changes in women's social role, whether related to demographic shifts, political campaigns, legislation, developments in contraception, or more general shifts in attitudes to sexuality and gender roles. Women's magazines have not only responded to all these changes, they have also played a significant part in shaping some of them. Although their history has not been static, it has also not been one of steady development. However, we would assert that the broad lines of their development and their central formal features were all in place by the early twentieth century. In what follows we focus on two aspects of that development: economic changes in the publishing of women's magazines and changes in the 'dominant' definitions of sexual difference with which they work.

The business of women's magazines

By 1914 the production of women's magazines was 'a considerable industry' in its own right and so it has continued until the 1980s (Braithwaite and Barrell, 1988, p. 11). Throughout the twentieth century in both Britain and America, the publishing industry has maintained a separate sector producing magazines addressed to women readers *as* women (since women clearly read other forms of printed matter that may not recognise their gender as the determining factor in their 'choosing' to read one text over another). Of course, the role of this sector has fluctuated both in size and in influence. In both world wars, but especially the second, the scale of production was relatively stagnant. In fact, the allocation of print in the Second World War was based on pre-1939 circulation figures, so not only did the amount diminish because of rationing, but the relative sales were frozen too. Nevertheless women's magazines played an important role during the Second World War in Britain as disseminators of information and morale-boosters. However, they did not yet occupy the major place in publishing they were to take in the post-war years.

An immediate period of relative quiet after both world wars, was followed by major restructuring in the industry. In the 1920s a number of middle-class magazines launched in the 1890s were ended, including *Women at Home* and *Woman's World*. Twenty-five new titles were published, including a number aimed at the working class. *Peg's Paper* (1919), for example, was a new version of a familiar genre, the fiction magazine aimed at the working-class girl. However, it was not until the 1930s that the future pattern of the trade was firmly established with the arrival of the new-style domestic or 'service' weeklies – *Woman's Own* launched by Newnes in 1932, *Woman* by Odhams in 1937, and *Woman's Illustrated* by Amalgamated Press in 1936. The first two were to dominate the sector for the next fifty years. However, the old-style domestic magazine from the 1890s, including *Home Chat* and *Home Notes*, survived until the 1950s. The disappearance of these late-Victorian magazines at that point was part of another general post-war shift. The boom in women's magazines in the late 1950s and 1960s both shaped and was shaped by the ideology of 'never had it so good', when domestic economy (both national and household) was understood to have declined in favour of energetic consumption.

It was not the number of different magazines, or even the number of sub-divisions of the 'target group' of women consumers, which made the women's magazine sector as a whole so important to the print industry in this period. Indeed, there were *fewer* magazines aimed at women in the late 1960s than there had been in the 1930s. However, existing titles drew a readership which was much larger, both statistically and proportionally, than that of their forebears. In 1964 a substantial majority of women from all social classes admitted to reading at least one of the weekly domestic or 'service' magazines – 60 per cent of the upper and middle class (ABC1), 71 per cent of lower middle class (C2), and 63 per cent of the working classes (D and E) (White, 1970, p. 169). With this kind of command of the market among those who were identified as controllers of family expenditure and consumption, women's magazines were not only themselves big business, but were increasingly a prime target for other businesses which recognised their value as advertising sites.

Enormous as these figures are by the standards of the 1890s, by 1964 circulation figures for the major weeklies were down from their all-time high of the late 1950s and early 1960s. A long period of decline in sales had begun. In the early 1960s over fifty million British women (50.2m) read a women's weekly and thirty-four million read a monthly. By 1987 the numbers were down to nearly twenty-four million (23.9m) and nearly forty million respectively (National Readership Survey quoted in Braithwaite and Barrell, 1988, p. 153). The major decline, then, began with the weeklies, whereas the monthlies enjoyed an overall increase in readership. However, according to the same survey, even the monthlies' figures indicate a proportional decline in readership (figures for the 1980s show a steady drop from 50 per cent of women reading any monthly in 1980 to 45 per cent in 1987). This is the context for the various attempts from the mid-1960s onward to reverse the trend through revamping old titles and launching new ones aimed at 'new' sections of the market. These attempts to revive the economic fortunes of the magazine press have inevitably been entangled in the ideological debate about the 'new' woman and, even if to a lesser extent, the 'new' man.

Femininity has always been taken as the common ground for definition of the readership of women's magazines, but what it means to be feminine once again has been a matter of disagreement and even outright dispute. In the 1890s domestic magazines had been launched which invoked but did not address the 'New Woman'. In the 1960s the new 'New Woman' was similarly caricatured in the women's press as denying her femininity (a myth neatly encapsulated in the image of bra-burning). This might put her outside the general appeal to womanhood made in the domestic magazines, but declining sales in a context of increasing prosperity and perhaps even more important, the belief that the contraceptive pill had revolutionised women's relationship to their own sexuality, all forced magazine publishers to look again at their definitions of femininity.

Some existing magazines, like *Woman's Mirror*, were re-designed with the aim of appealing to the post-1960s woman, but without a great deal of success (Winship, 1987, p. 48). *She* had pioneered a new-style, non-domestic magazine in the mid-1950s, but it was *Nova*, launched in the mid-1960s, which was hailed as the first of the publications for the 'New Woman'. Despite its initial success, *Nova* was not financially viable in the long term. It was still on the station book-stalls in 1972, however, when two more new magazines were launched in Britain, very different in appeal, appearance and aims, but both also claiming to address the 'post-sixties' emancipated woman. *Cosmopolitan*'s British and American versions were targeted at the single, sexually active woman, while *Spare Rib* spoke to and for the Women's Liberation Movement. Both have survived into the 1990s. However, even such apparently bold departures from the traditional domestic magazine did not substantially affect the shape of the mass industry in women's periodicals, which continued to define their readers as homemakers, involved in both the practical and emotional work of sustaining family. The difficulty of defining the new femininity, or even deciding if it exists, is therefore shown not only by the radical difference between *Cosmopolitan* and *Spare Rib*, or by the decline and eventual collapse of *Nova* in 1975, but above all by the persistence of these older patterns of publishing. Indeed, the rush of new launches in the 1980s in Britain, which we discuss in the next chapter, can be read as yet another re-working of the old formulas with little to indicate that either feminism or a new 'post-feminist' femininity has arrived.

None of this activity has halted the long-term fall in the sales of women's magazines through the 1970s and 1980s. However, as the figures quoted above show, even with this apparent inexorable decline, magazines of this type are still important financially and culturally. In 1985, £180 million, around a third of the total expenditure spent by consumers on magazines, was spent on women's magazines (Mintel Survey, 1986, p. 81). Since we know that buyers and readers are not identical groups, it seems even more significant that substantial proportions of women (and men) still claimed in the same year to 'look at' these magazines every week or every month. In 1985 over a fifth of all women (21.9 per cent) and a twentieth of all men (4.5 per cent) claimed to have looked at *Woman's Own*. Nor is magazine reading, according to the statistics for that year, confined to one class. Although the readership profiles for different magazines obviously vary, the practice of 'looking at' them was shared by all social groups and, interestingly, by both women and men. Male readership was approximately a fifth of female readership of weeklies, and rather more of some monthlies (Mintel Survey, 1986, p. 81). The huge success in the late 1980s of the newly launched monthly *Prima* and the weeklies *Bella* and *Best* shows that the magazine for women continues to be popular with readers, profitable for publishers and useful to advertisers. To sum up, we may say that, since 1914, the women's magazine sector has gone through various changes within an overall pattern of rise and then slow decline but, nevertheless, since the early years of the century it has continued to be a 'considerable industry'.

The developments in the structure of this industry could not have been foreseen in 1914 and yet at least two of the most important determinants of that structure were already present. As we showed in the last chapter, the foundations of the mass press in the late nineteenth century were laid with the emergence of large publishers who financed multiple publications from a mixture of private capital and stock flotation. Women's magazines played an important part in this process. As the twentieth century went on, this sector was increasingly shaped by the rivalries of publishing empires evolved from these turn-of-the-century businesses. Amalgamation of smaller presses in the 1920s made possible giant publishing companies, especially those of Newnes, and Odhams Press. The rivalry of these two, publishers respectively of *Woman's Own* and *Woman*, dominated the industry through to the 1950s. In 1961, Amalgamated Press won the battle with Odhams, who had already taken over Newnes and Hulton's. The result was the giant IPC which has continued to command the market through the 1970s and 1980s.

The growth of ever larger publishing empires, which often provide their own competition, has not been confined to firms of British origin. The entry into British publishing of foreign-based firms has been perhaps the most important factor in the recent history of the industry. Like the British publishing giants, these firms have in the last two decades become multinationals whose interests are neither confined to one country nor to one product, be it print, paint, or washing-machines. Here again, the roots of this development lie as far back as the early years of the twentieth century, when North American publishers began to see the advantage of using the capital and publishing expertise acquired in one country as a basis for entry into the market elsewhere. The first appearance of a British edition of *Vogue* in 1916, in the middle of the war, was an important landmark in the history of the women's magazine publishing sector. Even more significant in retrospect had been the entry of Hearst, the American publishing tycoon, into the British market in 1911 with the purchase of the then rather grandiosely named National Magazine Company. Hearst's attempts to reproduce American-style publication in Britain before the war were unsuccessful, but in the 1920s the National Magazine Company's launch of a British edition of *Good Housekeeping* (1922) substantially changed the magazine market in Britain (Braithwaite and Barrell, 1988, pp. 13–14). It was followed by *Harper's Bazaar*, also from Hearst, *True Story* and *True Romance*. These fiction magazines competed successfully with the traditional millgirl and shopgirl fiction, a legacy of the nineteenth-century publishing industry. An analogous transformation of British women's magazine publishing through the importation of North American innovation took place in the 1960s with the launch of British versions of *Family Circle* and *Living*, and in the 1970s with *Cosmopolitan*, whose innovations we have already mentioned. In the 1980s, European-based publishers entered into the British market, especially from Germany. It is a pattern which is at once new and familiar.

The dominance of increasingly large firms, often multinationals with diversified interests, has not completely squeezed out the small company devoted to one magazine. The success in the 1970s of *Slimming*, 1969 brainchild of two journalists working from their home, is taken as the classic case. From a very different position, *Spare Rib* has outlasted many more conventional titles, despite its defiance of the capitalist mode of finance, and its commitment to co-operative editorial and production methods. However, *Slimming* sold to Argus Publications in 1979, and, while *Spare Rib* has survived, other broadly 'alternative' women's magazines have failed to establish themselves. *Women's Review*, a serious arts and feminist-oriented magazine, began with high hopes in 1985 and folded eighteen months later.

Those multinationals which control women's magazines view them as simply another product to be sold along with others. Since the introduction of the Audit Bureau of Circulations in 1931, there has developed an increasingly sophisticated set of techniques, not just for verifying circulations, but for checking spending patterns and identifying target consumers. In the 1930s magazines began to research into their readership through the use of questionnaires. This process became more systematic in the 1950s and, in 1956, the advertisers' own Joint Industry Committee for National Readership Surveys began to undertake research and publish its results. However, it would be a mistake to think that as a result of the increasing sophistication of research techniques, women's magazines have been tailored to reflect the needs or desires of women readers in a direct and straightforward way. Reader profiles and circulation figures are primarily produced in order to sell space to advertisers, rather than sell magazines to readers.

Advertising

The centrality of advertising to the twentieth-century women's magazine press was cemented in the 1890s when the ladies' papers were able to keep their price to sixpence instead of the shilling they would have had to charge if they had depended on cover price alone. This proportion of advertising revenue to cover price profits is almost exactly the same as that quoted for *Cosmopolitan* (Winship, 1987, p. 38). Also in the 1890s, magazines had begun to include pages of advertisements in the body of their text rather than confining them to the beginning and end, and, even more important, to link commodity consumption with their production of models of 'ideal' femininity on the one hand and visual pleasure on the other. These early beginnings were taken up in different ways in the twentieth century. The 'ladies' papers' declined in importance after the First World War, but the kinds of advertising they pioneered spread to the rest of the women's press. Full-page advertisements with entertaining copy and interesting images became more general, though they did not oust the smaller, often closely written, line advertisements, reliant on verbal repetition rather than visual appeal (Meech, 1986, p. 15). In the 1920s and '30s, women's magazines continued to develop the use of advertising, but they were still regarded by advertisers as insignificant by contrast with newspapers and general interest magazines, and could not command the same volume of advertising and revenue as other periodical literature. This was to change in the 1950s, when increasing national prosperity combined with a rise in sales of women's magazines in particular, revolutionised advertising both generally and locally. The role of educating women as consumers, which magazines adopted after the war, fitted well with advertisers' aims to persuade them to spend more on domestic appliances, clothes, convenience food and cosmetics. The intermingling of advertising and editorial copy, the pressure on readers to take the magazine's 'friendly advice' on how to be a good consumer, the development of more sophisticated techniques for persuasion, all these profoundly affected the structure of the women's magazine. As Cynthia White identifies, 'starting in the mid-1950s the balance of power between editorial and advertising departments began to swing in favour of the latter in response to increasing pressure from higher management' (White, 1970, p. 157). Janice Winship reports a significant single event in this process: the decision by the editor of *Woman* in 1956 to agree with British Nylon Spinners, who had booked a double page colour advertising spread, that there would be no article which prominently featured natural fibres in the same issue (Winship, 1987, p. 40). It is now taken for granted that advertisers will pay more for strategic positioning (adverts for food alongside the cookery section, for example).

Below-the-line promotions, or 'advertorials', either for a single advertiser or for partnership advertisers selling similar products, make it increasingly difficult to distinguish between advertising and editorial copy, particularly as this kind of promotional feature is usually written by the magazine's own journalists employing their own house style. Moreover, many magazines also run their own 'special offers', selling goods directly to their readers, and thus unambiguously positioning them as consumers. Some magazines take this one step further by selling goods which encourage readers to define themselves as the 'ideal' reader (the *Cosmo* or

Company girl), products identified as part of the magazine's favoured 'lifestyle' which frequently advertise the magazine itself through the use of the corporate logo. Many theorists of 'post-modern culture' or of 'late capitalism' identify consumer choice as *the* key motif of the age. Attention to the ways in which 'consumption' has been gendered in this process has, however, been relatively neglected. We have seen that, as early as the eighteenth century in the history of the women's magazine, women readers were being positioned as consumers. In the nineteenth century the identification of consumption with leisure became complicated by the overt correlation of consumption and *work*. Nevertheless, consumption and production retained their implicit gender associations and, throughout the twentieth century, it is clear that consumption and femininity continue to inscribe and define one another in the women's magazine, though in complex and, frequently, contradictory ways.

The shift in advertising toward increasing reliance on visual images points to another element in the complex interplay of the business of women's magazines and the work of femininity. As in the nineteenth century, rivalry in women's magazines in the twentieth century has continued to pivot on the quality of the production of high-quality visual material – but on the colour print as opposed to the pictorial fashion-plate. The emergence of the two 'big weeklies', *Woman* and *Woman's Own*, in the 1930s cannot be explained without reference to their use of the new colour-gravure process. *Woman* was the first magazine printed entirely by this process, thoroughly eclipsing its rivals. A large part of the impact of *Cosmopolitan* was, and is, dependent on its visual appeal, achieved not so much through new technical processes as through the extensive use of glossy colour photography and by its selfconscious play with the range of visual tricks made possible by colour photo-copying machines and other modern technologies (Winship, 1987, p. 100). The long-term effects of the electronics revolution on the women's magazines are still to be assessed. Yet, whatever uncertainties there are, it seems likely that there will always be pressure to produce a magazine as visually attractive as one's competitors. *Spare Rib* moved to a glossy cover in 1985. The importance of this step for a serious and avowedly feminist magazine should not be underestimated.

In a culture of consumption, represented most powerfully by the advert, the appearance of a women's magazine is not simply a matter determined by the modes of technology or finance employed in its production. It is also, crucially, a matter of how readers define themselves and are defined by the magazine. The question of visual appeal is a central concern here. For most of the period we are discussing, illustration of fashions that offer 'models' for the readers, were reproduced in high-quality pictures. Most importantly, the covers of women's magazines with their obligatory female model or famous person become the outward sign of the concern with appearance which characterises both medium and message.

The work of femininity

Just as twentieth-century developments in the organisation and financing of the industry can be traced to the nineteenth-century press, so too can their internal shape, mix of ingredients, and generic traditions. By 1900 most of the characteristic elements of the late-twentieth-century women's magazine were already being used in different combinations in *Home Chat, Woman, Woman at Home, The Gentlewoman* and other magazines of the period. There were the short stories and serials (almost always romantic), the articles on housekeeping, childcare and family relationships, the recipes, the fashion-plates and pull-out dress patterns, the letters pages addressing 'personal' problems, dress, appearance or medical matters, the illustrated articles about the famous and royal, the competitions, the gossip columns, the advertisements for aids to beauty and home.

These generic features did not remain static, of course. A comparison of Annie Swan's letter page from *Woman at Home* in 1901 with that of Evelyn Home in *Woman* in 1951 and, in turn, that of Irma Kurtz in *Cosmopolitan* in 1981, reveals striking differences in subject matter and tone. However, the convention of the letters page itself in which the 'auntie' figure offers advice to individual readers has persisted. Not only that, it has maintained its importance as an essential element of the woman's magazine. Similarly, the visual pleasure offered by the ladies' paper of the 1890s is very different from that of today's glossies, which can print high-quality colour pictures on every page. Nevertheless, the importance of the good-quality picture, in which the woman is the primary subject, persists.

The illustrated interview or article about a personality is a particularly good example of this generic continuity through difference. These have continued to be staples of the press generally, but carry particular weight in women's magazines. The format, an invention of the 'new' journalism of the late nineteenth century, has been progressively extended to include new groups of the famous. In the inter-war period, the cinema provided a novel figure, that of the film star, as a source of fantasy for readers and copy for journalists. Apart from the special film journals, like *Women's Filmfare* (launched in 1935), other magazines could use the familiar interview or biographical article to bring the stars to their readers. The growth of television after the Second World War may be one of the reasons why magazine sales in general have slumped, but it has also given an old convention new content. Soap-opera stars share covers and interview space with film stars and, of course, members of the Royal Family.

The treatment of female Royals demonstrates the ways in which traditions are re-worked in the pages of the women's magazine. Princesses, we have argued, have featured at different times and in different guises in the women's magazine since the early eighteenth century. It was in 1950 that *Woman's Own* bought the story of the royal nanny, 'Crawfie'. This not only gave a huge boost to sales (according to the magazine they went 'up to 500,000 overnight'), it also took the royal interview and story into new territory (Winship, 1987, p. 40; Braithwaite and Barrell, 1988, p. 44). The promise of revelations about the intimate and, especially, the sexual lives of the Royal Family has been a constant element in much of the British press, but in women's magazines it has a particular selling power. The fascination with the Royal Family, especially the women (Princess Anne succeeded Margaret Rose and Princess 'Di' has overtaken them all), has extended to the United States, Europe and Australia.

Yet, despite the change in emphasis from reverence to prurience, the central meaning of the interview or 'bio-pic' remains – it gives the reader access to the 'truth' about the great and famous. The 'truth' here is always understood as that of the personal as opposed to the public persona. Such articles therefore tap into that continuing opposition between the feminine as the personal, private world of intimate relationships, and the masculine public world of big business and politics. Moreover, that personal world is valued as 'more true' than the public one. The implicit argument is that the real self is the self revealed in personal intimacy, increasingly in the modern women's magazine, understood as sexual behaviour. The continuing importance of this kind of article for women's magazines, like other features such as the letter page and fashion-plate, is not just a symptom of reader conservatism or journalistic laziness. It is related to continuities in gender definitions and representations of the self, masculine or feminine, that the magazine both produces and draws upon in contemporary culture.

Because the magazine is a mixture of kinds of writing rather than simply one kind, journalists and editors have also been able to rework not just the individual elements, but their combination and weighting. For example, romantic fiction, or at least fiction which centres on heterosexual relationships in the context of romantic love and marriage, has been a staple of the women's magazine since the eighteenth century, before the Beetons enshrined it on their opening page. From the 1890s' *My Lady's Novelette* through *Peg's Paper* in the 1920s to *True Romance* in the 1970s, a tradition of magazines almost wholly devoted to such fiction commanded a loyal audience. Since the ladies' papers of the 1890s there have been certain categories of magazines which have down-played fiction, but it has remained an ingredient of the classic·magazine recipe. Interestingly, the importance of fiction of this traditional kind seems to have declined in the 1980s. Sales of fiction magazines have decreased since the early 1970s. However, magazines as different as *Just Seventeen* and *Woman's Own* have begun to produce special fiction issues, taking fiction out of the regular magazine into a separate ghetto. It may be that the narrative role which romantic fiction has played in magazines over the last hundred and fifty years is more satisfactorily dealt with in the 1980s by other elements – the true stories of readers' lives, the mini-narratives of advertisements, the 'make-overs' in which readers are transformed with new clothes, hairstyle and make-up.

The constant re-working of inherited tradition is not, of course, confined to literary or generic convention. The ideal of femininity, and the place of the magazine in relation to its female reader, are the two poles around which the whole cosmos of women's magazines revolves. And here, too, there is both constant movement and relative stasis. In the rest of this section we take up the question of continuity and discontinuity by bringing together discussion of convention or genre, and those two central aspects of the women's magazine – the representation of the feminine and the representation of the magazine.

Women's magazines throughout this century have consistently fought to centre definitions of the feminine on the domestic. In the battle over what constitutes women's work, few magazines have opposed the position that women's first duty is unpaid labour in the home, even where she does undertake paid work outside it. After the First World War, the combined effects of women's contribution to the war effort, the success of the long struggle for the vote, and the brutal statistics of death amongst the male population which showed many more women than men of marriageable age in the population, were not enough to change the magazines' emphasis on homemaking as the *only* suitable work for women. The very insistence might demonstrate that women's domestic priorities were no longer self-evident.

Good Housekeeping (launched in 1922) embodied the principle of homemaking as a full-time job with its own kind of professionalism. The 'Good Housekeeping Seal' not only guaranteed a certain quality, it carried the idea of standards into the area of homemaking and consumer choice. The use of the vocabulary of professionalism was not entirely new in domestic magazines. It had been central to the Beetons' concept of 'household management'. What was new, however, was that middle class women were not only managing their households, they were having to do the cleaning and cooking previously performed by domestic servants. *Good Housekeeping* and the service magazines of the 1930s were, therefore, engaged in a double process of encouraging high standards of household management and providing work-manuals of basic skills.

In the Second World War, the pressing need to recruit women into a range of jobs outside the home made itself felt through the women's magazines, which worked closely with the British government throughout the war. However, the stress on the importance of women's domestic role did not disappear. Instead, it was redefined in terms of national, as distinct from simply family, interest. Women's significance as household managers in a time of rationing and shortage was a persistent theme. Nevertheless, large numbers of married women inevitably did work outside the home, and many enjoyed it. Once again in the post-war reconstruction, these women found little support in the magazines, which advocated a return to an exclusive concentration on homemaking as the feminine norm. Work could only be a prelude to women's proper career as wife and mother. In the 1950s, as we have already indicated, domestic work was increasingly linked to consumption, as advertisers joined in the pressure on housewives to make their homes ever cleaner and more efficient, through the acquisition of new domestic appliances and home commodities.

New, or at least more powerful, links were established between the work of femininity and consumption in relation to that other and potentially contradictory aspect of femininity, that of female beauty. Ever since the first fashion plate had appeared in a magazine and certainly since the Beetons had combined the fashion plate and the paper pattern, the magazine for women had carried the double message that beauty was natural and even essential to femininity, but that it had to be worked at. In the period after the Second World War, magazines increasingly extended the work of beautification beyond the traditional areas of dress and fashion, or care of the hair and complexion, into the purchase and skilful application of make-up and beauty products. 'Make-up' became not only respectable but essential for feminine beauty. Cosmetic advertisements and advice on their use in advertorials thus brought together consumption and the representation of woman as object of the gaze, linking both to the work of femininity.

Domestic labour in the context of the family has, then, been central to the definition of themselves which magazines offered their readers. But many of those readers had in fact been in paid labour, working-class women consistently and middle-class women increasingly, especially in the 1970s and 1980s. Magazines did not ignore this aspect of their readers' lives. The tension between the demands of the home and the need or desire for paid labour has been one of the women's magazines' recurring preoccupations ever since the early years of the century when *Home Chat* initiated articles such as 'The Daughter who Stops at Home' on the woman who cares for aging parents while her sisters go out to work (vol. 3, 29 October 1904, pp. 279–80). Nor did even the most dedicated of the household magazines of the 1950s suggest that women's interests should be entirely confined to the domestic: *Good Housekeeping* as well as *Woman* ran articles on social issues, as long as they were 'non-political'. But what Betty Friedan has called 'the problem without a name', that questioning of her existence, felt but unarticulated by domestic women of the United States in the mid twentieth century, remained unvoiced in the mass of women's magazines long after *The Feminine Mystique* had been overtaken in the international women's liberation movement, which it helped to launch (Friedan, 1965).

As we have already suggested, the impact of the women's movement of the 1960s and 1970s on women's magazines was complex. *She* in the 1950s, *Nova* in the 1960s, *Cosmopolitan* in the 1970s, *Options* and *Elle* in the 1980s, all aimed to break with the traditions of the domestic magazine, while distancing themselves from the women's movement as such. However, none of these magazines took the world of paid work as the ground for an alternative definition of the feminine. The representation of the woman reader as 'housewife' has been closely linked with the representation of the magazine as work manual. The traditional genres of paper patterns, recipes and household tips persist, and have been revitalised in those journals of the late 1980s such as *Prima* and *Essentials*, precisely because our definitions of the feminine are so tied up with the domestic.

The nineteenth-century model of the double nature of home-making as physical and moral or spiritual also persists. Nowhere is this more clearly seen than in the advice columns. The form of the personalised letter and personalised response both enacts and addresses the idea of feminine responsibility. The difference between Annie Swan's pages on 'Love, Courtship and Marriage' and Irma Kurtz's letter column can be explained in part by the growth of secularism in the century between 1890 and 1980. Religious and specifically Christian moral discourse has given way to the discourses of humanist morality and increasingly to popularised psychology. This was evident not just in the letters pages, but generally. Where *Home Chat* in 1900 could run a regular article called 'In the Shadow of the Cross', *Woman's Weekly* recruited the 'Man who Sees' in the 1920s, to write a column on general matters of morality. The column still appears. Tom Crabtree of *Cosmopolitan* offers a very different vocabulary in which pop psychology reworks moral choice as self-development. This secularisation may also be expressed in the movement of horoscopes from the cheap working-class journals like *Peg's Paper* into the middle-class weeklies and glossy monthlies.

Another change evident in the magazines, especially in the letters pages, is that sexual questions and the problems of family relationships come to be more explicitly and perhaps more sympathetically addressed in the years following the Second World War. In the 1930s, sex education became more widely available but the general context remained one of silence and ignorance (White, 1970, pp. 109–10) In the early 1970s, *Cosmopolitan* sought to break with the model not only of the domestic woman, but also of the woman whose sexuality was determined by family responsibilities, rather than her own pleasure. However, even in the pages of *Cosmopolitan* the assumption that relationships are women's responsibility and part of their 'work' persists. Questionnaires for readers on their sexual performance may present themselves as more liberated than the quizzes of the 1950s about the fulfilment of housewifely duties, but, while they redefine what is desirable in a woman, they still offer the reader an idea of femininity as a goal to be worked for and understand women as objects of male desire. The discourses of sexual liberation which magazines like *Cosmopolitan* have made their own not only draw on the male-dominated sex manuals of the 1960s, they relate to the older tradition of magazines as work-manuals. The tangled relations of work and pleasure which characterised the domestic magazine re-emerges in the pages of *Cosmopolitan* in the 1970s recast into the sphere of sexuality.

The assumption of femininity as simultaneously natural and culturally acquired through labour sets up a complex tension for the reader. On the one hand she is addressed as already 'woman' – this is, after all, the ground on which she is identified as a reader. On the other hand, there is a clear gap between what is and what the magazine claims she 'ought' (to desire) to be. Femininity, therefore, becomes a both a source of anxiety and a source of pleasure because it can never be fully achieved. The magazines perpetuate this myth of femininity and offer themselves as a solution. The magazine will be friend, advisor and instructor in the difficult task of being a woman. This characterisation of magazines as the reader's friend is perhaps the one single most persistent element in women's periodicals' self-representation over every period we have discussed. This tone of intimacy was fundamental to the magazine on its first emergence in the eighteenth century and dominated those of the 1890s. The launching of *My Weekly* and *Woman's Weekly* in the period immediately before the 1914–18 war and the introduction of a 'more democratic approach' with *Woman* in the late 1950s and early '60s were also key moments in the evolution of the women's magazine's fiction of 'community' (Braithwaite and Barrell, 1988, p. 143; White, 1970, p. 159).

The idea of the magazine as 'friend', therefore, implicitly addresses the problem of femininity as one shared by all women, but explicitly isolates the woman at home as an individual responsible for her own conduct and being. Further, these magazines not only assume an exclusively heterosexual femininity, they also assume a shared set of cultural values – white, British, middle-class – each articulated through notions of ideal femininity in similar but distinctive ways.

In the 1980s, certain magazines addressed to non-white women were launched, including *Chic* and *Black Hair and Beauty*. *Spare Rib* brought into the open the racism of magazine publishing, including its own past. These changes have not, however, so far extended to the mainstream women's magazine. The relations between femininity and class have not simply been those of exclusion. The clear class distinctions reflected by the periodicals of the 1890 to 1914 period gave way in the 1930s to the popular weeklies with an appeal which did, to some extent, succeed in crossing class barriers. The readership statistics already quoted for the boom period of the late 1950s and 1960s show why the idea that femininity transcended class difference could be assumed. In the 1970s and 1980s, a discourse of 'style' has replaced that of class in the women's magazine, and generation has come to play an important part in differentiating readerships. In the next chapter we consider how far difference is acknowledged by magazines of the 1980s and how far femininity is still represented as both the ground for identity, and the cause of identity anxiety.

5

Contemporary magazines, contemporary readers

Part one: readers and reading

In this chapter, as in previous ones, we analyse a select sample of magazines in order to pursue the question of the women's magazine's distinctive working of gender ideology. In this case, however, instead of drawing our sample from an extended period, we concentrate on a selection of magazines (listed in the Appendix) from a single year, 1988. We are also able here to draw on our discussions with other groups of women about their relation to and readings of the magazines we chose for our sample, where such reader research was impossible with regard to earlier periods. Here, then, by drawing on the practices of close reading and reader research, we hope to elaborate on some of the more general argument we have outlined earlier and demonstrate the complexity of the relations between those economic, ideological and social factors that go into 'reading' magazines in late-twentieth-century culture.

There was a point in 1988 when we felt we were being overtaken by events. We found it difficult to keep up with the proliferation of new titles being issued in Britain – *Bella*, *Best*, *Prima*, *Essentials*, *More!*, *Riva*, *New Woman* and *Me*. We wondered whether we were seeing the beginning of the end of the form whose development we had traced in the eighteenth and nineteenth centuries. Did these new magazines really depart from the formulas, themes and contradictions we had identified as constitutive of the form to date? As our discussion has indicated, we understand the women's magazine as a historically specific form. We therefore recognised the possibility that we were witnessing a

126

major transformation of the genre. However, these 'new' magazines prove, we would argue, to be remarkable for their adherence
to the patterns and formulas of the past, despite their immediate
visual 'difference' from their contemporaries. There are discontinuities but these are often re-workings or re-mixes of old
continuities. Above all, at the centre of the new magazines, as of
the old, lies that fundamental division of masculine and feminine,
and the endeavour to give content and value to the 'femininity'
they market. This process is essential if magazines are to function
as organs of advertising and sales, targeted at women in terms of
their common femininity. However, in the late 1980s, it continues
to be a difficult task, giving rise to the ambiguities and contradictions that have come to be typical of the form. These contradictions do not, of course, ultimately harm the magazines. For
reasons we have already discussed, magazines can comfortably
carry contradictory discourses, whereas a single prose essay or a
book like this one must at least present the illusion of coherence.

Our sample of 1988 magazines was collected over three months
– March, June and September. We do not offer content analysis
here, but rather reading and interpretation around a number of
central and shared features, ideological and formal, of the texts,
informed by our wider reading of magazines past and present. It
might be argued that a proper analysis would confine itself strictly
to the sample in order to produce an objective and dispassionate
account from a purely empirical position. As we argued in our
first chapter, however, we would insist that any critical reading or
data collection or textual analysis which presents itself as value- or
theory-free is *mis*representing itself. Second, and more important,
we are interested in magazines as they are read by historical
readers, including ourselves. We have, therefore, read the 1988
sample, as we read the eighteenth- and nineteenth-century ones,
with our own social selves to the fore. We have also been able to
draw on the experience of other historical readers, the women we
interviewed and with whom we discussed the magazines. We do
not claim that this data is fully representative – the sample is small
and neither systematically chosen nor controlled. We do not offer,
then, a survey of reading practices of women in Britain in 1988,
but rather intend the material to be suggestive, indicative of some
of the ways in which women readers can and do talk about their
consumption of the form.

The groups which participated in the project were as follows: an already existing university women's group (about ten members came to the session): a group of six pensioners from a church in a midlands town, an already existing support and discussion group of five youth, community and social workers in London: and a sample of ten students from a northern urban polytechnic. Participants filled in a simple questionnaire designed to elicit age, occupation and marital status, as well as which magazines, if any, they bought or read, and their tastes and habits in reading more generally. Discussion took place over tea and coffee in sitting-rooms with a tape-recorder on the table over a period of about two hours. In each case the interviewer posed the following five questions in the same order, providing some structure for discussion: Do you *buy* magazines? Do you *read* them? When and where do you read them? What bits do you generally read first? What do you like about them, and are there bits you never read or don't like? Some of the magazines from our 1988 sample were on the table and participants looked at them as they talked. Extracts from the transcripts are referenced, along with the page number from the transcript as follows: P – pensioners group; U – university women's group; W – youth, community and social work group; Po – polytechnic group.

In order to make the analysis of our sample of magazines more manageable we grouped them into categories. After lengthy discussion of the most profitable means of categorisation we returned to that used by the publishing industry and the readers themselves; the magazines we collected for the sample have implied readers across the age range and among different social classes. We looked, then, at magazines for teenagers (*Patches* and *Just Seventeen*), traditional weeklies (*Woman's Own* and *Woman's Weekly*), glossy monthlies (*Cosmopolitan, Chic* and *New Woman*) and the new domestic magazines (*Bella* and *Best*). Where appropriate, we will be introducing other magazines not systematically acquired for the purpose of the sample, but illuminating with regard to specific questions raised by them.

Readers' discussion implicitly or explicitly used these categories also. The pensioners, for example, thought of 'women's magazines' as the traditional weeklies and expressed interest in the new domestic magazines, which some of them had begun to buy:

Doris: I think *Bella* does come out, does it? every week. I'm not quite sure . . . we had the first one free, did you realise that? (this to EF) we had the first one free through the door. [P1]

They rejected the glossies as not for them, however:

Catherine: I never thought of these, I didn't count these, I thought they were er, in between, *Cosmopolitan* I thought men *or* women
EF: no, it's def –
Joan: it's definitely a woman's book
Rosalind: I wouldn't know where to start
Catherine: you couldn't hold it could you? [P1]

These readers, then, define 'women's' magazines as those magazines that appear to refer to their social, economic and ideological reality. Those magazines that do not can only be understood as not specifically for women. As we pointed out in Chapter 1, women's magazines establish their address to women by virtue of exclusion (of their competitors) and representivity (the claim that only *they* speak for and to that undifferentiated social body, women).

Interestingly, in the course of our research we were inundated with piles of magazines, kindly donated or lent, by women who heard about our book. Some of the pensioners had collections which included issues from the 1950s and 1960s, and some dating back to the 1930s. We have already hinted that we are critical of any social or literary theory which postulates an ideal reader constructed and subjected by the text. The 'connoisseur's interest' exhibited by so many women who talked to us reinforces this critical approach. Women are both selective and loyal in their choice and use of their magazines. Nevertheless, magazines offer their readers particular definitions and understandings of what it is to be female. As our historical analysis has shown, women's magazines, like other cultural forms targeted primarily at women, focus firmly on that which is socially defined as 'women's world' – *Results* the domestic, the familial *or* the intimate, sexual and personal. Each magazine privileges a particular mix of women's experiences, and presents them not only as if they were women's *only* interest, but also as if they were interests shared by *all* women. In this book we seek to analyse the particular readings of femininity which have been and are now offered within the form of the women's magazine and to investigate the relations between those readings, the reader implied by the text, and the historical reader who 'consumes' or 're-reads' them herself.

Our discussions with readers show that they <u>are conscious of the magazines</u> as bearers of particular discourses of femininity <u>(domesticity, glamour, maternity)</u> and that the magazines' primary means of address to specific groups of women is through their use of commodity display:

> *Catriona*: no, I mean if you buy something like *Vogue* I mean what it's about is extravagance anyway, because [*inaud*], whereas something like *Woman* or *Best* I mean it's aimed at the family market, and so an awful lot of what it's putting forward is things like being economic in the home and how to shop cheaply, or make
>
> *Amy*: and how much you spend on those things kind of reflects how much you think how much you value yourself, maybe in a way, and also it reflects, it really reflects on your aspirations [laughter]
> *Catriona*: I don't know, if I want to go on a train, I wouldn't go for the cheapest one, but the cheapest one with a spine [laughter] [U3]
>
> *Joan*: a single person could have *My Home* and the married one *Woman and Home* and then later *Mother and Home* and *Home*
> *EF*: right, so you were supposed to
> *Joan*: yes, and there used to be *Home Chat* and *Home Notes*
> *Doris*: *Home Notes*, yes
> *Joan*: now, I don't know which way round that was, that was supposed to be when you got married [P4]
>
> *Maddy*: I don't buy a magazine to read about me, I buy a magazine because I want to change, and I want to look at a different world
> *June*: . . . in a way I like looking at the fashion and things and I suppose it's escapism as well, because I know I'll never buy anything like that, if you see what I mean [W6]

In these comments we can identify two distinct positions on the pleasures of the women's magazine for its readers, as a reflection of or 'time-keeper' for the particular circumstances of their lives at different times (women do not so much 'grow up' with magazines as 'grow out' of them, transferring allegiance from one title to another when the circumstances of their lives change), and as fantasy. These comments also show a consciousness of reading as a meaningful and socially structured practice: your self-identity as a married or a single woman is tied up with your choice of magazine, your public appearance is affected by whether you buy

[margin annotation: Results/comments]

Woman or a magazine 'with a spine'. Yet, the younger women all expressed criticism of the magazines' content:

> *Lisa*: it's not actually that they're mindless [*inaud*] I spose it's more what Linda was saying, that they can be full very much of particular stereotypes, and they're very much kind of limiting your horizons . . . [W6]

> *Katie*: you spend all your time reading these magazines, learning how to make yourself look beautiful and all you can expect is to get shouted at by workmen, and the whole message is actually in there [U10]

The complaint of 'stereotypes' was the most common one articulated by these younger women readers and, in particular, as Katie comments above, that even if it were possible to attain the 'ideal' self imagined by the text it would not render the 'happiness' it supposedly promises.

Despite the clear-sighted criticism offered by a number of readers, it is not our view that the constructions of femininity we find in magazines are harmless and innocuous. This is a position that has been taken by some theorists of popular culture, especially in response to moral panic about the effects of violence on television or in comics on young children (Barker, 1989). While we reject any straightforward causal relation between representation and behaviour, or the idea that these texts simply 'brainwash' their readers, we would argue that certain readings are privileged and that frequently the terms of our criticism can only remain within the terms of the magazine discourse itself. We may not agree with the versions of femininity offered in any particular magazine text, or in magazines in general, but our disagreement is a response to, a reaction to, these versions, rather than a re-shaping or a destruction of them. This is why we cannot conclude that the discourses of women's magazines are innocuous. The magazine determines the range of possible meanings and assumptions implicit in its own text, what kind of life is seen as a struggle, and what is easy, or can be taken for granted:

> *Angela*: . . . even now I know what's wrong according to a feminist perspective, if I'm really tired I'll buy them [W2]

> *Lisa*: . . . I'd been to this conference and it'd been really heavy all day, and I got on the train to come back, you know just before I got on

the train, I really fancied reading something quite light and in fact I bought *Cosmopolitan* [W4]

The magazines' representations of femininity are offered in a form which is, above all, *easy* to deal with, process, interpret. This means that our task is not only to analyse these representations, but also to look critically at how they work, and examine the conditions which give them this air of obviousness (even as we reject 'the obvious').The ability to make sense of a text – be it a film, novel, or conversation – relies on the operation of certain generic codes and conventions, which are easily recognised by readers, and it may be precisely this 'ease', rather than the contents themselves, that ensure the text's influence.

Of course, the register or genre is not wholly determining of reader interpretation. For example, feminists have offered re-readings of popular cultural forms such as soap-opera and 'film noir', as peculiarly 'feminine' forms that offer positive images of women or fantasies of female power. If feminism were a 'preferred' framework through which to apprehend the world, if might be that readers and analysts could come to associate femininity, wit and strength and that this configuration of associations would become sedimented in women's own lives. Crucially, for this new configuration to be established not only the reading but the plot, form and content – the production of the text – would have to change. Just as the proto-feminist reading of film noir may be stymied if, in the end, the heroines are always dead or dying, so in our view this essentially recuperative process of reading against the grain of the text has limited applicability to women's magazines of any historical period. However, *critical* re-reading which seeks out, beyond positive images of the female self, contradictions and problems, is of value.

We recognise that the critical assessments offered by readers of magazines that we report here were produced in a particular context, that of a researcher eliciting information about their reading, more likely to generate critical readings. It is possible that on other occasions women read magazines quite uncritically or naively. This is where the limits of social research methods become clear: how can we possibly gain access to such 'naive' readings, if they do indeed exist? Simply posing the question, 'What do you think about that?' or 'Do you like that?' pushes the respondent into a mode of discourse which is analytical and critical (unless she says 'Don't know' or 'Nothing' in which case the researcher is none the wiser).

The context or setting, then, produces a large number of, in the terms of Richardson and Corner (1986), 'displaced' and 'mediated' readings, rather than 'transparent' ones. The 'transparent' reading is that which works in co-operation with the text, adopting the stance of the implied reader encouraged by the text, such as Doris's below:

> *Doris:* . . . it's this lady, and the tears came into my eyes when I was reading it, well, because this is how young mums feel now, and she went into premature labour and the baby was stillborn, and she felt this nurse, I've come to take him away, and they fought to keep it so they could bury it properly [P9]

By contrast, a mediated reading negotiates with the forms and conventions of the genre, recognising its message and reporting it without necessarily expressing agreement or empathy with it:

> *Phil:* the thing that really annoys me is, they always set things up to be answering certain questions – 'Why are we so cruel?' well it makes it that we are . . . [W7]

A displaced reading adopts the position of implied reader in order to criticise it, commenting that someone else, if they were reading this, would think that such and so:

> *Marie:* . . . cos if you're thirteen and you don't do that you're going to think that's what you ought
> *Katie:* I mean, don't they, I mean if they're girls surely they can remember what it was like to be thirteen and the power of suggestion is like really strong, cos if when you are thirteen, and this is how things should be, that you should be stopping at every pram – they'll assume girls do [U10]

Here, the group members express fear about the effect of the magazine on a thirteen-year-old with the implication that they themselves are not so affected, as they are able to *see through* the workings of the magazine and its message.

Despite the exigencies of the setting, not all the groups criticised the magazines. The pensioners neither criticised them, nor produced displacement readings, unlike the students and youth-workers. This difference might be accounted for by class or generation. An interesting difference between the students and the youth workers emerged. The youth workers used what we would call a theoretical vocabulary of stereotypes:

FASHION & STYLE.

> *Linda*: I never read them . . . I'm quite anti- them really cos I just think they're you know, they've all got pictures of women on the front that look really sort of together, and they've got all wonderful hair and make-up and it just, in every way it's set up to make women look inadequate, which they're not . . . [W5]

> *Lisa*: they can be very full of particular stereotypes, they're very much limiting your horizons [W6]

> *Angela*: I feel sad that magazines reinforce a lot of women stereotypes, but I don't feel that they actually cause those women to have the stereotypes . . .
> *Maddy*: they're a very strong reinforcing agent aren't they? [U11]

By contrast, the students used both a different language and identified different areas of conflict and criticism:

> *Katie*: but I think the worst things about women's magazines is they teach you to see yourself as an object . . . they make you aware of bits of your body, bits, you feel kind of unrelated to them, because you're assessing them through someone else's eyes . . . [U11]
> *Penny*: it's all about, look [*reads from* Patches] 'use our tips for terrific silky skin, then slip into style pyjamas and go to bed with Rob Lowe . . .' [*gasps and screams of laughter*]. This is for thirteen-year-olds!
> *Katie*: they're just turning you into like proto-consumers [U10]

We are inclined to put this difference down to age distinction and specifically to developments in the disciplines of literary and social theory which may have informed the students' approach, in which the idea of stereotype is now largely rejected. It is, however, still an important concept for teachers and youth workers in their pedagogic practice.

Either way, a critical and reflexive tone was constantly present in both the students' and youth-workers' discussions. Perhaps as a result they proved more eager to 'defend' or 'explain' their magazine reading and the pleasures it extends to them:

> *Harriet*: I buy them sometimes to cheer myself up, it's a luxury
> *Penny*: yes, because they're quite expensive

Harriet: instead of going out and buying clothes which is even more expensive, you can go and buy a magazine, it's a self-indulgence [U11]

Helen: they are a form of escapism, cheer me up when ill etc. I sometimes think I can learn from them – how to cope in certain situations. I can see why they may offend some women, but these things don't bother me. They relax me, and that for me is the main thing. In reading about other people's problems I can forget my own [Po6]

The pensioners' discussion lacks this sort of reflexiveness, making few attempts to analyse exactly what the pleasure of liking consists in, why (rather than when) they read magazines. It may be that they do not consider that reading magazines is an activity that requires explanation, whereas the others, aware that in feminist and critical circles it may be disapproved of, adopt a more defensive position. Obviously, however, the pensioners differed in what they liked and disliked in the magazines:

Catherine: in the – um – *Woman's Weekly* 'The Man Who Sees' I think's a bit tedious
Joan: oh yes
Catherine: isn't he tedious? [P12]

Joan: and in *People's Friend* I like the things people write up and say, like 'why is a thing called something?' and they investigate it [P9]

Our interpretation of readers' discussion is, as we have said, intended to be suggestive rather than exhaustive. Some of the fragments of discussion we have reproduced display a significant and ubiquitous feature of these sessions; women like laughing at and mimicking the conventions of the magazine form:

Joan: ah yes, I like that
Doris: a special day you had
Catherine: 'A Day I'll Never Forget'
Doris: yes, well, 'The Day I'll Never Forget'
Joan: they invite you to write in
Rosalind: yes, 'A Holiday of a life time'
Joan: they went and stayed at a farmhouse and she went into premature labour [laughter]
Joan: her husband had to deliver the baby [P9]

Maddy: but the stuff I read would be, you know, 'how to cope with stress at work'. I'd turn to, or – um – 'how to get healthy in four days' or 'change your lifestyle with a pear – it'll do everything' [laughter] [W7]

Reading in our culture is, for the most part, assumed to be an individual and silent activity. Its construction in this form has been a political process. Evidence to the Select Committee Enquiry prior to the Public Libraries Act of 1950 articulated concern that people were not reading, despite reading and study groups in pubs and other public places. Reading in these groups was public and noisy and therefore had to be denied even as it was acknowledged (Corrigan and Gillespie, 1977) Reading of this kind has not been entirely banished from our cultural practice – teenage girls read *Jackie* in groups in school breaks, for instance. Our discussion got pretty noisy too (with the result that the tapes were not easily transcribed in places):

> go on, what's that one?
> what's it say? what's it say?
> read it
> this is typical of a magazine problem page for someone to have a good laugh
> what's it say? [U6]

We shall have more to say about this kind of pleasure in magazines later. For now, we want simply to attend to the possible criticism that we seem to be granting an authenticity to readers' negotiations with magazines which we have denied to the critics. Certainly, the insertion of verbatim speech from the groups adds a note of authenticity and interest which would otherwise be missing from our discussion. It is, after all, a familiar ploy of the magazines who use the voice of 'real people' in the shape of letters, 'true experiences', the make-over, to add interest, lightness and realism as well as break the dominance of the editorial or authorial voice. The reader's voice breaks that authority only to confirm it, of course. Readers who are featured in magazines do not dissent from the values and meanings carried by the whole. The grandmother who has her hair cut and lightened affirms the aesthetics and value system of the magazine. The reader's voice in this book has a similar stylistic function, adding authenticity and interest, breaking our authorial dominance, but not vitiating or undermining our project.

Part two: contemporary magazines

In the rest of this chapter we organise sections thematically. Again we would introduce a note of methodological self-consciousness here. The headings under which we discuss our sample of magazines (sexuality, home and family, etc.) would, we believe, be acceptable to other critical readers, though they might wish to add others or order them differently. There will, inevitably, be echoes here of the argument in previous chapters. It is open to the sceptic to suspect that the discovery of continuity in themes and style is not so much an empirical finding as an act of projection on our parts. We would answer that we have looked for difference and, throughout, been struck by similarity.

Femininity and masculinity

'Every time I go into [the newsagents] I look and I think, I do actually look to see if there's something I like in that section, but I just see it simply as a bank of women's faces that doesn't fit in with me' comments one of the youth workers we taped. If, as we agree, women's magazines are about being female, and the problems of being female, their almost exclusive emphasis on heterosexual relationships positions women wholly in relation to men. Men feature in magazines as desirable, but also threatening, dull, unsatisfying, unfaithful and so on. Yet, while some magazines have male contributors who either articulate some notional 'male' point of view, or expose the male psyche, men as such are in fact peripheral to the magazine as both producers and consumers. Women's concern, according to most magazines, is with personal and emotional relationships, primarily with husbands or partners, but also with children, family and friends. The work of maintaining healthy personal relationships is women's work. While the glossies are keen to promote themselves as the champions of the young, free and single woman, their endorsement of the single state is never more than ambiguous. It may be promoted as something to enjoy, rather than endure, but only 'while it lasts'. The 'single' state (without a man) is a temporary condition. In the more traditional magazines, being single is usually understood to be a problem, both explicitly and implicitly in that their address to readers assumes a partner and/or children. Contemporary teenage girls' magazines typically centre around the highly restricted themes of boys and pop culture, with the more traditional, such as *Jackie* and *Patches*, still reliant on what has been termed 'the ideology of romance' for their main copy (McRobbie, 1978b). Every girl, apparently, wants a boyfriend, sooner or later, and the magazines offer advice on how to acquire, and sometimes keep, the desired object. Boys can be divided into two types: good boys are kind, considerate and moral; bad boys are selfish, inconsiderate, sexually predatory and untrustworthy. Boys of both sorts are in lamentably short supply and this puts girls into competition with each other. Female friendships occasionally figure as a source of solidarity in the prose and photo-fiction which are the staples of these magazines, but they are usually introduced as a means to the end of ensnaring the current 'hunk' or as a source of consolation upon failure.

Other aspects of adolescent femininity do feature in the magazines, notably school or, more rarely, work, and leisure interests, but all are secondary to romantic interest. School is primarily a place to meet boys, and leisure time is occupied with making oneself attractive to boys. Apart from shopping for clothes and make-up, girls' major leisure interests, if one were to take the magazines as sociological evidence, are listening to music and amassing information about favourite pop, television and film stars. These are either female role models (like Kylie Minogue or Debbie Gibson) or, more usually, handsome hunks (like Bros, Wet Wet, Wet and Rob Lowe).

An alternative, and from our own perspective, more positive version of adolescence is presented in *Just Seventeen*, in which the traditional culture of romance is to some extent displaced. Relationships with boys still feature, but as a fairly small part of the whole, and are treated with some cynicism. The magazine assumes that its readers are first and foremost interested in *style*. Originally produced as a free giveaway accompanying the music magazine *Smash Hits*, *Just Seventeen* provides extensive coverage of music and other media of teenage popular culture, notably television and cinema. Unlike its fellow teenage girls' magazines, it acknowledges that homosexuality and lesbianism exist, and also assumes its readers are interested in 'social issues'. It provides some coverage of careers (rather than jobs), offering, in our sample, case-studies of both traditional and non-traditional female occupations (women in the fire service and in secretarial work, for instance).

Moving up the age range to magazines aimed at adults, there are discernible differences, as well as enduring similarities, between titles. The traditional weeklies *Woman's Own* and *Woman's Weekly* revolve around the representation of femininity as domesticity. This is particularly pervasive in *Woman's Weekly*, which has an average reader's age of fifty, and mixes articles on homecraft, notably knitting, with romantic fiction. Unashamedly conservative, it presents 'the domestic' as cosy, comfortable and largely unproblematic. Homecrafts are less central to *Woman's Own*, although they do feature, but the emphasis is squarely on marital relationships. The implied reader is married with children; she may have a job outside the home, but it is less important than the maintenance of a stable home-life. *Woman's Own*, however, does recognise that home-life and domesticity are not automatically and everywhere stable and secure: domestic violence, illness, death, divorce, criminality are all presented as both threats and object lessons to the maintenance of 'family'.

Best and *Bella* look quite different from the established weeklies and are much more 'factual', crammed with short items, including news, celebrity gossip and a barrage of handy hints and tips. They seem, in fact, reminiscent of the nineteenth-century domestic manual, privileging instruction over entertainment and, despite the inclusion of jokes and gossip, abandoning the more intimate tone of the traditional weeklies. Femininity is understood as the sum of the individual woman's practical skills, whether efficiency in running a home, or competence in the office. Children figure here more centrally than men, who are largely absent, except in the fiction (which has a surprising preponderance of thriller, mystery and 'twist in the tale' narratives as opposed to romance) and, inevitably, the problem-page. Neither magazine devotes much attention to romance, although *Bella* offers one short romantic story each week, or to discussions of personal relationships.

By contrast, the monthly glossies we looked at, *Cosmopolitan* and *New Woman*, both dedicate considerable space to discussion of personal and sexual relations. In *Cosmopolitan*, femininity is equated with youth, ambition, and success in both 'career' and 'personal' life, offering its readers the prospect of being serious, but sexy. Sound advice on careers, finance, property and so on are set alongside articles on how to look glamorous and desirable. Perhaps more than any other contemporary women's magazine, *Cosmopolitan* manages a staggeringly contradictory model of femininity. Domesticity takes a fairly low profile, rearticulated in the shape of articles on food and homes that express 'personal style'. Women's careers are given serious attention, but are always secondary to relationships, with partners in particular, but also with friends or parents. 'Relationship', though, remains a code-word for men, who are endlessly analysed and 'exposed'. While *Cosmopolitan* searches for the 'new man', insisting that men must change in order to suit the 'new' competent and self-interested woman, its constant exposure of the shortcomings and psychic deformities of the contemporary man suggests that it is its readers who must adapt and compromise, armed with the artillery of anthropological insight into the 'opposite sex' provided by the magazine.

New Woman, launched as the first 'post-feminist' magazine, shares many of the characteristics of *Cosmopolitan*, but with a somewhat different inflection. Femininity in *New Woman* may be about success, but 'a new woman is fun to be with, not a formidable challenge – someone who is softer, more feminine than the myth of superwoman', someone who 'puts the quality of [her] relationships before everything else' ('Editorial', issue 1, August 1988). Like *Cosmopolitan*, however, *New Woman* seeks to deproblematise men by getting inside the male psyche, offering articles on 'What Men Really Think About Sex' (August 1988) or 'At Last – What Really Makes A Woman Sexy' (September 1988) by those who know, the men themselves.

All the magazines discussed so far, like the vast majority of magazines currently available in Britain, present a normative model of femininity which is almost exclusively white. The glossies occasionally employ light-skinned black models in fashion-plates but by and large the world of women's magazines is not only heterosexist and middle-class, but also excludes the experience of black women. Race is rarely an issue, and *never* a political issue. Some magazines are willing to incorporate some aspects of cultures other than the dominant one, notably with regard to fashion and food, presented as new forms or objects of consumption for their assumed white female readers, but this is the extent of their 'multiculturalism'. The only magazines which consistently address issues of racial difference are those aimed overtly, if not exclusively, at a black audience. Amongst these are several devoted to black hair and beauty, but it is *Chic* that comes closest to the familiar mix of instruction and entertainment of the mainstream 'white' women's magazine. Clearly targeted to women of African or Afro-Caribbean origin, it shares the aspirational tone of the other glossies. It frequently features black women who are 'high-flyers', successful and influential in politics, business or the media, advertising itself as for 'The Woman Of Purpose'. Once again, despite the inclusion of political issues (black British MPs, women and eating disorders) and some suggestion that 'Black' is a political category, the dominant model of femininity remains essentially one of individual achievement in three areas of life: career, relationships and personal appearance.

Sexuality

Definitions of female (and male) sexuality are central to our cultural constructions of the feminine. Magazines aimed at teenage girls are frequently read by those as young as nine and ten, who are already receiving clear signals about sexual identity and behaviour from these texts. *Patches* and *Jackie* rarely address teenage female sexuality directly; rather they displace it into a rhetoric of romantic love. Adolescent romance in *Patches*, at least so portrayed in the photo-stories and prose fiction, is extremely chaste, involving nothing more sexual than a kiss as the favoured resolution. The moral messages are, however, quite clear: in order to be good a girl must be neither sexually provocative nor demonstrative. There are clear demarcations between good and bad girls, just as between good and bad boys. Bad boys are undeniably attractive, but they will always abuse and disappoint. Good boys are at first dull, but turn out to be saviours. It is important that girls learn to distinguish between these two types. Sometimes girls can be proactive in engineering romantic encounters, although an important feminine skill lies in concealing this from boys. Even when girls do take the initiative they are still encouraged to appear passive. Sexuality is either denied, or represented as a threat to romantic success.

Similar definitions of sexuality are to be found in romantic fiction magazines aimed at older readers, such as *Loving*, *True Romance* and *True Monthly*. The first two are wholly concerned with romantic love and the search for the 'right' man. *True Monthly*, by contrast, invests less in the conquering power of romantic love, presenting a highly punitive vision of female sexuality. Women in these stories are frequently duped by bad men – seduced, raped and prostituted. Men fall into the familiar division of heroes and villains. Sexuality is dangerous, and if women give in to sexual desire they will live (or not) to regret it. The only alternative to this pain and regret is to be rescued by the good man, who is inevitably less glamorous and exciting – that is, less sexual – than the villain.

Sexuality is less clear cut in the pages of *Just Seventeen* where it is addressed both as fun – 'Do You Think You're Sexy?' (7 September 1988) – and as a matter worthy of serious discussion. The magazine offers considered counsel on all matters relating to sexuality, and recognises that emergent sexuality can be equally problematic for boys and girls. A section of the problem-page is given over to answering questions from boys. The magazine is also unusual in so far as it frequently presents homosexuality and lesbianism as legitimate forms of sexuality:

> We live in a society which is geared towards heterosexuality, and the subsequent prejudices against gay people should be seen for what they are – ignorant. Homosexuality is not a problem: other people's reaction to it is. (30 March 1988)

Just Seventeen may not be prescriptive about sexual behaviour, but its discussions adopt a familiar didactic rhetoric of 'responsibility':

> When it's between two people who both want to express their feelings in a physical way, sex is neither right nor wrong. But one-night stands do carry certain risks that you're less likely to encounter when sex is part of a loving, caring relationship. (28 September 1988)

The emphasis on long-term relationships as either the most fulfilling or most appropriate context for sexual expression is shared by nearly all the magazines in our sample. The glossies are more inclined to celebrate sexuality outside of the context of 'relationships', but Janice Winship points out that *Cosmopolitan* treats sexuality in isolation from all other forms of social activity (Winship, 1987, p. 133). In fact, it does seem to us that *Cosmopolitan* sometimes engages with broader debates about sexuality:

> Even today, the woman who loses her virginity to the wrong loud mouthed lout can find herself ostracised as a slag; the wife who wants a night out with the girls a 'scrubber'; and the career woman branded by the jealous as someone who 'slept her way to the top'. Yet for the man who uses prostitutes, or just generally puts it about, there are only compliments: he becomes a stud, one of the lads. Even the man who rapes can claim he was 'led on': for men, supposedly, are never to blame for their sexual activities – only women can thus be divided into the 'good' and the 'fallen'. (September 1988)

It should be added, however, that most articles are by no means so clear about sexual inequalities and double standards. As Winship notes, the glossies prefer to discuss and emphasise sexual difference, rather than inequality, and to advocate understanding and compromise from both parties as a resolution to sexual conflict. The editorial stance of *Cosmopolitan* is avowedly to promote 'an understanding, rather than a battle, between the sexes' (June *1988*). *Cosmopolitan* and *New Woman* both define female sexuality as heterosexual and active. Sexual attractiveness, and its achievement, is given a high priority, hence the proliferation of articles, from a male point of view, about what makes a woman 'sexy'.

From its position as a magazine for women who care most about the quality of their relationships, *New Woman* promises a great deal by way of information and advice on love and sex. In fact very little, and certainly nothing new, is delivered. The emphasis is still on long-term relationships, particularly the means to keep them sexually exciting. The responsibility for maintaining and improving relationships is, of course, women's. There is an ever present tension between the celebration of high-charged short-term erotic affairs ('Big Sexual Encounters', September 1988) and more sensible, if less passionate, on-going relationships. Not only do the magazines imply that it is unrealistic to expect sexual passion on a grand scale to last, but also that this might be undesirable. In the traditional weeklies, sexuality is largely subsumed under the topics of domesticity and maternity. In *Woman's Own*, for example, the problematic nature of sexuality is only addressed directly in the problem-page where women are most likely to be advised to 'work harder' at an existing relationship, rather than seek fulfilment outside it. Stable, companionate relationships which endure are valued more highly than short-lived excitement. This is also true of *Woman's Weekly*, although the ideology of romance retains a firmer hold here. The magazine carries a comparatively high proportion of romance fiction in which virginal heroines still succumb to masterful heroes. Heroines may be allowed to be 'independent' in some respects; they may have some kind of career, but they are not truly fulfilled until they find the right man. The new weeklies, with their emphasis on domesticity, homecare and, in the case of *Best*, fashion, devote little attention to sexuality as such. They do carry short features on family relationships, particularly on the rights and wrongs of parenting. Sexuality here figures only as maternity, or it is medicalised and dealt with only as a health issue.

Home and family

Our preceding chapters have illustrated the process through which domestic ideology became central to adult women's magazines. The weeklies in particular speak to women primarily as wives, mothers and homemakers. A glance down the contents list of almost any contemporary magazine will confirm the endurance of this perception of women's role. If teenage girls' magazines are structured through an ideology of romance, women's magazines shift the emphasis into the ideology of the family, maternity and domesticity. Although the family does sometimes figure in teenage girls' magazines, either as a source of generational conflict or as an important support system, it is fairly marginal. In weekly magazines aimed at adult women, romantic love is largely replaced by an apparently more mature mode of caring: women are charged with the responsibility of reproducing and maintaining the family, both in practical and emotional terms. Women's magazines since their first appearance have presented themselves as handbooks for their readers. Guidance takes the direct form of a recipe: ideas, skill instruction, ingredients, tools or utensils and methods for specific activities such as cooking, decorating and gardening, presented in a narrative, attractive and easily consumable form. They also, on a wider level, provide a particular construction of family life and women's position within it. All the weeklies we read (*Bella, Best, Woman's Own, Woman's Weekly*) present domestic work as women's responsibility. They typically focus on the non-repetitive, 'skilled' aspects of domestic labour, effectively concealing its routine and often thankless nature. Yet, at the same time, to fulfil their didactic and counselling function, they must address the less satisfying aspects of women's caring role. This they do by pointing out that a happy home and a happy, healthy family are not givens but, like everything else worth having, must be worked for.

Cookery, knitting, sewing and other homecrafts are presented not as work but as leisure, with the implication that all women (or at least all readers) share an interest in and enjoyment of such activities. *Bella* and *Best*, in particular, devote a great deal of space to features such as 'Home and Gardens', 'In The Kitchen', 'To Knit, To Sew, To Make' (*Best*) and 'Recipes and Diets', 'Your Home', 'Things To Do' (*Bella*). Gardening and Do-It-Yourself are brought into the purview of women's responsibility. Given the criticisms levelled at magazines, that they concentrate on a narrow range of feminine activities, it could be viewed as enlightened of *Bella* to use illustrations of women carrying out 'home' tasks socially defined as male. However, it is significant that while changing roles for women involve the incorporation of areas of work traditionally defined as men's responsibility, there is little indication that this is balanced by a changing role for men, taking on feminine tasks. *Bella* and *Best* look distinctively different from the established weeklies, in particular in their use of colourful and multiple inset pictorial material and small text. It may be that their elaborate multiplication of homecare material is as much a work of fantasy as the romantic fiction that remains a staple feature of other magazines. Readers read about these tasks (be it romance or knitting) when they have neither time nor opportunity to undertake them, gaining pleasure from consuming them in the magazine form rather than producing them in their own lives. However, at least on the surface, the emphasis on practical advice, step-by-step guides, pull-out-and-keep recipes and patterns, elevates domestic work into a full-time occupation, and themselves into trade manuals for the professional homemaker and mother. Yet by presenting this work as leisure they deny and conceal it.

Domesticity is less central to the definitions of femininity in *Cosmopolitan* and *New Woman*, but still, if covertly, influential. Both include sections on food and cooking, made to accord with the perceived or idealised lives of their readers. Thus, they often utilise unusual, 'exotic' or expensive ingredients, connecting 'cookery' with 'entertainment'. Cooking, like other forms of consumption presented in the glossies, is an expression of personal style and taste. This might be seen as tantamount to a return to the eighteenth-century women's magazines' focus on 'accomplishment', performed to impress, as ornament and display, rather than out of necessity. In this sense, cooking becomes a completely different activity from that of the nightly calorie-counted and budgeted family meal of the weeklies. Domestic work is neither a science nor a profession here, but an art, an expressive and creative leisure activity.

While the magazines are inclined to disguise a great deal of domestic labour as leisure (even those which also disguise it as science or profession), they are interestingly less reluctant to present the maintenance of happy family life as something which requires a substantial amount of work. Although the discourse of political economy has no place in any of these magazines, that of pop psychology is all-pervasive, elevating the routine and pain recognised as a part of many women's lives to a specialised function which only women can fulfil. The weeklies, in particular, operate within an ethos which sees family life as women's primary source of satisfaction. The family unites women; it is the common denominator not just between readers, but also between readers and editors, readers and celebrities, even readers and royalty. Discourses of the family render class and racial differences either invisible or irrelevant.

The letters pages of *Woman's Own*, *Woman's Weekly*, *Bella* and *Best* are particularly instrumental in creating this commonality, largely through humour. Children, partners and sometimes pets (also treated as family members) are funny, infuriating, but always essentially lovable. Men are characterised in a similar mode to children – somewhat forgetful, imperfectly socialised and helpless individuals. This is a reassuring portrayal, validating women's role. If this is what men are like, then women are always needed to direct and support them through their lives.

The letters page sets up an intimate and comfortable world of shared concerns. This contrasts sharply with that other traditional forum for reader correspondence, the agony column. Here, the negative side of family life and personal relationships is articulated. Common themes emerge from the letters: dissatisfaction with marriage, lack of sexual fulfilment, inconsiderate or abusive partners, lack of success in finding a partner. Problems seem all too recognisable, yet despite the repetition of the same issues week after week, there are few attempts to draw out from them any sense of commonality or shared experience. A unique exception to this is *Best*, where responses from readers are printed the following week, rather than counselling from an 'expert' agony aunt. Yet, still, wherever problems arise, they are treated as individual failures or inadequacies, and the family as an institution is rarely brought into question. *Best* readers/advisers frequently comment 'the same thing happened to me . . .', but they present this as coincidence – there is no suggestion that women's problems may have political origins, be politically structured, or politically transformable.

It is not only in the problem-page that magazines overtly acknowledge that, for some women, personal relationships and family life do not always run smoothly. Features on individuals, usually 'ordinary people' but occasionally celebrities, whose lives have been beset by personal trauma or tragedy, are presented as entertainment, but carry powerful moral messages. They focus on individual stoicism and bravery in the face of adversity, taking the form of mini-narratives or personal testimonies. Subject-matter frequently verges on the sensational, and has a strong emotive appeal. This use of narrative is particularly favoured by *Woman's Own*, as the following extract from a 'Shock Report' on domestic violence, presented in the recognisable register of popular fiction, illustrates:

> The screams were silent, so no one heard. They went on and on, running through her body like bolts of lightning, but no one knew. The

tears flowed like mountain streams, but no one saw them . . . . (19 March 1988)

Even *Bella* and *Best*, despite their 'factual' or practical focus, rely heavily on the narrative of personal testimony:

When Tony came out of hospital I said to Ken 'This isn't the end, you know, it's only the beginning' . . . I refuse to sit here in tears. You have to fight. (*Bella*, 4 June 1988)

We have seen that narrative fiction has been a staple feature of the women's magazine since its inception and that the rise of the magazine may be allied to that of the novel, the literary form of the bourgeoisie, and frequently associated with the female reader and a feminisation of culture in general. The history of the relationship of literary form and the linked processes of ensuring class and gender hegemony continues to be relevant to the twentieth-century magazine. The conventional divisions of period-ical genres run along gender lines – newspapers for men, magazines for women. Empirical and analytic forms of reporting characterise the former, ideal and emotive novelisation the latter. This suggests an underlying connection between women and narrative, which includes but extends beyond the explicitly fictive. 'Triumph over tragedy' stories serve to comfort readers about the relative security of their own lives. But, as Winship points out, readers are not invited to question the causes of these experiences (Winship, 1987, pp.70–1). Story and analysis are separated; empathy is encouraged in place of political action.

Leisure, lifestyle and consumption

Apart from representing domestic labour as women's leisure, contemporary magazines also incorporate a whole range of material which could be more strictly categorised as leisure. Magazines themselves occupy a significant place in women's lives, in so far as they are read in 'leisure time', fragmented and nebulous as this may be, and afford pleasure to their readers. While there are obvious differences between women in terms of their access to time and other resources, in general women's leisure is substantially more home-centred than men's. Watching televi-sion and reading are the two most popular (in the sense of most

frequent) leisure pursuits for women (Green, Hebron and Woodward, 1990). Weekly magazines in particular capitalise heavily on
the popularity of television, notably on those programmes aimed
at and enjoyed by a predominantly female audience. Interviews
with soap-opera stars, for example, often concentrate on their
home and family life, and frequently cross over into other areas of
magazine content, with the inclusion of celebrity recipes, fashion
and beauty advice.

There are differences in the way the various categories of
magazine define and address women's leisure pursuits. The
conventional weeklies construct female leisure narrowly – television, reading fiction, listening to music, self-beautification (including shopping), knitting and sewing, are the sum. The glossy
monthlies add 'eating out', and allow that their readers may also
be interested in the fine arts and 'serious' literature. However, a
common theme unites the coverage of leisure across the entire
range of magazines, from those for teenagers to *Woman's Weekly*.
Female leisure is inextricably bound up with (commodity) consumption.

In recent years the advertising and publishing industries'
discourse of consumption has constructed itself and revolved
around a crucial category, that of 'lifestyle'. Readers are offered
advice on how to choose the goods, and sometimes the attitudes
and beliefs, which combine to produce a desired lifestyle.
Shopping is not only elevated to the status of being the ultimate
leisure experience, it is also the ultimate form of self-expression.
This is an area where magazines have no reserve about offering
help and advice in the shape of special promotions, product tests,
endorsements and recommendations. They legitimate specific
choices from a bewildering range of goods and, in doing so,
provide an appropriate context for advertisers.

Consumption has different inflexions, through editorial and
advertising copy, depending on the assumed target audience or
'market segment' of the magazine. The traditional women's
weeklies speak to women primarily as controllers of the 'family'
budget, but also as individuals who are interested in their
appearance. The newer weeklies have a similar emphasis, but
include more product and consumer tests, transforming commodity consumption into a scientific and professional occupation, and
promoting a broader range of goods. Cars and motor accessories

are featured in *Best*, but their treatment remains gender specific. Cars featured are small and economical rather than the expensive power motors featured in 'men's' magazines such as *GQ* and *Arena*. Weekly magazines include clothes for children and for men in their fashion pages, assuming that keeping the family clothed as well as fed is women's responsibility.

If the weeklies situate readers primarily as domestic consumers, the glossies' appeal is both more individualistic and narcissistic. Comparatively expensive fashion and beauty products dominate; illustrations are lavish and stylish, with editorial content often barely distinguishable from advertising. If these magazines represent beauty as fashion, style and individuality, they also effectively encourage women to look similar to each other by advocating certain styles of clothes, make-up, interior design, and expressly denigrating and rejecting others ('*out* go last year's dull browns...'). Consumption of household goods is equally a matter of appearance and display of the right artifacts, however impractical. The glossies aim at consumers who are at least aspirational, if not affluent. The right consumer durables, taste and trappings, are the hallmarks of success. To take this one step further, and the remarks of readers bear this out, reading (or being seen to read) the right magazine is as important as the possession of any other commodity, in the establishment of social identity.

The notion that identity is achieved through consumption is equally prevalent in young women's magazines. Those which concentrate on romance, such as *Patches*, privilege self-beautification in particular. *Just Seventeen*, by contrast, is more akin to the glossies and the music press in its commitment to a culture of style, tying consumption in with other areas of teenage leisure, such as television, cinema and video. Its most obvious link is with pop music. Readers are encouraged to emulate their favourite stars – 'Bros Fashion' (11 June 1988) and 'Celebrity Slap' (29 June 1988) – who are presented as style arbiters – 'The Blue Mercedes Guide to Shopping' (2 March 1988). Despite variants in the range and type of consumer durables that any one category of magazine will market, all employ the feminine image as the major medium. As women we are taught that the secret of our success, whether in bedroom or boardroom, is in our physical appearance. Women are still, by and large, perceived in terms of closeness to or distance from culturally specific notions of feminine beauty. An important role for the magazine, therefore, lies in encouraging women to aspire and strive towards meeting this ideal. No woman should feel complacent – there is always scope for improvement. Self-beautification is perhaps the point at which the dual functions of the magazine – instruction and entertainment – converge and become most coherent. Each of the magazines in our 1988 sample offers a particular 'look', or range of 'looks', for the reader to emulate. Perhaps in recognition of women's varied roles, there is no longer, if there ever was, a single feminine image. At the level of hairstyles, clothes and make-up, contradictory elements are brought together. Yet underlying this are strong messages about what constitutes an acceptable look for different types of women. This plurality of looks, of superficial styles, is firmly rooted in two key assumptions: first, that all women share a major preoccupation with the way in which they look; second, that all women can improve their appearance by the application of time and effort and through the purchase of certain products. In *Just Seventeen* this might be a pair of shoes just like Kylie's, in *Cosmo* it might be an expensive perfume to wear with the dress-for-success suit, and in *Woman's Own* it might be a piece of jewellery to brighten up last year's frock. Finally, however, the result is the same – 'improvement' in appearance leads to self-improvement in other areas of life.

Nowhere is this more clear than in the magazines' enduring obsession with women's weight. Other fads and fashions may come and go, but body weight is always under scrutiny. Apart from the occasional real life reader or celebrity, the women depicted in magazines are uniformly slim, down to those featured in *Patches'* photo-love stories. While this preoccupation has recently come to be articulated through a discourse of 'health' as opposed to beauty, slenderness continues to be the key indicator of sexual attractiveness. One exception may be the magazines for older women, such as *Woman's Weekly*, which runs a weekly column of fashion for the 'fuller figure'. Various kinds of slimming diets are the stock-in-trade of both traditional and new weeklies, and frequent features of the glossies. Even magazines aimed at younger readers offer the occasional diet, although here the emphasis is more often on exercise as a means of weight control. The very profitable trade in specialist slimming magazines is not lost on the producers of more general women's magazines.

In teenage girls' magazines and in the glossy monthlies the emphasis on self-beautification is essentially unproblematic. It is presented as another form of leisure, but leisure as investment, where the pay-off will be the ability to compete successfully for men. For older women the emphasis is less on catching a man than keeping him. However, magazines also recognise that women who have many competing demands on their time may have neither the energy nor inclination to spend it on improving their appearance. Additionally, not all readers have the economic resources to buy the products which will effect the necessary transformation, so in order to maintain their interest they are offered cheap and cheerful beauty tips. And for those readers who consider themselves in need of more than standard advice, there is always the possibility of the magazine intervening in a more direct way to perform the 'make-over'. It is significant that it is one of the new weeklies which has introduced this old occasional stand-by of its more traditional competitors as a regular feature:

> Lesley, 35, is a busy housewife and mother of Adam, six. She admitted she doesn't have much of a beauty routine and was happy for us to sit back and go to town on her. (*Bella*, 14 March 1988)

> Lynne, 30, has no time for herself. She's too busy looking after Peter and their six children . . . and if anyone deserved a day off and a chance to enjoy a little pampering it was Lynne. Doesn't she make a glamorous mum! (*Bella*, 4 June 1988)

Here, again, the double pleasures of the magazine, as fantasy and reflection, entertainment and instruction, are offered in a single feature. 'Make-over' candidates are perhaps our clearest indicator of the implied reader of the magazine. Significantly, it is the weeklies, rather than the glossies, that exploit the make-over most frequently. These magazines seek to recognise the realities of many women's lives (tedium, hard work, denial of self) and offer them the prospect of transformation without loss of validation of their worth.

Employment

If leisure, as consumption or disguised as domestic work, has a high profile in all women's magazines, the same cannot be said of paid work. The majority recognise that many women are employed outside the home, either through necessity or because they want to be. However, in so far as the magazines still present themselves as primarily concerned with women's domestic role, paid employment is effectively all but ignored. *Woman's Weekly* rarely has any discussion of issues related to employment, and *Woman's Own* has no regular slot devoted to it. The Derek Jameson column sometimes carries short features, such as 'Secretaries Unite' (18 June 1988), taking a lighthearted but critical approach to the chauvinism of men and women:

> There is no difference whatsoever between a woman and a man doing the job. As in so many fields, the only thing that separates the sexes in car showrooms is the prejudice in the minds of some men – and women (*Woman's Own*, 25 June 1988)

Social inequalities in the labour market are reduced to a question of individual 'chauvinism', which women as well as men are guilty of, and anti-sexism, rather than feminism, underpins the discussion. Jameson's lighthearted comments are frequently ambiguous, apparently pro-women, but aim to diffuse gender difference and inequality rather than confront them. Elsewhere, *Woman's Own*'s coverage of paid work is largely concerned with the problems that women face in combining domestic responsibility and employment ('Help! Who Can I Ask To Look After My Child?', 6 September 1988).

Bella and *Best* both offer weekly columns on paid work, usually consisting of a spotlight on a particular job, but marginal in the context of the publication as a whole. Coverage often takes the form of an interview with a woman about her job, together with some factual information. If the range of jobs covered is broad, they are in general understood *as* jobs, rather than careers – an important distinction. Again, paid employment is secondary to women's primary careers as wives and mothers. Magazines recognise the reality of paid employment for women, but do not make it a focus of their concern.

Women's magazines aimed at a younger market, and also at women less likely to be married at an early age due to educational or class advantage, give far more coverage to paid work. Implied readers here have careers, not jobs, put a high value on paid work, and want to succeed. *Cosmopolitan*, in particular, promotes the idea of the motivated, energetic working woman, most obviously in its monthly column titled 'Career Ahead'. The key to women's success in work is here understood as a combination of assertiveness and effective communication. Articles focus on middle-class occupations, and are illustrated by photographs of young models, well-groomed and trim in executive fashion, conducting meetings and directing their colleagues. There is little mention of discrimination against women in the workplace. Problems can be coped with, it is suggested, through appropriate training. *Cosmopolitan* acts out its own message through the organisation of its own (non-profit-making) training days, as well as listing other courses or training events not directly connected with the magazine. In line with its rather schizophrenic appeal, the more structural problems that face women workers – lack of childcare provision, poor pay and conditions in part-time work – are dealt with elsewhere in the magazine.

Chic's approach is more consistent, frequently making reference to discrimination in employment – reasonably perhaps, as it can assume that its readers are likely to encounter the double oppression of racism and sexism in their experience of paid employment. The September 1988 issue contains a full article on discrimination in employment on grounds of both race and sex. In line with its overall rationale, *Chic*'s 'solution' is primarily effected through the presentation of strong role models for readers to emulate.

Feminism and politics

On the surface, feminism and politics are rarely discussed in women's magazines, but even those titles which deny any kind of involvement with feminism or other political positions nevertheless have to negotiate with them. In our sample, *Patches* and *Woman's Weekly* are the most explicit in their denial of feminism. While they operate at opposite ends of the age range, both are deeply committed to a dominant ideology of romance which proves profoundly reactionary in its positioning of women. Both work within a narrow, traditional definition of femininity which constructs women as passive and wholly preoccupied with aspirations or achievements in the realm of the personal. Of course, one of the achievements of feminist discourse during the 1970s and 1980s has been to validate the importance of 'feminine' qualities such as care, nurturance, emotion, and so on. We do not aim to criticise this 'reclamation' of the feminine, but to point out that *Patches* and *Woman's Weekly* construct femininity as *exclusively* nurturing and, by extension, accommodating to the needs of men, whether material or emotional. There is no question, in *Woman's Weekly*, that women may not be fulfilled by a solely domestic role, nor do they make many concessions to women's lives outside of it. Further, in *Patches* and romantic-fiction magazines such as *True Monthly*, these qualities of nurturance and sympathy are not presented as extending to other women. Women compete for male attention and affection, viewing and experiencing each other as rivals.

Other magazines have a less simple relation to feminism. However unsatisfactory we might find much of the content of *Woman's Own* and *Cosmopolitan*, there can be little doubt that feminism has had some impact. In both the traditional and the newer weeklies there seems to have been an acceptance and incorporation of some basic feminist principles (what we might term 'the acceptable face of feminism'). *Woman's Own*, *Bella* and *Best* are more accurately labelled 'anti-chauvinist', critical of men's crasser expressions of misogyny and prejudice. They are not, however, 'anti-sexist'; the difficulties and problems women face in the workforce or at home are, by and large, represented as part and parcel of being a woman, and never related to broader patterns of discrimination and inequality that might be fought and changed. One area where feminism has made a significant and observable impact is that of health. *Woman's Own*, in particular, has been very voluble in raising readers' awareness of the importance of cervical smear tests and regular breast examination.

Given the progressive coverage of sexuality and employment in *Just Seventeen*, the magazine has a surprisingly ambiguous relation to feminism. It does touch on inequality and discrimina-tion, highlighting sexual double standards, distinctions between jobs traditionally defined as male and female, and so on. But this is undercut by content found elsewhere in the same issue, particularly the prose fiction. A notable example from our sample is a two part story titled 'An Independent Girl' which works with peculiarly reductive stereotypes of feminism, and equates 'inde-

pendence' with loneliness and unfriendliness. The central character, in response to being cheated on by a boyfriend, joins a
women's group:

> Judy was determined to succeed in her new life as an independent girl.
> She had joined a women's group and had vowed never to rely on a man
> for any reason ever again. . . . In time she would get used to the
> women's group. In fact, they were having some kind of meeting that
> very evening. She would go along and launch herself into the swing of
> things. How she longed for a nice frivolous party, for a long session in
> front of the make-up mirror, and a stunning new dress! Shame on you
> Judy, she said to herself, you've given up all that sort of thing. (*Just
> Seventeen*, 23 March 1988)

After refusing offers of help from, and an invitation to dinner by,
the boy next door, she is encouraged by one of her women
neighbours to give him a chance. He pretends to lose his door-
key, so she invites him into her flat: 'After all, if she let him wait in
her flat she would simply be doing him a favour. . . . It was a
sacrifice she would have to make, whether her feminist friends
would approve or not' (30 March 1988). She finds she enjoys his
company: 'After a while she couldn't deny it any more. She liked
him, she wanted him there, he cheered her up . . . . Judy discovered
what had been missing from the flat, and it wasn't missing any
more' (30 March 1988). Judy's flight into feminism is, then,
understood as purely responsive, a reaction to her boyfriend's
infidelity. Feminism and women's groups are equated with hatred
of men, and lack of 'fun' (feminists never wear make-up or dress
up for parties). This definition ultimately renders feminism
irrelevant to Judy's life and, by implication, the lives of the
readers of *Just Seventeen*.

The monthly glossies vary in the degree of enthusiasm they
show for feminism. *Cosmopolitan*'s particular brand of aspirational feminism has been well documented elsewhere (Winship,
1987, pp. 115–22). The magazine operates in a framework which
encourages women to stand up for their rights, but the strategies
for achieving equality are presented as individual rather than
collective. The overall structure of the magazine allows scope for
single articles to be more radical than this dominant liberalism,
however. A number of regular and some occasional contributors
attempt to move the debate around gender inequality away from

individual solutions to question structural social divisions in gender or more general social inequity:

> Nearly 43 percent of women who work do so on a part-time basis, and in many instances, these women are employed with little or no opportunity for progression. There is no training and few career prospects. Part-timers find themselves in the lower grades, overlooked by their colleagues, employers and sometimes by their union. ('The Perils Of Part Timing', June 1988)

> As the welfare state is eroded, women's lives are becoming harder. We may worry about friends stuck on National Health Service waiting lists, fret that our smear tests are not being properly processed, or wonder if we should walk down our badly lit roads at night. But it is only when you look at the extent of the cuts that you realise just how heavily women are being penalised. ('Why the Cuts Hurt Women Most', June 1988)

Both these extracts, but especially the latter, reveal the magazines' address to political issues through the medium of 'human interest', but also point to the fact that, on occasion, they can and do criticise government policy. What is questionable, however, is the impact of such pieces within the overall context of the magazine. Even when writers explicitly declare their feminism, they rarely deviate from the model, personified by the editor herself, of being feminist but suitably feminine.

New Woman surprises by its ability to present large amounts of material that cry out for feminist analysis, and yet doggedly to avoid its implementation. For example, an article on the 'Myth Of The Modern Marriage' details a great deal of empirical evidence about the domestic division of labour, but provides no broader context than the claim to provide a 'snapshot' of modern marriage. The conclusion lays responsibility firmly on the individual: 'The struggle is not so much between man and woman (though that sometimes comes into the equation) but within each man and woman, working out their own life, struggling within the marriage' (March 1988).

Chic is, perhaps unsurprisingly, consistent in its coverage of the politics of race, but less so with regard to the politics of gender. Race is presented as a unifying bond, sometimes as a political construction, but this is less true of gender. We have already suggested that *Chic* shares the aspirational feminism typified by

Cosmopolitan. It has regular contributions from male writers, some of whom are critical of what they perceive as more extreme feminist principles. An article on why men are adulterous takes radical feminist writer Andrea Dworkin as its starting-point, and the author opens by derogating Dworkin's physical appearance before going on to consider whether her opinions have any validity ('Why Men Have Affairs', September 1988). Other contributors are more comfortable with feminist discourse: 'Sex is used to sell products, and the expression of sexuality has come to reside almost exclusive in the female body' ('Your Body Or Your Prison', June 1988).

All the glossies are fascinated with the modern or 'post-feminist' construction of masculinity, although none would use that terminology, referring instead to the 'phenomenon' of the 'New Man'. '*Cosmo* Man' was one of the first attempts to figure this pioneering breed. Rowena Chapman remarks that the construct arises neatly out of *Cosmopolitan*'s discourse of equality and as a parallel to its construction of the 'career woman' (Chapman, 1988, p. 209). It is certainly the case that images of masculinity have shifted during the last few years, helped along by style magazines such as *Arena* (targeted at a male readership), *The Face* and *Blitz*. The terrain of masculinity has been re-drawn, not least through the address to men as consumers. It is significant that men, like women, are now encouraged to buy a whole range of products in order to beautify themselves and to acquire the elusive 'style' which is the magazines' stock-in-trade.

There is, however, an equally significant difference, not only in terms of kind but means, in the marketing of products to men. While women are encouraged to buy mostly in the hope of making themselves desirable to men, the appeal to male consumers is largely narcissistic. That is, men seem to be constructed as objects of pleasure, and even desire, for themselves. This is obviously a possible way of accounting for women's relation to the representations of women in magazines as well, as we discussed in Chapter 1, but this reading is much less defensible in the case of women. Women's magazines, in the main, overtly insist that women's primary duty and orientation is to men. In her discussion, Chapman points out that the construction of the 'New Man' has involved the colonisation of traditionally feminine characteristics, at the same time as magazines such as *Cosmopolitan* encourage (career) women to adopt more masculine attributes in the pursuit of individual success. She argues that the construction of the 'New Man' ultimately serves men's interests. They may adopt a 'position of superiority as [a] proto-female' in contrast with women characterised as proto-male: 'Whoever is the most powerful appropriates the most attractive value-system' (Chapman, 1988, pp. 247–8). Feminism having reclaimed and revalued feminine attributes and values so successfully, men, still the most powerful class, may seek to appropriate them. Feminist women who have cultivated independence and assertiveness are (as ever, but more so) characterised as unnatural, uncaring, selfish.

Because of their emphasis on the domestic, on personal and familial relationships, few of the magazines engage with broader political issues. Certainly none would alienate potential readers by aligning themselves consistently with a single political party, although they may question social division and political policy by examining their impact on women's lives. We have already noted that the weeklies dwell on stories of personal tragedy, yet rarely relate them to underlying political processes and trends. *Woman's Own* ran features on the Zeebrugge ferry disaster and the King's Cross fire without discussing safety standards, concentrating on experiences of personal loss as a result of such tragedies. There is, here, a clear assumption that readers would not favour the inclusion of overtly 'political' content, and that the omission of such content is not in itself a political act.

Some 'celebrity' interviews do give voice to the political concerns of well known individuals. An interview with actress Glenda Jackson in *Best* refers to her strong socialist principles (9 September 1988). A *Woman's Own* interview with Sean Connery takes the title 'Why Mrs Thatcher's Got It Wrong', but his criticism is actually fairly mild. Politicians themselves are treated as celebrities and interviewed accordingly: 'Well, would you have a shower with this man?' is the caption accompanying an interview with the British Labour MP, Ron Brown. Brown is given considerable space to expound his opinions and concern over the rightward shift of the Labour Party in the late 1980s. However, it is *Woman's Own*'s moderate stance that has the last word:

'The House of Commons isn't really my place. My place is with the people of Leith and their basic honest values'. As they await the next election, there may be many people in the Labour Party who eagerly agree with him. (4 October 1988)

When political issues are discussed, albeit in terms of their impact on women's lives or those of their families, there are opportunities for some more hard-hitting journalism. *Bella* conducted an enquiry into 'Poverty In Britain' in October 1988, with emphasis on the north–south divide, drawing in quotations from Labour and Conservative politicians as well as 'ordinary people'. Expert sources such as the Low Pay Unit and the Scottish Council for Voluntary Service gave factual evidence of the divide, and the claim of regeneration in the Welsh valleys from Conservative minister, Peter Walker, is undercut by a closing statement from a redundant Welsh steelworker: 'Jobs have gone and the face of Wales has changed. So there's a big shopping centre in the valleys. Who's got the money to spend in it? Certainly not me' (8 October 1988). Through the medium of the survey or report, the weekly women's magazines in particular frequently rail against social injustice, particularly where it involves a perceived threat to the family. They also address topical issues and relate them to the specificities of women's situation. Thus an article on ecology entitled 'How Green Is Your Shopping Trolley?' presents a wide-ranging and intelligent discussion of issues, under the cover of a domesticating and trivialising introduction. What is going on here, of course, is that even in the political arena, women are addressed as *consumers*. Of course, this approach has the advantage that readers feel they are on familiar ground; issues can be presented as relevant to them (ecologically sound products ensure family welfare, but are considerably more expensive and a drain on the family purse). Yet it is significant that although increasing materialism and the adulation of consumption may be criticised in specific articles, the publication in which the articles appear can find no other way to address women than as consumers.

While individual articles may be critical of specific political positions and decisions, the general ethos of the weekly magazine is of a vague and unspecified 'social concern'. Some injustices are highlighted, but little indication of possible solutions is given. It is here that the absence of any notion of civic, public or collective virtue, to which we pointed in Chapter 1, is especially glaring. The world of politics is ultimately distant from that of 'real life', the world of women. There is no indication that readers might apply pressure for change through political process, or influence political decision-making through participation. There is no discussion of the processes by which political reality and policies are produced, and of the ways in which citizens might join in their production. Perhaps this is why ecology emerges as an increasingly important issue, as an arena in which persons can 'act' without threat to the essentially passive identity of consumer, so vital to the magazines' economic and ideological continuance.

Part three: ideological pleasures

We have argued that women's magazines in their address to women postulate a set of shared and common interests, concerns, tastes and circumstance. This process of the construction of women as a homogeneous group has had a crucial structuring role in the forging of modern class identity. In our analysis of magazines past and present, we have identified a range of discourses of femininity carried in the magazines. In this section we want to consider further the specific interaction of such gender ideologies and pleasure in the women's magazine.

From the beginning of this project and in the course of the seminars which generated it, we were conscious that the duality of ideology and pleasure posed a problem. In the field of cultural theory these two poles have generally been understood in opposition to each other. While theorists of popular culture celebrate its pleasures, those of mass culture condemn the stupefying effect of its ideological straitjacket. For some theorists, pleasure is connected with sexuality and disruption, opening a space for authenticity and freedom; for others, such pleasures are simply further symptoms of false consciousness. Analysts of women's magazines find themselves caught between an emphasis on the pleasures of the form and an exposition of its subliminal and unseen ideological effect. We would argue that all pleasure is socially constructed – what counts for an individual or group as pleasurable depends on the culturally and socially determined range of meanings and values available to them in discourse. We must, then, reject the principle that pleasure can be 'pure' or 'authentic', and also recognise that the construction and maintenance of any social order entails the construction and maintenance of certain pleasures that secure consent and participation in that order. That any cultural form is both pleasurable *and* ideological is, then, neither surprising nor worrying – what else could pleasure be? and how else could ideology work? Women's magazines themselves do not, of course, acknowledge the socially constructed nature of pleasure. Rather, in addressing women as an a-historical, naturally occurring, and homogeneous group they presume that women's pleasures are similarly a-historical, naturally occurring and homogeneous. Yet, paradoxically, it is only through consumption of the magazine that we can gain access to this 'natural' womanhood. Men tell us that they read women's magazines in order to find out about women; more bizarrely, *women* read women's magazines to find out about women. Further, our analysis shows that although women's pleasure is *represented* as homogeneous and unified by the dominant editorial voice of the magazine, it is precisely in heterogeneity and contradiction that individual readers take their pleasure from the text:

> *Roma*:   this one [*Prima*] I pick up cos there's all sorts of odd bits
> *EF*:   so you read that differently?
> *Roma*:   yes, I just pick it up and dip into it
> *EF*:   when?
> *Roma*:   odd five minutes [P4]

> *Lisa*:   . . . . I mean, I think one of the things I quite like is, that you can actually make your own sort of menu up, um if you, you know, you can read something requires a bit of mental stimulation, and then you can read a recipe or look at the fashion page [W7]

Magazines, then, offer the pleasure of difference and multiplicity, carrying severely contradictory, if not incoherent, discourses of femininity simultaneously.

The discourses of women's magazines are forged through the exploitation and, again frequently contradictory, meshing of discourses that co-exist elsewhere in modern culture. The conservative discourse of separate spheres and female passivity co-exists with a liberal discourse of women as autonomous beings with independent rights and pleasures. Domesticity is constructed both by the 'scientific' discourse of social science, and by the more traditional discourses of the household as place of production and affective kinship ties. Sexuality is constructed both by a Christian ascetic discourse of distaste and fear which renders it dangerous and disruptive, and by newer sexological discourses which construct 'normal' or healthy sexuality as orgasmic, and autonomous from other forms of human connection such as love, kinship and friendship. In some magazines this in turn co-exists with a feminist position critical of, if not repudiating, a heterosexuality in need of transformation if it is to fulfil women's needs and with liberationist discourses which celebrate sexuality as the highest form of human experience. The eighteenth-century bourgeois representation of femininity as leisured co-exists with newer class discourses of women as participants in the sexual division of labour.

These contradictions are, however, viable. In order to maintain gender or class hegemony, they do not have to be disguised, smoothed over, or explained away. Rather, as readers we are free to consume what we will and reject what we will not. This leads us to another aspect of the pleasure of the women's magazine, its status as commodity. The 'choice' of which magazine to buy, read and display is understood as a choice about social identity. Furthermore, magazines are indispensable guides to decisions about further patterns of consumption as a register of social being. This is most clearly seen in the magazine recipe, which might be understood as a symbol of the pleasures of consumption afforded by the magazine more generally. We consume in order to produce and in order to exchange. Recipes have a traditional status as items of gift exchange between women, an expression of shared culture. In women's sharing of magazines on a regular and ritualistic basis, this meaning of the recipe still endures:

> *June*: when I go and see my mum she's got, you know, on a circuit, like she buys one and my, her neighbour buys one, and they swap over and then it goes to someone else and you know it does the rounds [W3]

Perhaps the more interesting significance of the recipe as a metaphor for the world of women's magazines as a whole, is the way in which it purports to offer a recipe for femininity itself. On the micro scale, every element of femininity is discussed by way of a list of ingredients, utensils and method. In this way, family relations, political and civic relations, pork chops in white wine, a slim and healthy you for Christmas, a cleaner environment, the avoidance of cancer or endometriosis, orgasmic sex, a secure lifetime of love, and a designer sweater are all of the same order – all things to make at home, or buy ready-made for the home. The pleasures of consumption include the pleasures of participation and belonging, but also those of use and transformation, as the success of a newly 'practical' emphasis in the new women's weeklies such as *Best* and *Bella* would seem to illustrate. All these pleasures, however, must, for the majority of women's magazines, be taken in the privacy of one's own home, and the bosom of the biological family.

A further significant pleasure of the magazine is visual:

EF: so if you're going to buy one it would be one of the glossy –
several: yes, mm
Amy: because of the luxury
Rebecca: it's more pleasing to look at them
Penny: you look at the pictures
Rebecca: yes the pictures are actually, for some reason it's pleasurable to look at them [U1]

Roma: it's good value, it's seventy-five pence, it was, it's now eighty-five, but it, look at the quality of the printing [*Prima*]
Doris: oh yes, I see that
Roma: it's very good value I think
Joan: and of course patterns are expensive anyway
Roma: yes
Joan: and you've got –
Roma: and *look* at that (*shows a picture of a cherry flan on a cookery page*) [P5]

For the younger women, here visual pleasure is about luxury, whereas the older concentrate on the pleasure gained from economy ('good value'). In both cases, 'seeing' is also a form of 'consuming' the commodity, however. But these comments do not explain women's pleasure in looking at other women. Given Roma's remarks, we must not underestimate the pleasure of seeing food, or bottles of perfume, or sun-soaked holiday vistas represented in the magazine, as well as the bodies of women. But we are inclined to argue that the representation of the commodity and the female body cannot be so easily separated as different forms of visual pleasure. Woman is the *sign* for the commodity. If a woman poses by a car, it is a sure sign that the car is for sale.

Caressing a bottle of perfume, she makes its commodity status plain. She has the dual identity of buyer and bought, subject and object.

The question arises whether the pleasure of the woman reader who looks proceeds from her enjoyment in adopting a 'dominant' or 'masculine' subject position in relation to objects, commodities, women. Our answer to this question is 'yes – but. . .', for women's dominion is never secure. We must take into account here not only the ideal reader posited or constructed by the magazine text, but also the social or historical reader and her negotiation with this 'preferred' reading. The ideal metaphorical equation of subjectivity with masculinity and objectivity with femininity must be assessed in relation to material practice or, in other words, the social reality of women's and men's lives. The woman reader who enjoys looking at objects – whether the female model or other feminised and commodified things – does so only in the knowledge that she too is a woman (feminised and commodified). Pleasure, as we have argued in Chapter 1, is not solely about the experience of danger – the seizing of a fleeting fantasy of absolute dominion. It is also about safety. In looking at pictures of women, the woman reader not only experiences the heady thrill of gaining subjectivity through objectification, but she also looks with an artisan's eye. Like the picture on the front of a knitting pattern, consulted to see how to interpret the instructions inside, representations of women in women's magazines offer blueprints or *illustrations* of the recipe for femininity offered by other aspects of the text.

This pleasure in safety is to be had from many elements of magazines, not least in the forging of a homogeneous domestic community in contrast with the threats and confusions of the world outside it. That world is constantly on the margins of the magazine's field of vision, understood both as threat and *unreality*. This distinction between public and private spheres is always liable to disruption, however. We can never, literally, feel safe in our homes. The security and warmth of the domestic space is threatened by pollution, illness, poverty and a number of other social ills attended to by women's magazines. The public world penetrates the private. Women are battered and raped, children are born handicapped, sexual experience is a disappointment. Women's magazines endeavour to cope with this unhappy knowledge in a variety of ways, but it must be remembered that it is precisely in this revelation of the threat from outside (all these are, after all, understood as elements foreign to, not the product of, home and family) that most pleasure can be taken from the present safety within.

A possibility that we must take seriously, having enumerated the pleasures of women's magazines, is that in reality they disappoint, or, at least, that these pleasures are ambiguous. Some of the women who contributed to our discussions did express disappointment, along these lines:

> *Penny*: if I read someone else's, that I haven't paid for, I usually find quite a lot in it, whenever I buy it I always feel dissatisfied cos somehow, you always, you flick through it, and you think, 'Oh, I really wanted – ', you read the problem page, then you read this, that and the other, and then you feel slightly dissatisfied I always think [U4]

> *Linda*:   . . . there's the other factor, that the things are too short for me, they're too bitty, and I only ever look at the pictures, I never really read the articles [W5]

For others, reading magazines seemed to afford a peculiarly 'feminine' kind of pleasure – that is, there was confusion as to whether it was undertaken out of pleasure or duty:

> *Roma*:   because I feel I *must* read every bit through, unless there's a serial I don't like, but I feel duty bound to *read it*, and I don't hand it to Joan until I've read it, and I tick the corner, and, oh, do the crossword [P4]

The pleasure of heterogeneity enters here, if ambiguously. Roma can reject a serial that she does not like. Its narrative continuity makes it, in some sense, a separate enterprise from the rest of the magazine. The context of reading also makes a difference to women's sense of 'duty' in completing the magazine:

> *Maddy*:   if I've bought it for a train journey I solemnly read it from cover to cover
> *EF*:   starting at the front?
> *Maddy*:   straight through, and I loathe the way articles are dotted about
> *Angela*:   I hate that too, I hate having to go to the back
> *Lisa*:   so you don't skip things

Maddy: no, if I've bought it for a journey and I feel slightly, you know, 'I've spent this money, and I've got to read it', well, it's odd isn't it, you buy something for relaxation, then you read it like an exercise [W8]

These extracts suggest several sources of dissatisfaction. One lies precisely in the heterogeneity of the magazine format, the impression that the reader may pick and choose, concur with some discourses and reject others, sometimes simply by not reading them. This very heterogeneity means that no one discourse is worked through satisfactorily, giving an air of superficiality. In its 'bittiness', the magazine seems to fail in its function of *affirmation*. The woman reader does not ultimately find herself, or her ideal self, mirrored in its pages, but fragments of that imagined self. We might, then, understand the ambiguous pleasures of magazine reading to be congruent with those of addiction. The answer to being disappointed is not to reject the substance itself, but to try again, or try another. The continued pursuit of femininity becomes a duty or quest, entailing, almost, the dissolution of pleasure.

We have seen that femininity proves unobtainable because it is contradictory. Beauty should above all be natural, but it has to be manufactured and laboured after. Women aspire to be autonomous and powerful, but they are also objects, of their own gaze and that of men. Femininity is both virtuous, and self-indulgent and wanton. Domesticity is idealised as a realm of skilled craft production, scientific and rational management, but the domestic sphere is the site of *final* consumption. The home is a place of leisure, but also a place of work. And finally, domestic bliss is fraught with danger.

Women's world is never complete, but always in the making. So, too, the attainment of femininity is women's sisyphean labour. The magazine, like the femininities it produces, never fully satisfy. As we have seen, for some women this is a positive feeling. They look forward to the magazine's arrival every week. For others, it leaves a feeling of being let down. In both cases, however, revisits are regular.

We have been at pains to point out in all cases the exclusions that the seemingly heterogeneous and open-ended form of the women's magazine still performs, in particular the glaring absence of certain discourses: feminist, socialist, critical. Readers have to negotiate, one way or another, with the discourses that are present, and that negotiation is a complex one. On the one hand, readers look at the femininities on offer in a spirit of curiosity:

> *Maddy:*   I get quite curious, I mean I've bought *Prima, Best, Marie-Claire*, I mean I've bought one copy of practically all the new ones that've come out because just to see what they're like, and to see what other people are reading. . . . I look for stuff that might revolutionise me and make me look like the woman on the cover [W5]

They also, however, approach magazines critically, as we discussed in the opening section of this chapter. Intimate knowledge of the genre, to the point of being able to mimic its conventions and tone, ensures that the constructions of femininity in the magazine's pages are predictable. The pleasure of ease and recognition is, we would argue, the major ideological pleasure of the magazine.

The point we are making here is that the discourses of femininity in circulation in popular women's magazines are tied to social institutions – marriage, the market, medicine – which make life 'easy' for us, in the sense that they are familiar and have made us what we are. Women's magazines speak to our social existence in comforting ways. Our historical analysis has pointed to the social formation of both these taken-for-granted institutions and modern discourses of femininity. What has been socially formed can, of course, be socially transformed. But we must not underestimate the relative ease of some female existences, bolstered politically, economically and ideologically by institutions and discourses such as the women's magazine, as opposed to others. Feminism requires, like other discourses, to be rooted in social institutions. The making of feminism is a sisyphean labour also, and one for which, at present, we lack the multiple instructions and skills elaborated in the women's magazine that serve to confirm, in tandem with other discourses and institutions, the limited and limiting definitions of 'feminine' identity available in contemporary culture.

Conclusion

This book has attempted to offer an analysis of the social function and ideological work of the women's magazine in modern patriarchal and capitalist culture. We have seen that the women's magazine has undergone a variety of major transformations in terms of its content and form since its first appearance in the late seventeenth century, but that it has also retained a remarkable continuity in terms of its address to readers and its social function. Most importantly, we have argued that the pleasures of the magazine for its women readers cannot be understood as 'innocent', nor separated from their ideological function in women's lives. There has not been time or space fully to develop some of the issues we have raised and this conclusion serves as an attempt to open out, rather than foreclose, further consideration of the women's magazine as a feminocentric popular form.

We begin, however, by seeking to offer some generalisations about the constitution and cultural role of the women's magazine that emerge from this study. There are a number of obvious and major changes that have taken place in the form since John Dunton published the first number of his short-lived *Ladies' Mercury* in 1693. Above all, women's magazines now form a separate industry controlled and maintained by large and powerful conglomerates such as IPC and Condé Nast. These multi million-pound businesses, for which magazines are only one of a number of their products, are now working in an international market. So, for example, *Cosmopolitan* is produced under licence in every continent, and *Good Housekeeping*, launched in the United States in 1885 and successfully exported to Britain in 1922, now has Japanese, Australian and South American versions (Braithwaite and Barrell, 1988, p. 150). *Bella*, produced by a German-based firm (Bauer) appears simultaneously under different names in Britain and America.

These multinational firms, however, maintain the aura of amateurism that characterised the very first magazines for women; they enshrine the fiction that any reader of the magazine may become a writer of it. If Dunton's or Robinson's correspondents in the seventeenth and eighteenth centuries received no remuneration for their efforts, the readers of *Woman's Weekly* can only expect to receive six pounds for their contributions to the letter page ('Lovely to Hear from You'), whereas the regular editors of features, fashion, cookery and so on are salaried. Paradoxically, increasing professionalism in the industry has also meant that contemporary women's magazines are a more genuinely collective and democratic product than their predecessors. A large number of professional women (and men) – from models, to agony aunts, to chief editors – contribute to the production of each monthly or weekly text and, as we have seen, although each magazine strives to produce its own distinctive identity (the glossy, the teen magazine, etc.), there is no perceived need to be internally consistent. Indeed, magazines flourish by offering a diverse number of positions or identities within their pages, usually in the shape of the different 'characters' of its regular contributors, who may hold quite contradictory 'opinions' on particular women's issues. Despite this diversity, however, we have argued that magazines do offer dominant or preferred readings, a point to which we will return below.

The form of the women's magazine, like its contributors, has both diversified and become more professional. In Chapter 3 we noted that it was the nineteenth century, by no means coincidentally the period in which British imperialism flourished and industrialisation became the determining force for social change, that saw the establishment of advertising as the major source of revenue for the women's magazine and a shift from a narrative to a pictorial emphasis within the form. The magazine first developed as a form of cheap and easily consumable narrative fiction in the shape of the single-essay periodical. The compulsion to 'narrativise', particularly through the confessional letter, remains a powerful one in the women's magazine, but with technological advances in printing and photography it has come to take more complex forms. The photo-love-story (staple of the teen magazine until the appearance of *Just Seventeen*), the fashion feature that builds itself around a 'story', the 'rags to riches' make-over, all testify to the pervasive power of narrative, and, in particular, romance narrative, as the structuring agent or generic continuity of the women's magazine.

However, the proliferation of visual media as a means of 'narrating femininity' raises some complex issues about the extent to which women are encouraged to objectify, rather than identify with, other women in the modern magazine. The physically undifferentiated 'heroine', whose romantic trials and triumphs in the eighteenth- and nineteenth-century serial kept the reader riveted, has been displaced, at least in the glossy monthlies, by the 'supermodel', the woman who commands a fortune by embodying contemporary womanhood, the 'face' of the year or decade. The unexpected recent success of the new weeklies such as *Best*, *Bella* and *More*, which virtually abandon the serial and, in some cases, offer little or no narrative fiction, might suggest that female fantasy in the women's magazine is now served by the pleasure of observing the 'commodity' – from the latest kitchen gadget to the supermodel – rather than that of consuming romance fiction.

Our study has also revealed some significant changes in the perceived readership of women's magazines through the centuries and hence an increased specialisation in terms of editorial address. We would argue that the women's magazine has, since its inception, presented bourgeois femininity as normative. However, mass literacy has inevitably meant that it must seek to address and embrace women who cannot be classified as middle class. In the three periods we have covered most extensively here – the eighteenth, late nineteenth, and late twentieth centuries – the relation of gender difference to class difference has been differently inflected. This is most clearly seen in the contrast between the eighteenth-century magazine's emphasis on bourgeois femininity as leisure and the nineteenth-century magazine's representation of bourgeois femininity as labour. The decline of the appellation 'lady' and increasing use of that of 'woman' is evidence of this shift in class determinations with regard to gender in the field of the women's magazine.

Moreover, in the nineteenth century we have noted that the magazine's bourgeois construction of femininity becomes intimately bound up with questions of nationhood, a concern that inevitably came to dominate the women's magazine in those periods in the first half of the twentieth century when Britain's female population was mobilised for the war effort. Since the 1970s, there has been some marginal address to the question of racial difference among female readers in the development of magazines for women of Afro-Caribbean and Asian origin. However, the existence of such magazines has done nothing to challenge the hegemonic power of middle-class values and white femininity in the mainstream magazines. This book has gone some way to a consideration of the complex relations between discourses of race, class and gender as they are articulated in the women's magazine, but, because of its generalist emphasis, has not been able to do full justice to the question. We hope it may provide a basis for further work on a more detailed and specific level than we have attempted.

Despite the changes in content, readership and editorial address briefly outlined above, we have been in the main struck by the remarkable continuities in the women's magazine from the late seventeenth century to the present day, to which we now turn. Women's magazines posit a collective and yet multivalent female subjectivity, which they simultaneously address and construct. In so doing, despite the often contradictory nature of this collective subjectivity, there are clear limits and boundaries to the variety of 'readings' and 'interpretations' available in the text. Although, unlike the *Lady's Magazine* of the late eighteenth century, most women's magazines of today can and do address women's rights to orgasmic heterosexual sex, labour outside the home, or financial independence, by their very nature they continue to function within an ideology of 'separate spheres' – an ideology that, as we have seen, consistently tends to relocate women within domestic and private frameworks. Orgasm thus makes a woman a better partner for her man, labour outside the home makes family or private life more exciting or more egalitarian, financial independence ensures that children can be supported despite the feckless nature of the opposite sex.

From their inception, women's magazines have posited female subjectivity as a problem, and themselves as the answer, offering themselves to female readers as a 'guide to living', a means of organising, responding to, and transforming their experience as women. However, they also, as a result of their claim to 'represent' rather than direct or influence the female social body, find themselves reproducing those very contradictions and paradoxes they ostensibly promise to resolve. Women's magazines have been and remain structured by this significant tension between their self-representation as a 'voice' for women and as a 'leader' of them. This tension is echoed in that between the magazine's function as a disseminator of fantasy and aspirational 'ideals' for women and as a means of representing the reality of women's lives in all their diversity, difficulty and confusion. On the micro level we can see this conflict acted out in the material on 'royalty' which occupies so large a space in modern weeklies: the women of the Royal Family are presented as 'just like us', facing the same problems of juggling priorities – children and 'work', retaining their husbands' attentions, expressing their creative impulses as well as their nurturing abilities – but they also appear as models and patrons of the most expensive fashions, as international travellers, 'superconsumers' on a scale unobtainable, if not unimaginable, for any reader of the magazine.

This confusion between the women's magazine as fantasy machine and as social realist text continues to bedevil any attempt to assess the ideological effects on its readers. Put simply, is it possible to ascertain whether readers consider the representations of femininity offered in the magazine 'true'? And, if they do, should we be seeking to do away with the form altogether, rather than writing a book about it, sensitive to its pleasures? As we have noted, most experienced readers of women's magazines are well acquainted with their codes and conventions and are inclined, particularly those readers who consider themselves 'educated' or 'intellectual', to seek to explain away or excuse their continued loyalty to a conservative form by insisting that they read it only as fantasy or escape.

We obviously cannot lay the blame for women's oppression at the door of women's magazines. This would be tantamount to confirming their own understanding of female liberation as a matter of 'personal' transformation rather than political action. There are many more influential economic, social and cultural causes for women's low pay and low status throughout the world. However, we would argue that the form's conservatism lies precisely in the fact that it cannot conceive of economic, social, cultural or political change as means of resolving the gender contradictions and inequities it addresses. Despite the fact that women's magazines are produced collectively and offer diverse perspectives on the condition of 'women', they are remarkably consistent in the resolutions they offer to the 'problem' of being female. Women are repeatedly told that their problems can only be dealt with through individual, rather than collective, responsibility. Agony columns, readers' letters, single articles, do, of course, insist on the commonality of women's experience. For every reader with a problem, there is another to tell her than she has 'been through the same thing'. Ultimately, however, women are informed that they must 'help themselves' and thus, implicitly, that their problems are their responsibility and may be of their own making. In other words, women's magazines are so structured, ideologically and formally, that they cannot offer political resolutions to what they consistently define as 'personal' problems.

It could be argued that it is this 'personalised' politics that differentiates women's magazines from other magazines and from the newspaper as periodical literature. 'Serious' and 'news' features have become more common in the major women's weeklies. Such articles attempt to offer a 'woman's' perspective on world politics by focusing on humanitarian issues and, in particular, on individual women's experiences of war, famine, and political oppression. As a result, the magazine, as elsewhere, rarely connects the disparate issues it addresses, presenting its 'news' coverage as single problems with single solutions, and seeking to stimulate its readers to sentimental identification and moral outrage, rather than political resistance. Fundamentally, then, women's magazines cannot recognise the collective noun 'woman' as a political category, since the interests of 'woman' are always already conceived of as 'personal'.

There are, of course, positive aspects to the women's magazine's insistent identification of femininity with the 'personal', the 'individual' and the 'private'. Evidently, the women's magazine, in privileging what it defines as emotional, sexual and personal issues and in specifying that these areas are women's priority and primary concern, puts women at the centre of all experience. Men exist only at the margins of this world, most strikingly in the fashion-plate where they usually appear only in the background or at the side of the picture admiring the self-confident woman who strides toward the camera. Men are, of course, a constant reference point; much of women's activity, as defined by the magazine, is directed toward 'humanising', modifying, responding suitably to men's anti-social behaviour. But, in so doing, the magazine reverses the conventional hierarchy of gendered subjects in cultural representations – masculinity functions as the 'not-feminine', the 'other' of woman, whether it is represented as dangerous or familiar. The women's magazine, like the romantic fiction so central to its formation, converts the public/private divide, habitually used to repress women, into an asset: 'Marking the boundaries between public and private spheres is a key part of the process of securing female subordination. But in romance this female, domestic space, this very powerlessness and dependence, are promoted to the foreground as a form of power and value and self-fulfilment' (Batsleer *et al.*, 1985, p. 95).

Would it be possible, then, to produce a popular magazine for women that identifies and analyses the subject 'woman' as a political category? The feminist monthly, *Spare Rib*, has maintained its own relatively small corner of the market on precisely this basis. *Spare Rib* interestingly shares many of the conventions and difficulties we have identified in its more conventional counterparts, but frequently addresses them directly rather than glossing over them. Its 'news' articles, like those in *Woman* although with a different emphasis, seek to identify a 'woman's angle' on political conflict; its reviews of contemporary books, plays, films and television, like those in *Cosmopolitan*, seek out positive images of femininity. Most significantly, in recent years *Spare Rib*'s letter pages have been largely taken up with the problem of the magazine's capacity to represent and express diversity amongst women (in particular ethnic and racial difference, differences of sexual orientation, and 'party' political difference). Unsurprisingly perhaps, of all the women's magazines, *Spare Rib* comes closest to admitting that such 'diversity' may in fact be conflict, that the homogenising category 'woman' can serve in some contexts to repress, rather than promote, political resistance.

The argument of this book would suggest that we cannot look at the women's magazine in isolation from the other cultural phenomena that women consume in order to 'make sense' of their experience as women, or through which they acquire gender identity and gender difference. Nor, even if it were possible, could we expect that a wholesale conversion of the women's magazine into a feminist medium would transform social structures on its own. Ideological apparatuses are, after all, only 'relatively autonomous'. The magazines we have looked at in this study do render under analysis what we might term a 'resisting reading', exposing the ideological and social contradictions that problematise the business of 'becoming female' for women. However, it is clear that women readers do not consume the women's magazine in order to be intellectually or politically challenged. Indeed, most women's magazines foster the idea that they are an 'easy' read. Their heterogenous form exposes the paradoxical nature of constructions of female identity (women should be thin but their first love is the chocolate cake, they should have 'careers' but childcare is their individual responsibility), but the 'preferred' reading does not call women readers' attention to such paradoxes. Rather, they are encouraged to consume each element of the magazine as a separate entity. Few women, as we have noted, read their magazines from cover to cover, beginning to end. Nor, it is clear, does the exposure of ideological contradiction necessarily result in revolutionary activity.

Despite these reservations, we would stress that the women's magazine must be understood as a cultural form in which, since its inception, definitions and understandings of gender difference have been negotiated and contested rather than taken for granted or imposed. Women's magazines are in the main produced and published for profit, not spiritual or feminist gain, but their form does offer a unique opportunity for debate and exchange. We have pointed out that the collective and egalitarian structure of the magazine (the interchangeability of writer and reader) is, to some extent, a fiction, but it is not entirely so. Throughout their history, women's magazines have offered their readers a privileged space, or world, within which to construct and explore the female self. In this respect, they are, indeed, 'women's own'.

Appendix: list of magazines

The following magazines are those discussed in most detail in Chapters 2 and 3, and those which constituted our sample in Chapter 4. This is not, therefore, a comprehensive list, nor does it cover all the magazines which have been consulted for this book.

Late seventeenth and eighteenth century

The Athenian Mercury, 1691–7, ed. John Dunton.
The Ladies Mercury, 1693, ed. John Dunton.
The Tatler, 1709–11, eds Joseph Addison and Richard Steele. Donald F. Bond (ed.) 1987, 3 vols, Oxford: Clarendon Press.
The Spectator, 1711–14, eds Joseph Addison and Richard Steele. Donald F. Bond (ed.) 1965, 5 vols, Oxford: Clarendon Press.
The Female Tatler, 1709–11.
Gentleman's Magazine, or Monthly Intelligencer, 1731–, vols 1–.
The Female Spectator, 1744–6, ed. Eliza Haywood, London: T. Gardner.
The Parrot. With a Compendium of the Times, 1746, ed. Eliza Haywood.
Ladies Magazine, or the Universal Entertainer, 1749–53, ed. Jasper Goodwill.
Lady's Magazine, or Polite Companion for the Fair Sex, 1759–63, ed. Oliver Goldsmith.
Lady's Museum, 1760–61, ed. Charlotte Lennox.
Lady's Magazine, or Entertaining Companion for the Fair Sex, 1770–1830, ed. G. Robinson, London: Robinson & Roberts.

Late eighteenth and nineteenth centuries

The Family Magazine, or a Repository of Religious Instruction and Rational Amusement, 1789–, Mrs. Trimmer.
Lady's Magazine and Museum of Belle Letters, 1832–7 (a merger of *The Lady's Magazine*, 1770–1832, pub. monthly from London, Dean & Munday and *The Ladies' Monthly Museum, or Polite Repository of Amusement and Instruction*, 1789–1828), then

177

Court Magazine and Monthly Museum and Lady's Magazine, 1838–47.
*La Belle Assemblée, or Bell's Court and Fashionable Magazine Addressed
    Particularly to the Ladies*, 1806–32, London: J. Bell, then
Court's Magazine and Belle Assemblée, 1832–48, then
La Belle Assemblée, or Ladies' Fashionable Companion, 1848–59.
The Mother's Magazine, 1834–49, eds Mrs A. G. Whittelsey and Rev. D.
    Mead, reprinted London: James Paul, from American edn.
Englishwoman's Domestic Magazine, monthly 1852–79, ed. Samuel Bee-
    ton, then merged with
The Illustrated Household Journal, 1880–1, then merged into
Milliner, Dress-maker and Draper, 1881–.
The Queen, an Illustrated Journal and Review, 1861–3, ed. Samuel Beeton,
    sold to Cox and absorbed
The Ladies' Newspaper and Pictorial Times to become *Queen, The Ladies'
    Newspaper*, 1863–.
English Woman's Journal, 1858–64, became
English Woman's Review of Social and Industrial Questions, 1866–1910, ed.
    Jessie Boucherett, then C. A. Biggs, then Helen Blackburn and Antoinette
    Mackenzie.
The Lady's Pictorial, 1881–1921.
The Gentlewomen, 1890–1926.
Woman: for all Sorts and Conditions of Women, 1890–1912, ed. Arnold
    Bennett (1890–1894).
Woman at Home: Annie Swann's Magazine, 1893–1920, ed. Robertson
    Nicholl, London: Hodder & Staughton, merged with
Home Notes, 1894–1957, London: Pearson, merged with
Woman's Own, 1957–.
Home Chat, 1894–1957, London: Harmsworth.
Woman's Weekly, 1911–.

1988 SAMPLE

Teenage Girls' Magazines:

Patches: weekly, cover price 32p. 31 pp.
Owned by D. C. Thompson Ltd.
Launched 1970: Circulation 74,102.
Just Seventeen: weekly, cover price 50p. 47 pp.
Owned by Emap Metro Publications Ltd.
Launched 1983: Circulation 278,039.

Monthly glossies

Chic: monthly, cover price £1. 74pp.
Owned by Ratepress Ltd.
Launched 1984: Circulation – no figures available.
Cosmopolitan: monthly, cover price £1. 240pp.
Owned by National Magazine Company Ltd.
Launched 1972: Circulation, 375,894.
New Woman: monthly, cover price £1. 150pp.
Owned by News International.
Launched 1988: Circulation – no figures available.

Weeklies

Woman's Own: weekly, cover price 37p. 66pp.
Owned by Newnes/IPC Magazines.
Launched 1932: Circulation 1,1113,080.
Woman's Weekly: weekly, cover price 34p. 71pp.
Owned by Fleetway/IPC Magazines.
Launched 1911: Circulation 1,325,742.
Bella: weekly, cover price 29p. 58pp.
Owned by Bauer UK.
Launched 1987: Circulation – no figures available.
Best: weekly, cover price 40p. 74pp.
Owned by G & J of the UK.
Launched 1987: Circulation est. 1 million.

Note: cover prices and figures refer to the time of survey; where prices
rose during the survey period, the higher price is quoted.

Bibliography

Abercrombie, Nicholas *et al.* (1980) *The Dominant Ideology Thesis* (London: George Allen & Unwin).

Adburgham, Alison (1972) *Women in Print: Writing Women and Women's Magazines from the Accession of Queen Victoria* (London: George Allen & Unwin).

Adorno, Theodor and Horkheimer, Max (1977) 'The Culture Industry: Enlightenment as Mass Deception', in Curran, Gurevitch and Woollacott (eds), *Mass Communication and Society* (London: Edward Arnold, pp. 349–83).

Althusser, Louis (1971) 'Ideology and Ideological State Apparatuses', in *Lenin and Philosophy and Other Essays*, trans. Ben Brewster (London: New Left Books).

Althusser, Louis and Balibar, Etienne (1970) *Reading Capital* (London: New Left Books).

Altick, Richard D. (1957) *The English Common Reader: A Social History of the Mass Reading Public 1800–1900* (Chicago: Chicago University Press).

Anderson, Paul Bunyan (1931) 'The History and Authorship of Mrs. Crackenthorpe's *Female Tatler*', *Modern Philology*, vol. 27, pp. 354–60.

Armstrong, Nancy (1985) *Desire and Domestic Fiction: A Political History of the Novel* (Oxford: Oxford University Press).

Ashley, Bob (1989) *The Study of Popular Fiction: A Source Book* (London: Printer Publishers).

Baehr, Helen (ed.) (1980) *Women and Media* (Oxford: Pergamon Press).

Barker, Martin (1989) *Comics: Ideology, Power and the Critics* (Manchester: Manchester University Press).

Barrell, John (1983) *English Literature in History 1730–80: An Equal, Wide Survey* (London: Hutchinson).

Barrett, Michèle (1980) *Women's Oppression Today: Problems in Marxist-Feminist Analysis* (London: Verso).

Barthes, Roland (1972) 'Myth Today', in *Mythologies*, trans. Annette Lavers (London: Jonathan Cape).

—— 1976, *The Pleasure of the Text*, trans. Richard Miller (London: Jonathan Cape).

—— 1983, *Selected Writings*, ed. Susan Sontag (London: Fontana).

Batsleer, Janet, Davies, Tony, O'Rourke, Rebecca and Weedon, Chris *(1985) Rewriting English: Cultural Politics of Gender and Class* (London: Methuen).

Beauvoir, Simone de (1960) *The Second Sex*, trans. H. M. Parshley (London: Four Square Editions).

Beetham, Margaret (1990) 'Towards a Theory of the Periodical as a Publishing Genre' in L. Brake, A. Jones and L. Madden (eds), *Investigating Victorian Journalism* (London: Macmillan).

Bell, David (1960) *The End of Ideology* (Glencoe: Free Press).

Benjamin, Walter (1970) 'The Work of Art in the Age of Mechanical Reproduction', in Hannah Arendt (ed.), *Illuminations*, trans. Harry Zorn (London: Jonathan Cape) pp. 219–54.

Bennett, Tony (1982) 'Theories of the Media, Theories of Society' in Gurevitch, Bennett, Curran and Woollacott (eds), *Culture, Society and the Media* (London: Methuen).

—— (1986) 'The Politics of the "Popular" and Popular Culture', in Bennett, Colin Mercer and Janet Woollacott (eds), *Popular Culture and Social Relations* (Milton Keynes and Philadelphia: Open University Press) pp. 6–21.

Benton, Ted (1981) 'Realism and Social Science', *Radical Philosophy*, no. 27.

—— (1984) *The Rise and Fall of Structuralist Marxism: Althusser and his Influence* (London and Basingstoke: Macmillan).

Berger, John (1972) *Ways of Seeing* (London: BBC).

Betterton, Rosemary (ed.) (1987) *Looking On: Images of Femininity in the Visual Arts and Media* (London: Pandora Press).

Bowley, Rachel (1986) 'Secsexecs', *Oxford Literary Review: Sexual Difference Special Issue*, vol. 8, nos 1–2, pp. 105–12.

Boyce, G. (1978) 'The Fourth Estate: Reappraisal of a Concept', in Boyce, John Curran and P. Wingate (eds), *Newspaper History from the Seventeenth Century to the Present Day* (London: Constable, pp. 19–40).

Braithwaite, Brian and Barrell, Joan (1979) (2nd edn 1988) *The Business of Women's Magazines: The Agonies and Ecstasies* (London: Associated Business Press).

Cameron, Deborah (1985) *Feminism and Linguistic Theory* (London: Macmillan).

Cecil, Mirabel (1974) *Heroines in Love 1750–1815* (London: Michael Joseph).

Chalmers, Alan (1982) *What is This Thing Called Science?*, 2nd edn (Milton Keynes: Open University Press).

Chapman, Rowena (1988) 'Mad About the Boy', *New Socialist*, May/June.

Cockburn, C. (1981) 'The Material of Male Power', *Feminist Review*, no. 9, pp. 41–59.

Connell, Myra (1981) 'Reading Romance', unpub. MA thesis, University of Birmingham CCCS.

Corner, John (1983) 'Textuality, Communication and Media Power', in Davis and Walton (eds), *Language, Image, Media*, pp. 266–81.

Corrigan, Phillip and Gillespie, Val (1977) *Class Struggle, Idle Time and Social Literacy* (London: Routledge & Kegan Paul).

Culler, Jonathan (1983) *On Deconstruction: Theory and Criticism after Structuralism* (London: Routledge & Kegan Paul).

Curran, James, Gurevitch, Michael and Woollacott, Janet (eds) (1977) *Mass Communication and Society* (London: Edward Arnold).

Darlow, T. H. (1925) *William Robertson Nicholl: Life and Letters* (London: Hodder & Stoughton).

Davidoff, Leonore and Hall, Catherine (1987) *Family Fortunes: Men and Women of the English Middle Class 1780–1850* (London: Hutchinson).

Davis, Howard and Walton, Paul (eds) (1983) *Language, Image, Media* (Oxford: Basil Blackwell).

Davis, Lennard (1983) *Factual Fictions: The Origins of the English Novel* (New York: Columbia University Press).

Delphy, Christine (1984) 'The Main Enemy', in *Close to Home: A Materialist Analysis of Women's Oppression* (London: Hutchinson) pp. 57–77.

Doughan, David (1987) 'Periodicals by, for, and about Women in Britain', *Women's Studies International Forum*, vol. 10, pp. 261–73.

Downie, J. A. (1969) *Robert Harley and the Press: Propaganda and Public Opinion in the Age of Swift and Defoe* (Cambridge: Cambridge University Press).

Dworkin, Andrea (1982) *Pornography: Men Possessing Women* (London: Women's Press).

Eagleton, Terry (1984) *The Function of Criticism* (Oxford: Basil Blackwell).

Eco, Umberto (1984) 'On Fish and Buttons: Semiotics and the Philosophy of Language', *Semiotics*, vol. 48, pp. 97–117.

Ellegard, Alvar, *The Readership of the Periodical Press in Mid-Victorian Britain* (Goteburg: Goteburg University Press).

Ellmann, Richard (1987) *Oscar Wilde* (London: Hamish Hamilton).

Elster, Jon (1985) *Making Sense of Marx* (Cambridge: Cambridge University Press).

Fergus, Jan (1986) 'Women, Class and the Growth of Magazine Readership in the Provinces', *Eighteenth Century Culture*, vol. 16, pp. 41–56.

Ferguson, Marjorie (1978) 'Imagery and Ideology: The Cover Photographs of Traditional Women's Magazines', in Tuchman, Kaplan

Daniels and Benét (eds), *Hearth and Home: Images of Women in the Mass Media.*

—— (1983) *Forever Feminine: Women's Magazines and the Cult of Femininity* (London: Heinemann).

Feuer, Lewis (1975) *Ideology and the Ideologists* (Oxford: Basil Blackwell).

Firestone, Shulamith (1980) *The Dialectic of Sex* (London: Women's Press).

Fish, Stanley (1975) *Is There A Text In This Class?* (Cambridge, Mass: Harvard University Press).

Foucault, Michael (1981) *The History of Sexuality: An Introduction* (Harmondsworth, Middlesex: Pelican).

—— (1980) *Power/Knowledge: Selected Interviews and Other Writings 1972–77* (Brighton: Harvester).

Frazer, Elizabeth (1987) 'Teenage Girls Reading *Jackie*', *Media Culture and Society*, vol. 9, pp. 407–25.

—— and Cameron, Deborah (1988) 'Knowing What to Say: The Construction of Gender in Linguistic Practice', in Ralph Grillo (ed.), *Social Anthropology and the Politics of Language* (*Sociological Review/Monograph 36*), pp.25–40.

Freeman, Sarah (1977) *Isabella and Sam: The Story of Mrs. Beeton* (London: Victor Gallancz).

Friedan, Betty (1965) *The Feminine Mystique* (Harmondsworth: Penguin).

Gammon, Lorraine and Marshment, Margaret (eds) (1988) *The Female Gaze: Women as Viewers of Popular Culture* (London: Women's Press).

Garfinkel, Harold (1969) *Studies in Ethnomethodology* (Englewood Cliffs NJ: Prentice Hall).

Gerbner, George (1957) 'The Social Role of the Confession Magazine', *Social Problems.*

Glazer, Nona (1980) 'Overworking the Working Woman: The Double Day in a Mass Magazine', *Women's Studies International Quarterly*, vol. 3.

Goldgar, Bertrand A. (1976) *Walpole and the Wits: The Relation of Politics of Literature 1722–42* (Lincoln and London: University of Nebraska Press).

Gorham, Deborah (1982) *The Victorian Girl and the Feminine Ideal* (London: Croom Helm).

Griffin, Christine (1982) 'Cultures of Femininity: Romance Revisited', *Occasional Papers (Women's Series)*, Birmingham CCCS, no. 69.

Gurevitch, Michael, Bennett, Tony, Curran, James and Woollacott, Janet (eds) (1982) *Culture, Society and the Media* (London: Methuen).

Graham, Walter (1936–7) 'Thomas Baker, Mrs. Manley and the *Female Tatler*', *Modern Philology*, vol. 34, pp. 267–72.

Gramsci, Antonio (1988) 'The Study of Philosophy' in David Forgacs (ed.), *A Gramsci Reader: Selected Writings 1916–35* (London: Lawrence & Wishart) pp. 324–47.

Green, Eileen, Hebron, Sandra and Woodward, Diane (1990) *Women and Leisure* (London and Basingstoke: Macmillan).

Greer, Germaine (1971) *The Female Eunuch* (London: Paladin Grafton Books).

Hall, Stuart (1977) 'Culture, the Media and the "Ideological Effect" ', in James Curran *et al.* (eds), *Mass Communication and Society* (Milton Keynes: Open University Press) pp. 315–48.

—— (1980) 'Encoding/Decoding' in Hall *et al.* (eds), *Culture, Media, Language: Working Papers in Cultural Studies* (London: Hutchinson) pp. 972–9.

—— and Jefferson, Tony (eds) (1976) *Resistance through Ritual: Youth Sub-Cultures in Post-War Britain* (London: Hutchinson).

Harrington-Smith, John (1951–2) 'Thomas Baker and the Female Tatler', *Modern Philology*, vol. 69, pp. 182–8.

Hebron, Sandra (1983) '*Jackie* and *Woman's Own*: Ideological Work and the Social Construction of Gender Identity', Occasional Paper, Sheffield City Polytechnic.

Hindess, Barry, Hirst, Paul, Cutler, Antony and Hussein, Athar (1977 and 1978) *Marx's Capital and Capitalism Today*, 2 vols (London: Routledge & Kegan Paul).

Hodges, James (1957) 'The Female Spectator: A Courtesy Periodical', in Richmond P. Bond (ed.), *Studies in the Early English Periodical* (Chapel Hill: University of North Carolina Press) pp. 151–82.

Holland, Norman L. (1975) *Five Readers Reading* (New Haven and London: Yale University Press).

Holland, Patricia (1983) 'The Page Three Girl Speaks to Women Too', *Screen*, vol. 24, no. 3 (May/June), pp. 84–102.

Hollis, Patricia (1970) *The Pauper Press* (Oxford: Clarendon Press).

Hunter, Jean (1977) '*The Lady's Magazine* and the Study of English-women in the Eighteenth Century', in Donovan H. Bond and W. Reynolds McLeod (eds), *Newsletters to Newspapers: Eighteenth Century Journalism* (Morgantown: School of Journalism, West Virginia University) pp. 103–17.

Irigaray, Luce (1981) 'This Sex Which Is Not One' and 'When the Goods Get Together', in Elaine Marks and Isabelle de Courtivron (eds), *New French Feminisms* (Brighton: Harvester) pp. 99–110.

Iser, Wolfgang (1978) *The Act of Reading: A Theory of Aesthetic Response* (Baltimore and London: Johns Hopkins University Press).

Jacobus, Mary (1986) *Reading Woman: Essays in Feminist Criticism* (London: Methuen; and New York: Columbia University Press).

James, Louis (1982) 'The Trouble with Betsy', in J. Shattock and M. Wolff, *The Victorian Periodical Press: Samplings and Soundings* (Leicester: Leicester University Press) pp. 349–66.

Jameson, Frederic (1979) 'Reification and Utopia in Mass Culture', *Social Text*, no. 1, pp. 130–48.

—— (1981) *The Political Unconscious: Narrative as a Socially Symbolic Act* (London: Methuen).

Jauss, H. R. (1982) *Towards an Aesthetic of Reception* (Brighton: Harvester).

Johnson, Richard (1979) 'Three Problematics: Elements of a Theory of Working Class Culture', in John Clarke, Chas Critcher and Richard Johnson (eds), *Working Class Culture: Studies in History and Theory* (London: Hutchinson and Birmingham CCCS) pp. 201–37.

Kaplan, E. Ann (1984) 'Is the Gaze Male?', in Snitow, Stansell and Thompson (eds), *Desire: The Politics of Sexuality*, pp. 321–88.

Koon, Helene (1978–9) 'Eliza Haywood and the *Female Spectator*', *Huntingdon Library Quarterly*, vol. 42, pp. 43–57.

Lee, Alan J. (1976) *The Origins of the Popular Press 1855–1914* (London: Croom Helm).

Leman, Joy (1980) ' "The Advice of a Real Friend": Codes of Intimacy and Oppression in Women's Magazines 1937–55', in Helen Baehr (ed.), *Women and Media*, pp. 63–78.

Lloyd, Genevieve (1984) *The Man of Reason: 'Male' and 'Female' in Western Philosophy* (London: Methuen).

Lopate, Carol (1978) 'Jackie!', in Tuchman, Kaplan Daniels and Benèt (eds), *Hearth and Home*.

Lovell, Terry (1987) *Consuming Fictions* (London: Verso).

Lovibond, Sabina (1989) 'Is Feminism Against Pleasure?', unpublished paper, Oxford University.

Macdonnell, Dianne (1986) *Theories of Discourse: An Introduction* (Oxford: Basil Blackwell).

Madden, Lionel and Dixon, Diana (1975) *The Nineteenth-Century Periodical Press in Britain: A Bibliography of Modern Studies 1901–71* (Toronto: Victorian Periodical Newsletter, University of Toronto).

March-Phillips, Evelyn (1894) 'Women's Newspapers', *Fortnightly Review*, N.S., vol. 56.

Marcuse, Herbert (1968) *One Dimensional Man: Studies in the Ideology of Advanced Industrial Society* (London: Routledge & Kegan Paul, reprint 1986 Ark editions).

Marx, Karl (1859) 'Preface' to *A Critique of Political Economy*, reprinted in McLellan (ed.), *Karl Marx*, pp. 388–92.

—— and Frederick Engels (1932) *The German Ideology*, reprinted in McLellan (ed.), *Karl Marx*, pp. 159–91.

Mattelart, Michèle (1986) *Women, Media, Crisis: Femininity and Disorder* (London: Comedia).

Mayo, Robert (1962) *The English Novel in the Magazines 1740–1815* (London: Oxford University Press).

McLellan, David (ed.) (1977) *Karl Marx: Selected Writings* (Oxford: Oxford University Press).

McRobbie, Angela (1978a) 'Working Class Girls and the Culture of Femininity', in *Women Take Issue* (London: Hutchinson and Birmingham CCCS Women's Studies Group) pp. 96–108.

—— (1978b) '*Jackie*: An Ideology of Adolescent Femininity', *Occasional Paper*, Birmingham CCCS.

—— and Nava, Mica (eds) (1984) *Gender and Generation* (London: Macmillan).

Meech, Trica (1986) *The Development of Women's Magazines 1799–1945*, Catalogue of Exhibition and Account of Manchester Polytechnic's Collection ()Manchester Polytechnic.

Mepham, John (1979) 'The Theory of Ideology in Capital', in Mepham and David-Hillel Ruben (eds), *Epistemology, Science, Ideology, Issues in Marxist Philosophy*, vol. 3 (Brighton: Harvester).

Mercer, Colin (1986a) 'Complicit Pleasures', in Bennett, Mercer and Woollacott (eds), *Popular Culture*, pp. 50–68.

—— (1986b) 'That's Entertainment: The Resilience of Popular Forms', in Bennett, Mercer and Woollacott (eds), *Popular Culture*, pp. 177–95.

Mill, John Stuart (1912) 'The Subjection of Women', first published 1869: reprinted in *On Liberty, Representative Government and the Subjection of Women: Three Essays by John Stuart Mill* (Oxford: Oxford University Press), pp.425–548.

Minogue, Kenneth (1985) *Alien Powers: the Pure Theory of Ideology* (London: Weidenfeld & Nicholson).

Mintel Market Intelligence (1986) 'Magazines', *Mintel*, pp. 75–88.

Mitchell, Juliet and Rose, Jacqueline (eds) (1982) *Feminine Sexuality: Jacques Lacan and the École Freudienne* (London and Basingstoke: Macmillan).

Mitchell, Sally (1981) *The Fallen Angel: Chastity, Class and Women's Reading 1835–80* (Bowling Green, Ohio: Bowling Green University Popular Press).

Modleski, Tania (1984) *Loving with a Vengeance: Mass Produced Fantasies for Women* (New York and London: Methuen).

Morris, Meaghan (1988) *The Pirate's Fiancee: Feminism Reading Post-Modernism* (London: Verso).

Mulvey, Laura (1975–6) 'Visual Pleasure and Narrative Cinema', *Screen*, vol. 16, no. 3 (Autumn) pp. 6–18.

Mumby, F. A. (1930) (revised edn with Norrie, 1954) *Publishing and Book Selling: A History from the Earliest Times to the Present Day* (London: Jonathan Cape).

Murray, Janet H. (1985) 'Class versus Gender Identification in *The English Woman's Review* of the 1880s', *Victorian Periodical Review*, vol. 18, no. 4.

Myers, Kathy (1983) 'Understanding Advertisers', in Davis and Walton (eds), *Language, Image, Media*, pp. 205–25.

Nowell-Smith, Simon (1958) *The House of Cassell 1848–1958* (London: Cassell).

Palmegiano, E. M. (1976) *Women and British Periodicals 1832–76* (Toronto: Victorian Periodical Newsletter, University of Toronto).

Pateman, Trevor (1983) 'How is Understanding an Advertisement Possible?', in Davis and Walton (eds), *Language, Image, Media*, pp. 187–204.

Phillips, E. Barbara (1978) 'Magazine Heroines: Is Ms. Just Another Member of the Family Circle?', in Tuchman, Kaplan Daniels and Benèt (eds), *Hearth and Home*.

Plant, Marjorie (1974) *The English Book Trade*, 3rd edn (London: George Allen & Unwin).

Pollock, Griselda (1977) 'What's Wrong with Images of Women?', *Screen Education*, no. 24, pp. 25–33).

Poovey, Mary (1984) *The Proper Lady and the Woman Writer: Ideology as Style in the Works of Mary Wollstonecraft, Mary Shelley and Jane Austen* (Chicago: Chicago University Press).

Radway, Janice (1987) *Reading the Romance: Women, Patriarchy and Popular Literature* (London: Verso).

Rendall, Jane (1987) 'A Moral Engine'? Feminism, Liberalism and the *English Woman's Journal*', in Rendall (ed.), *Equal or Different: Women's Politics 1800–1914* (Oxford: Basil Blackwell) pp. 112–40.

Richards, I. A. (1929) *Practical Criticism: A Study of Literary Judgement* (London: Routledge & Kegan Paul).

Richardson, Kay and Corner, John (1986) 'Reading Reception: Mediation and Transparency in Viewers' Accounts of a TV Programme', *Media, Culture and Society*, vol. 8.

Richetti, J. J. (1969) *Popular Fiction before Richardson: Narrative Patterns 1700–39* (Oxford: Clarendon Press).

Sargent, Lydia (ed.) (1981) *Women and Revolution: The Unhappy Marriage of Marxism and Feminism* (London: Pluto Press).

Sayer, Derek (1979) *Marx's Method* (London: Harvester).

Sharpe, Sue (1976) *Just Like a Girl: How Girls Learn to Be Women* (Harmondsworth, Middlesex: Penguin).

Shevelov, Kathryn (1989) *Women and Print Culture: The Construction of Femininity in the Early Periodical* (London: Routledge).

Shorter, C. K. (1899) 'Illustrated Journalism: Its Past and Future', *Contemporary Review*, vol. 65.

Shuwer, P. (1966) *History of Advertising* (London: Leisure Arts Ltd).

Snitow, Ann, Stansell, Christine and Thompson, Sharon (eds) (1984) *Desire: The Politics of Sexuality* (London: Virago).

Sonnenschein, David (1970) 'Love and Sex in the Romance Magazines', *Journal of Popular Culture*, vol. 4.

—— (1972) 'Process in the Production of Popular Culture: The Romance Magazine', *Journal of Popular Culture*, vol. 6.

Sontag, Susan (1983) 'Writing Itself: On Roland Barthes', in Sontag (ed.), *Barthes: Selected Writings* (London: Fontana).

Stanley, Liz and Wise, Sue (1983) *Breaking Out: Feminist Consciousness and Feminist Research* (London: Routledge & Kegan Paul).

Stearns, Bertha Monica (1930) 'The First English Periodical for Women', *Modern Philology*, vol. 28, pp. 45–59.

—— (1933) 'Early English Periodicals for Women', *PMLA*, vol. 48, pp. 38–60.

Stewart, Penni (1980) 'He Admits . . . But She Confesses', in Baehr (ed.), *Women and Media*, pp. 105–14.

Taylor, Helen (1989) *Scarlett's Women: Gone with the Wind and its Female Fans* (London: Virago).

Thompson, John B. (1984) *Studies in the Theory of Ideology* (Cambridge: Polity Press).

Thompson, Sharon (1984) 'Search for Tomorrow: On Feminism and the Reconstruction of Teen Romance' in Vance (ed.), *Pleasure and Danger: Exploring Female Sexuality*, pp. 350–84.

Tompkins, J. P. (ed.) (1980) *Reader Response Criticism: From Formalism to Post-Structuralism* (Baltimore: Johns Hopkins University Press).

√Tuchman, Gay, Daniels, Arlene Kaplan, and Benèt, James (eds) (1978) *Hearth and Home: Images of Women in the Mass Media* (New York: Oxford University Press).

Vance, Carol (1984) 'Pleasure and Danger: Towards a Politics of Sexuality' in Vance (ed.), *Pleasure and Danger: Exploring Female Sexuality* (Boston: Routledge & Kegan Paul) pp. 1–28.

Vincent, David (1989) *Literacy and Popular Culture: England 1750–1914* (Cambridge: Cambridge University Press).

Walkerdine, Valerie (1984) 'Some Day My Prince Will Come: Young Girls and the Preparation for Adolescent Sexuality', in McRobbie and Nava (eds), *Gender and Generation*, pp. 162–84.

Watt, Ian (1957) *The Rise of the Novel: Studies in Defoe, Richardson and Fielding* (London: Chatto & Windus).

Watson, Melvin (1956) *Magazine Serials and the Essay Tradition 1746–1820*, Louisiana State University Studies Humanities Series no. 6 (Baton Rouge: Louisiana State University Press).

Weeks, Jeffrey (1985) *Sexuality and its Discontents: Meanings, Myths and Modern Sexualities* (London: Routledge & Kegan Paul).

Whicher, George Frisbie (1915) *The Life and Romances of Eliza Haywood* (New York: Columbia University Press).

White, Cynthia L. (1970) *Women's Magazines 1693–1968* (London: Michael Joseph).

Wiener, Joel (1969) *The War of the Unstamped: The Movement to Repeal the British Newspaper Tax* (Ithaca and London: Cornell University Press).

Williams, Raymond (1966) *Communications* (London: Chatto & Windus).

—— (1977) *Marxism and Literature* (Oxford: Oxford University Press).

Williamson, Judith (1986) *Consuming Passions: The Dynamics of Popular Culture* (London: Marion Boyars).

Wilson, Elizabeth (1985) *Adorned in Dreams: Fashion and Modernity* (London: Virago).

Winship, Janice (1978) 'A Woman's World: *Woman* – an Ideology of Femininity', in *Women Take Issue* (London: Hutchinson and Birmingham CCCS Women's Studies Group) pp. 133–45.

—— (1987) *Inside Women's Magazines* (London and New York: Pandora Press).

Index